George Alfred Henty, Walter Paget

With Moore at Corunna

George Alfred Henty, Walter Paget

With Moore at Corunna

ISBN/EAN: 9783744741620

Printed in Europe, USA, Canada, Australia, Japan

Cover: Foto ©ninafisch / pixelio.de

More available books at **www.hansebooks.com**

WITH MOORE AT CORUNNA

TERENCE FINDS THAT THE SEA-HORSE HAS BEEN BADLY MAULED
BETWEEN-DECKS.

WITH MOORE AT CORUNNA

BY

G. A. HENTY

Author of "With Cochrane the Dauntless," "A Knight of the White Cross," "In Freedom's Cause," "St. Bartholomew's Eve," "Wulf the Saxon," etc.

WITH TWELVE ILLUSTRATIONS BY WAL PAGET

NEW YORK
CHARLES SCRIBNER'S SONS
1912

PREFACE

From the termination of the campaigns of Marlborough—at which time the British army won for itself a reputation rivalled by that of no other in Europe—to the year when the despatch of a small army under Sir Arthur Wellesley marked the beginning of another series of British victories as brilliant and as unbroken as those of that great commander, the opinion had gained ground in Europe that the British had lost their military virtues, and that, although undoubtedly powerful at sea, they could have henceforth but little influence in European affairs. It is singular that the revival of Britain's activity began under a Government which was one of the most incapable that ever controlled the affairs of the country. Had their deliberate purpose been to render nugatory the expedition which — after innumerable vacillations and changes of purpose—they despatched to Portugal, they could hardly have acted otherwise than they did.

Their agents in the Peninsula were men singularly unfitted for the position. Then the Government divided the commands among their generals and admirals, sending to each absolutely contradictory orders, and when at last they brought themselves to appoint one to the supreme command, they changed that commander six times in the course of a year. While lavishing enormous sums of money, arms, clothing, and materials of war upon the Spaniards, who wasted or pocketed them, they kept their own army unsupplied with money, transport, or clothes. Unsupported by the home authorities,

PREFACE

the British commanders had yet to struggle with the faithlessness, mendacity, and inertness of the Portuguese and Spanish authorities, and were hampered with obstacles such as never beset a British commander before. Still, in spite of this, British genius and valour triumphed over all difficulties, and Wellesley delivered Lisbon and compelled the French army to surrender.

Then again, Moore, by his marvellous march, checked the course of victory of Napoleon and saved Spain for a time. Cradock organized an army, and Wellesley hurled back Soult's invasion of the north, and drove his army, a dispirited and worn-out mass of fugitives, across the frontier, and in less than a year from the commencement of the campaign carried the war into Spain. So far I have endeavoured to sketch the course of these events in the present volume. But the whole course of the Peninsular War was far too long to be condensed in a single book, except in the form of history pure and simple; therefore, I have been obliged to divide it into two volumes; and I propose next year to follow up the adventures of my present hero, who had the good fortune, with Trant, Wilson, and other British officers, to attain the command of a body of native irregulars, acting in connection with the movements of the British army.

Yours sincerely,

G. A. HENTY.

CONTENTS

CHAP.		PAGE
I.	THE MAYO FUSILIERS,	1
II.	TWO DANGERS,	20
III.	DISEMBARKED,	39
IV.	UNDER CANVAS,	57
V.	ROLICA AND VIMIERA,	75
VI.	A PAUSE,	94
VII.	THE ADVANCE,	112
VIII.	A FALSE ALARM,	131
IX.	THE RETREAT,	149
X.	CORUNNA,	167
XI.	AN ESCAPE,	185
XII.	A DANGEROUS MISSION,	203
XIII.	AN AWKWARD POSITION,	219
XIV.	AN INDEPENDENT COMMAND,	241
XV.	THE FIRST SKIRMISH,	259
XVI.	IN THE PASSES,	275
XVII.	AN ESCAPE,	294
XVIII.	MARY O'CONNOR,	312
XIX.	CONFIRMED IN COMMAND,	330
XX.	WITH THE MAYOS,	350
XXI.	PORTUGAL FREED,	369
XXII.	NEWS FROM HOME,	386

ILLUSTRATIONS

	PAGE

TERENCE FINDS THAT THE *SEA-HORSE* HAS BEEN BADLY MAULED BETWEEN-DECKS, ... *Frontispiece*, 30

TWO FRENCH PRIVATEERS BEAR DOWN UPON THE *SEA-HORSE*, . 24

"I SHOULD NOT HAVE MINDED BEING HIT, FATHER, IF YOU HAD ESCAPED," 94

"I AM TOLD THAT YOU WISH TO SPEAK TO ME, GENERAL," . 116

"WHAT DO YOU MEAN, TERENCE? . . . WE WOULD HAVE THRASHED THEM OUT OF THEIR BOOTS IN NO TIME," . . 156

"POOR OLD JACK! HE HAS CARRIED ME WELL EVER SINCE I GOT HIM AT TORRES VEDRAS," 186

TERENCE RECEIVES A PRESENT OF A HORSE FROM SIR JOHN CRADOCK, ... 220

"IN THE NAME OF THE JUNTA I DEMAND THAT AMMUNITION," SAID CORTINGOS, ... 232

"THE FRENCH CAVALRY RODE UP TOWARDS THE SQUARES, BUT WERE MET WITH HEAVY VOLLEYS," 268

"MACWITTY WAS STANDING COVERING THE TWO BOATMEN WITH HIS PISTOLS," 310

TERENCE BIDS GOOD-BYE TO HIS COUSIN, MARY O'CONNOR, . 350

"WHO ARE YOU, SIR, AND WHAT TROOPS ARE THESE?" SIR ARTHUR ASKED, SHARPLY, ... 368

WITH MOORE AT CORUNNA

CHAPTER I

THE MAYO FUSILIERS

HAT am I to do with you, Terence? It bothers me entirely; there is not a soul who will take you, and if anyone would do so, you would wear out his patience before a week's end; there is not a dog in the regiment that does not put his tail between his legs and run for his bare life if he sees you; and as for the colonel, he told me only the other day that he had so many complaints against you, that he was fairly worn out with them."

"That was only his way, father; the colonel likes a joke as well as any of them."

"Yes, when it is not played on himself; but you haven't even the sense to respect persons, and it is well for you that he could not prove that it was you who fastened the sparrow to the plume of feathers on his shako the other day, and no one noticed it till the little baste began to flutter just as he came on to parade, and nigh choked us all with trying to hold in our laughter, while the colonel was nearly suffocated with passion. It was lucky you were able to prove that you had gone off at daylight fishing, and that no one had seen you anywhere near his quarters. By my faith, if he could have proved it was you he would have had you turned out of the barrack gate, and word given to the sentries that you were not to be allowed to pass in again."

"I could have got over the wall, father," the boy said, calmly; "but mind, I never said that it was I who fastened the sparrow in his shako."

"Because I never asked you, Terence; but it does not need the asking. What I am to do with you I don't know. Your Uncle Tim would not take you if I were to go down upon my knees to him. You were always in his bad books, and you finished it when you fired off that blunderbuss in his garden as he was passing along in the twilight, and yelled out 'Death to the Protestants!'"

The boy burst into a fit of laughter. "How could I tell that he was going to fall flat upon the ground and shout a million murders, when I fired straight into the air?"

"Well, you did for yourself there, Terence. Not that the old man would ever have taken to you, for he never forgave my marriage with his niece; still, he might have left you some money some day, seeing that there is no one nearer to him, and it would have come in mighty useful, for you are not likely to get much from me. But we are no nearer the point yet. What am I to do with you at all? Here is the regiment ordered on foreign service and likely to have sharp work, and not a place where I can stow you. It beats me altogether!"

"Why not take me with you, father?"

"I have thought of that, but you are too young entirely."

"I am nearly sixteen, father. I am sure I am as tall as

many boys of seventeen, and as strong too. Why should I not go? I am certain I could stand roughing it as well as Dick Ryan, who is a good bit over sixteen. Could I not go as a volunteer? Or I might enlist; the doctor would pass me quick enough."

"O'Flaherty would pass you if you were a baby in arms; he is as full of mischief as you are, and has not much more discretion; but you could not carry a musket, full cartridge-box, and kit for a long day's march."

"I can carry a gun through a long day's shooting, dad; but you might make me your soldier servant."

"Bedad, I should fare mighty badly, Terence; still as I don't see anything else for you, I must try and take you somehow, even if you have to go as a drummer. I will talk it over with the colonel, though I doubt whether he has forgotten that sparrow yet."

"He would not bear malice, dad, even if he were sure that it was me—which he cannot be."

The speaker was Captain O'Connor of his Majesty's regiment of Mayo Fusiliers, now under orders to proceed to Portugal to form part of the force that was being despatched under Sir Arthur Wellesley to assist the Portuguese in resisting the advance of the French. He was a widower, and Terence was his only child. The boy had been brought up in the regiment. His mother had died when he was nine years old, and Terence had been allowed by his father to run pretty nearly wild. He picked up a certain amount of education, for he was as sharp at lessons as at most other things. His mother had taught him to read and write, and the officers and their wives were always ready to lend him books; and as, during the hours when drill and exercise were going on, he had plenty of time to himself, he had got through a very large amount of desultory reading, and, having a retentive memory, knew quite as much as most lads of his age, although the knowledge was of a much more irregular kind.

He was a general favourite among the officers and men of the regiment, though his tricks got him into frequent scrapes, and more than one prophesied that his eventual fate was likely to be hanging. He was great at making acquaintances among the country people, and knew the exact spot where the best fishing could be had for miles round; he had also been given leave to shoot on many of the estates in the neighbourhood.

His father had, from the first, absolutely forbidden him to associate with the drummer boys.

"I don't mind your going into the men's quarters," he said, "you will come to no harm there, but among the boys you might get into bad habits; some of them are thorough young scamps. With the men you would always be one of their officers' sons, while with the boys you would soon become a mere playmate."

As he grew older, Terence, being a son of one of the senior officers, became a companion of the ensigns, and one or other of them generally accompanied him on his fishing excursions, and were not unfrequently participators in his escapades, several of which were directed against the tranquillity of the inhabitants of Athlone. One night the bells of the three churches had been rung simultaneously and violently, and the idea that either the town was in flames, or that the French had landed, or that the whole country was up in arms, brought all the inhabitants to their doors in a state of violent excitement and scanty attire. No clew was ever obtained as to the author of this outrage, nor was anyone able to discover the origin of the rumour that circulated through the town, that a large amount of gunpowder had been stored in some house or other in the market-place, and that on a certain night half the town would be blown into the air.

So circumstantial were the details that a deputation waited on Colonel Corcoran, and a strong search-party was sent down to examine the cellars of all the houses in the market-place and for some distance round. These and some similar occurrences had much alarmed the good people of Athlone, and it was certain that more than one person must have been concerned in them.

"I have come, Colonel," Captain O'Connor said, when he called upon his commanding officer, "to speak to you about Terence."

The colonel smiled grimly. "It is a comfort to think that we are going to get rid of him, O'Connor; he is enough to demoralize a whole brigade, to say nothing of a battalion, and the worst of it is he respects no one. I am as convinced as can be that it was he who fastened that baste of a bird in my shako the other day, and made me the laughing stock of the whole regiment on parade. Faith, I could not for the life of me make out what was the matter, there was a tugging and a jumping and a fluttering overhead, and I thought the shako was going to fly away. It fairly gave me a scare, for I thought the shako had gone mad, and that the divil was in it. I have often overlooked his tricks for your sake, but when it comes to his commanding officer, it is too serious altogether."

"Well, you see, Colonel, the lad proved clearly enough that he was out of the way at the time; and besides, you know he has given you many a hearty laugh."

"He has that," the colonel admitted.

"And, moreover," Captain O'Connor went on, "even if he did do this, which I don't know, for I never asked him" ("Trust you for that," the colonel muttered), "you are not his commanding officer, though you are mine, and that is the matter that I came to speak to you about. You see there is no one in whose charge I can leave him, and the lad wants to go with us; he would enlist as a drummer, if he could go no other way, and when he got out there I should get the adjutant to tell him off as my soldier servant."

"It would not do, O'Connor," the colonel laughed.

"Then I thought, Colonel, that possibly he might go as a volunteer—most regiments take out one or two young fellows, who have not interest enough to obtain a commission."

"He is too young, O'Connor; besides, the boy is enough to corrupt a whole regiment; he has made half the lads as wild as he is himself. Sure you can never be after asking me to saddle the regiment with him, now that there is a good chance of getting quit of him altogether."

"I think that he would not be so bad when we are out there, Colonel; it is just because he has nothing to do that he gets into mischief. With plenty of hard work and other things to think of I don't believe that he would be any trouble."

"Do you think that you can answer for him, O'Connor?"

"Indeed and I cannot," the captain laughed; "but I will answer for it that he will not joke with you, Colonel. The lad is really steady enough, and I am sure that if he were in the regiment he would not dream of playing tricks with his commanding officer, whatever else he might do."

"That goes a long way towards removing my objection," the colonel said, with a twinkle in his eye; "but he is too young for a volunteer—a volunteer is the sort of man to be the first to climb a breach, or to risk his life in some desperate enterprise, so as to win a commission. But there is another way. I had a letter yesterday from the Horse Guards, saying that as I am two ensigns short, they had appointed one who will join us at Cork, and that they gave me the right of nominating another. I own that Terence occurred to me, but sixteen is the youngest limit of age, and he must be certified and all that by the doctor. Now Daly is away on leave, and is to join us at Cork; but O'Flaherty would do; still, I don't know how he would get over the difficulty about the age."

"Trust him for that. I am indeed obliged to you, Colonel."

"Don't say anything about it, O'Connor; if we had been going to stay at home I don't think that I could have brought myself to take him into the regiment, but as we are going on service he won't have much opportunity for mischief, and even if he does let out a little—not at my expense, you know—a laugh does the men good when they are wet through and their stomachs are empty." He rang a bell. "Orderly, tell the adjutant and Doctor O'Flaherty that I wish to see them. Mr. Cleary," he went on, as soon as the former entered, "I have been requested by the Horse Guards to nominate an ensign, so as to fill up our ranks before starting, and I have determined to give the appointment to Terence O'Connor."

"Very well, sir, I am glad to hear it; he is a favourite with us all, but I am afraid that he is under age."

"Is there any regular form to be filled up?"

"None that I know of in the case of officers, sir. I fancy they pass some sort of medical examination at the Horse Guards, but, of course, in this case it would be impossible. Still, I should say that, in writing to state that you have nominated him, it would be better to send a medical certificate, and certainly it ought to be mentioned that he is of the right age."

At this moment the assistant-surgeon entered.

"Doctor O'Flaherty," the colonel said, "I wish you to write a certificate to the effect that Terence O'Connor is physically fit to take part in a campaign as an officer."

"I can do that, Colonel, without difficulty; he is as fit as a fiddle, and can march half the regiment off their legs."

"Yes, I know that, but there is one difficulty, Doctor, he is under the regulation age."

O'Flaherty thought for a moment and then sat down at the table, and taking a sheet of paper, be began:

I certify that Terence O'Connor is going on for seventeen years of age, he is five feet eight in height, thirty-four inches round the chest, is active, and fully capable of the performance of his duties as an officer either at home or abroad.

Then he added another line and signed his name.

"As a member of a learned profession, Colonel," he said, gravely, "I would scorn to tell a lie even for the son of Captain O'Connor;" and he passed the paper across to him.

The colonel looked grave, and Captain O'Connor disappointed. He was reassured, however, when his commanding officer broke into a laugh.

"That will do well, O'Flaherty," he said; "I thought that you would find some way of getting us out of the difficulty."

"I have told the strict truth, Colonel," the doctor said, gravely. "I have certified that Terence O'Connor is going on for seventeen; I defy any man to say that he is not. He will get there one of these days, if a French bullet does not stop him on the way, a contingency that it is needless for me to mention."

"I suppose that it is not strictly regular to omit the date of his birth," the colonel said; "but just at present I expect they are not very particular. I suppose that that will do, Mr. Cleary?"

"I think that you can countersign that, Colonel," the adjutant said, with a laugh. "The Horse Guards do not move very rapidly, and by the time that letter gets to London we may be on board ship, and they would hardly bother to send a letter for further particulars to us in Spain, but will no doubt gazette him at once. The fact, too—which of course you will mention—that he is the son of the senior captain of your regiment, will in itself render them less likely to bother about the matter."

"Well, just write out the letter of nomination, Cleary; I am a mighty bad hand at doing things neatly."

The adjutant drew a sheet of foolscap to him and wrote:—

To the Adjutant-general, Horse Guards,
 Sir, I have the honour to inform you that, in accordance with the privilege granted to me in your communication of—

and he looked at the colonel.

"The 14th inst.," the latter said, after consulting the letter.

—I beg to nominate as an ensign in this regiment, Terence O'Connor, the son of Captain Lawrence O'Connor, its senior captain. I inclose certificate of Assistant-surgeon O'Flaherty, —the surgeon being at present absent on leave—certifying to his physical fitness for a commission in his Majesty's service. Mr. O'Connor having been brought up from childhood in the regiment is already perfectly acquainted with the work, and will therefore be able to take up his duties without difficulty. This fact has had some influence in my choice, as a young officer who had to be taught all his duties would have been of no use for service in the field for a considerable time after landing in Portugal.
 Relying on the nomination being approved by the commander-

in-chief, I shall at once put him on the staff of the regiment for foreign service, as there will be no time to wait your reply.

I have the honour to be

Your humble, obedient servant,

Then he left a space, and added:

Colonel Mayo Fusiliers.

"Now, if you will sign it, Colonel, the matter will be complete, and I will send it off with O'Flaherty's certificate to-day."

"That is a good stroke, Cleary," the colonel said, as he read it aloud. "They will see that it is too late to raise any questions, and the 'going on for seventeen' will be accepted as sufficient."

He touched a bell.

"Orderly, tell Mr. Terence O'Connor that I wish to see him."

Terence was sitting in a state of suppressed excitement at his father's quarters. He had a strong belief that the matter would be managed somehow, for he knew that the colonel had no malice in his disposition, and would not let the episode of the bird—for which he was now heartily sorry—stand in the way. On receiving the message he at once went across to the colonel's quarters. The latter rose and held out his hand to him as he entered.

"Terence O'Connor," he said, "I am pleased to be able to inform you that from the present moment you are to consider yourself an officer in his Majesty's Mayo Fusiliers. The Horse Guards have given me the privilege of nominating a gentleman to the vacant ensigncy, and I have had great pleasure in nominating your father's son. Now, lad," he said, in a different tone of voice, "I feel sure that you will do credit to my nomination, and that you will keep your love of fun and mischief within reasonable bounds."

"I will try to do so, Colonel," the lad said, in a low voice, "and I am grateful indeed for the kindness that you have shown me. I have always hoped that some day I might obtain a commission in your regiment, but never even hoped that it would be until after I had done something to deserve it. Indeed I did not think that it was even possible that I could obtain a commission until——"

"Tut, tut, lad, don't say a word about age! Doctor O'Flaherty had certified that you are going on for seventeen, which is quite sufficient for me, and at any rate you will see that boyish tricks are out of place in the case of an officer going on for seventeen. Now, your father had best take you down into the town and get you measured for your uniforms at once. You must make them hurry on with his undress clothes, O'Connor. I should not bother about full-dress till we get back again; it is not likely to be wanted, and the lad will soon grow out of them. If there should happen to be full-dress parade in Portugal, Cleary will put him on as officer of the day, or give him some duties that will keep him from parade. We may get the route any day, and the sooner he gets his uniform the better."

Two days later Terence took his place on parade as an officer of the regiment. He had witnessed such numberless drills that he had picked up every word of command, knew his proper place in every formation, and fell into the work as readily as if he had been at it for years. He had been heartily congratulated by the officers of the regiment.

"I am awfully glad that you are one of us, Terence," Dick Ryan said. "I don't know what we should have done without you. I expect we shall have tremendous fun in Portugal."

"I expect we shall, Dick; but we shall have to be careful. We shall be on active service, you see, and from what they say of him I don't think Sir Arthur Wellesley is the sort of man to appreciate jokes."

"No, I should say not. Of course, we shall have to draw in a bit. It would not do to set the bells of Lisbon ringing."

"I should think not, Dick. Still, I dare say we shall have plenty of fun, and at any rate we are likely, from what they say, to have plenty of fighting. I don't expect the Portuguese will be much good, and as there are forty or fifty thousand Frenchmen in Portugal, we shall have all our work to do, unless they send out a much bigger force than is collecting at Cork. It is a pity that the 10,000 men who have been sent out to Sweden on what my father says is a fool's errand are not going with us instead. We might make a good stand-up fight of it then, whereas I don't see that with only 6,000 or 7,000 we can do much good against Junot's 40,000."

"Oh, I dare say we shall get on somehow!" Dick said, carelessly. "Sir Arthur knows what he is about, and it is our turn to do something now. The navy has had it all its own way so far, and it is quite fair that we should do our share. I have a brother in the navy, and the fellows are getting too cheeky altogether. They seem to think that no one can fight but themselves. Except in Egypt we have never had a chance at all of showing we can lick the French just as easily on land as we can at sea."

"I hope we shall, Dick. They have certainly had a great deal more practice at it than we have."

"Now I think we ought to do something here that they will remember us for before we start, Terence."

"Well, if you do, I am not with you this time, Dick. I am not going to begin by getting in the colonel's bad books after he has been kind enough to nominate me for a commission. I promised him that I would try and not get into any scrapes, and I am not going to break my word. When we once get out there I shall be game to join in anything that is not likely to make a great row, but I have done with it for the present."

"I should like to have one more good bit of fun," Ryan said; "but I expect you are right, Terence, in what you say about yourself, and it is no use our thinking to humbug Athlone again if you are not in it with us; besides, they are getting too sharp. They did not half turn out last time, and, indeed, we had a narrow escape of being caught. Well, I shall be very glad when we are off; it is stupid work waiting for the route, with all leave stopped, and we not even allowed to go out for a day's fishing."

Three days later the expected order arrived. As the baggage had all been packed up, that which was to be left behind being handed over to the care of the barrack-master, and a considerable portion of the heavy baggage sent on by cart, there was no delay. Officers and men were alike delighted that the period of waiting had come to an end, and there was loud cheering in the barrack-yard as soon as the news came. At daybreak next morning the rest of the baggage started under a guard, and three hours later the Mayo Fusiliers marched through the town with their band playing at their head, and amid the cheers of the populace.

As yet the martial spirit that was roused by the struggle in the Peninsula had scarcely begun to show itself, but there was a strong animosity to France throughout England, and a desire to aid the people of Spain and Portugal in their efforts for freedom. In Ireland, for the most part, there was no such feeling. Since the battle of the Boyne and the siege of Limerick, France had been regarded by the greater portion of the peasantry, and a section of the population of the towns, as the natural ally of Ireland, and there was a hope that when Napoleon had all Europe prostrate under his feet he would come as the deliverer of Ireland from the English yoke. Consequently, although the townspeople of Athlone cheered the regiment as it marched away, the country people held aloof from it as it passed along the road. Scowling looks from the women greeted it in the villages, while the men ostentatiously continued their work in the fields without turning to cast a glance at them.

Terence was not posted to his father's company, but was in that of Captain O'Driscol, although the lad himself would have preferred to be with Captain O'Grady, with whom he was a great favourite. The latter was one of the captains whose companies were unprovided with an ensign, and he had asked the adjutant to let him have the lad instead of the ensign who was to join at Cork.

"The matter has been settled the other way, O'Grady; in the colonel's opinion he will be much better with O'Driscol, who is more likely to keep him in order than you are."

O'Grady was one of the most original characters in the regiment. He was rather under middle height, and had a smooth face, a guileless and innocent expression, and a habit of opening his light-blue eyes as in wonder. His hair was short, and stuck up aggressively; his brogue was the strongest in the regiment; his blunders were innumerable, and his look of amazement at the laughter they called forth was admirably feigned, save that the twinkle of his eye induced a suspicion that he himself enjoyed the joke as well as anyone. His good-humour was imperturbable, and he was immensely popular both among men and officers.

"O'Driscol!" he repeated, in mild astonishment. "Do you mean to say that O'Driscol will keep him in better order than meself? If there is one man in this regiment more than another who would get on well with the lad it is meself, barring none."

"You would get on well enough with him, O'Grady, I have no doubt, but it would be by letting him have his own way, and in encouraging him in mischief of all kinds."

O'Grady's eyebrows were elevated, and his eyes expressed hopeless bewilderment.

"You are wrong entirely, Cleary; nature intended me for a schoolmaster, and it is just an accident that I have taken to soldiering. I flatter meself that no one looks after his subalterns more sharply than I do. My only fear is that I am too severe with them. I may be mild in my manners, but they know me well enough to tremble if I speak sternly to them."

"The trembling would be with amusement," the adjutant grumbled. "Well, the colonel has settled the matter, and Terence will be in Orders to-morrow as appointed to O'Driscol's company, and the other to yours."

"Thank you for nothing, Cleary," O'Grady said, with dignity. "You would have seen that under my tuition the lad would have turned out one of the smartest officers in the regiment."

"You have heard of the Spartan way of teaching their sons to avoid drunkenness, Captain O'Grady?"

"Divil a word, Cleary; but I reckon that the best way with the haythens was to keep them from touching whisky. It is what I always recommend to the men of my company when I come across one of them the worse for liquor."

The adjutant laughed. "That was not the Spartan way, O'Grady; but the advice, if taken, would doubtless have the same effect."

"And who were the Spartans at all?"

"I have not time to tell you now, O'Grady; I have no end of business on my hands."

"Thin what do you keep me talking here for? haven't I a lot of work on me hands too. I came in to ask a simple question, and instead of giving me a civil answer you kape me wasting my time wid your O'Driscols and your Spartans and all kinds of rigmarole. That is the worst of being in an Irish regiment, nothing can be done widout ever so much blather;" and Captain O'Grady stalked out of the orderly-room.

On the march Terence had no difficulty in obtaining leave from his captain to drop behind and march with his friend Dick Ryan. The marches were long ones, and they halted only at Parsonstown, Templemore, Tipperary, and Fermoy, as the colonel had received orders to use all speed. At each place a portion of the regiment was accommodated in the barracks, while the rest were quartered in the town. Late in the evening of the fifth day's march they arrived at Cork, and the next day went on board the two transports provided for them, and joined the fleet assembled in the Cove. Some of the ships had been lying there for nearly a month waiting orders, and the troops on board were heartily weary of their confinement. The news, however, that Sir Arthur Wellesley had been at last appointed to command them, and that they were to sail for Portugal, had caused great delight, for it had been feared that they might, like other bodies of troops, be shipped off to some distant spot, only to remain there for months and then to be brought home again.

Nothing, indeed, could exceed the vacillation and confusion that reigned in the English cabinet at that time. The forces of England were frittered away in small and objectless expeditions, the plans of action were changed with every report sent either by the interested leaders of insurrectionary movements in Spain, or by the signally incompetent men who had been sent out to represent England, and who distributed broadcast British money and British arms to the most unworthy applicants. By their lavishness and subservience to the Spaniards our representatives increased the natural arrogance of these people, and caused them to regard England as a power which was honoured by being permitted to share in the Spanish efforts against the French generals. General Spencer with 5,000 men was kept for months sailing up and down the coast of Spain and Portugal, receiving contradictory orders from home, and endeavouring in vain to co-operate with the Spanish generals, each of whom had his own private purposes, and was bent on gratifying personal ambitions and of thwarting the schemes of his rivals, rather than on opposing the common enemy.

Not only were the English ministry incapable of devising any plan of action, but they were constantly changing the naval and military officers of the forces. At one moment one general or admiral seemed to possess their confidence, while soon afterwards, without the slightest reason, two or three others with greater political influence were placed over his head ; and when at last Sir Arthur Wellesley, whose services in India marked him as our greatest soldier, was sent out with supreme military power, they gave him no definite plan of action. General Spencer was nominally placed under his orders by one set of instructions, while another authorized him to commence operations in the south, without reference to Sir Arthur Wellesley. Admiral Purvis, who was junior to Admiral Collingwood, was authorized to control the operations of Sir Arthur, while Wellesley himself had scarcely sailed when Sir Hew Dalrymple was appointed to the chief command of the forces, Sir Harry Burrard was appointed second in command, and Sir Arthur Wellesley was reduced to the fourth rank in the army that he had been sent out to command, two of the men placed above him being almost unknown, they never having commanded any military force in the field.

The 9,000 men assembled in the Cove of Cork knew nothing of these things; they were going out under the command of the victor of Assaye to measure their strength against that of the French, and they had no fear of the result.

"I hope," Captain O'Grady said, as the officers of the wing of the regiment to which he belonged sat down to dinner for the first time on board the transport, "that we shall not have to keep together in going out."

"Why so, O'Grady?" another captain asked.

"Because there is no doubt at all that our ship is the fastest in the fleet, and that we shall get there in time to have a little brush with the French all to ourselves before the others arrive."

"What makes you think that she is the fastest ship here, O'Grady?"

"Anyone can see it with half an eye, O'Driscol. Look at her lines; she is a flyer, and if we are not obliged to keep with the others we shall be out of sight of the rest of them before we have sailed six hours."

"I don't pretend to know anything about her lines, O'Grady, but she looks to me a regular old tub."

"She is old," O'Grady admitted, reluctantly, "but give her plenty of wind and you will see how she can walk along."

There was a laugh all round the table; O'Grady's absolute confidence in anything in which he was interested was known to them all. His horse had been notoriously the most worthless animal in the regiment, but although continually last in the hunting field, O'Grady's opinion of her speed was never shaken. There was always an excuse ready; the horse had been badly shod, or it was out of sorts and had not had its feed before starting, or the going was heavy and it did not like heavy ground, or the country was too hilly or too flat for it. It was the same with his company, with his non-commissioned officers, with his soldier servant, a notoriously drunken rascal, and with his quarters.

O'Grady looked round in mild expostulation at the laugh.

"You will see," he said, confidently, "there can be no mistake about it."

Two days later a ship-of-war entered the harbour, the usual salutes were exchanged, then a signal was run up to one of her mast-heads, and again the guns of the forts pealed out a salute, and word ran through the transports that Sir Arthur Wellesley was on board. On the following day the fleet got under way, the transports being escorted by a line-of-battle ship and four frigates, which were to join Lord Collingwood's squadron as soon as they had seen their charge safe into the Tagus.

Before evening the *Sea-horse* was a mile astern of the rearmost ship of the convoy, and one of the frigates sailing back fired a gun as a signal to her to close up.

"Well, O'Grady, we have left the fleet, you see, though not in the way you predicted."

"Whist, man! don't you see that the captain is out of temper because they have all got to keep together, instead of letting him go ahead?"

Every rag of sail was now piled on to the ship, and as many of the others were showing nothing above their topgallant sails she rejoined the rest just as darkness fell.

"There, you see!" O'Grady said, triumphantly, "look what she can do when she likes."

"We do see, O'Grady. With twice as much sail up as anything else, she has in three hours picked up the mile she had lost."

"Wait until we get some wind."

"I hope we sha'n't get anything of the sort—at least no strong winds; the old tub would open every seam if we did, and we might think ourselves lucky if we got through it at all."

O'Grady smiled pleasantly, and said it was useless to argue with so obstinate a man.

"I am afraid O'Grady is wrong as usual," Dick Ryan said to Terence, who was sitting next to him. "When once he has taken an idea into his head nothing will persuade him that he is wrong; there is no doubt the *Sea-horse* is as slow as she can be. I suppose her owners have some interest with the government, or they would surely never have taken up such an old tub as a troop-ship."

CHAPTER II

TWO DANGERS

THE next day, in spite of the sail she carried, the *Sea-horse* lagged behind, and one of the frigates sailed back to her, and the captain shouted angry orders to the master to keep his place in the convoy.

"If we get any wind," O'Grady said, as the frigate bore up on her course again, "it will take all your time to keep up with her, my fine fellow. You see," he explained to Terence, "no vessel is perfect in all points; some like a good deal of wind, some are best in a calm. Now this ship wants wind."

"I think she does, Captain O'Grady," Terence replied, gravely. "At any rate her strong point is not sailing in a light wind."

"No," O'Grady admitted, regretfully; "but it is not the

ship's fault. I have no doubt at all that her bottom is foul, and that she has a lot of barnacles and weeds twice as long as your body. That is the reason why she is a little sluggish."

"That may be it," Terence agreed; "but I should have thought that they would have seen to that before they sent her to Cork."

"It is like enough that her owners are well-wishers of Napoleon, Terence, and that it is out of spite that they have done it. There is no doubt that she is a wonderful craft."

"I am quite inclined to agree with you, Captain O'Grady, for as I have never seen a ship except when the regiment came back from India ten years ago, I am no judge of one."

"It is the eye, Terence. I can't say that I have been much at sea myself, except on that voyage out and home; but I have an eye for ships, and can see their good points at a glance. You can take it from me that she is a wonderful vessel."

"She would look all the better if her sails were a bit cleaner, and not so patched," Terence said, looking up.

"She might look better to the eye, lad, but no doubt the owners know what they are doing, and consider that she goes better with sails that fit her than she would with new ones."

Terence burst into a roar of laughter. O'Grady, as usual, looked at him in mild surprise.

"What are you laughing at, you young spalpeen?"

"I am thinking, Captain O'Grady," the lad said, recovering himself, "that it is a great pity you could not have obtained the situation of Devil's Advocate. I have read that years ago someone was appointed to defend Old Nick when the others were pitching into him, and to show that he was not as black as he was painted, but was a respectable gentleman who had been maligned by the world."

"No doubt there is a good deal to be said for him," O'Grady said, seriously. "Give a dog a bad name, you know, and you may hang him; and I have no doubt the Old One has been held responsible for lots of things he never had as much as the tip of his finger in at all, at all."

Seeing that his captain was about to pursue the matter much further, Terence, making the excuse that it was time he went down to see if the men's breakfast was all right, slipped off, and he and Dick Ryan had a hearty laugh over O'Grady's peculiarities.

"I think, O'Grady," Captain O'Driscol said, two days later, "we are going to have our opportunity, for unless I am mistaken there is going to be a change of weather. Those clouds banking up ahead look like a gale from the southwest."

Before night the wind was blowing furiously, and the *Seahorse* taking green sea over her bows and wallowing gunwale under in the waves. At daylight, when they went on deck, gray masses of cloud were hurrying overhead and an angry sea alone met the eye. Not a sail was in sight, and the whole convoy had vanished.

"We are out of sight of the fleet, O'Grady," Captain O'Driscol said, grimly.

"I felt sure we should be," O'Grady said, triumphantly. "Sorra one of them could keep foot with us."

"They are ahead of us, man," O'Driscol said, angrily; "miles and miles ahead."

"Ahead, is it? You must know better, O'Driscol; though it is little enough you know of ships. You see we are close-hauled, and there is no doubt that that is the vessel's strong point. Why, we have dropped the rest of them like hot potatoes, and if this little breeze keeps on, maybe we shall be in the Tagus days and days before them."

O'Driscol was too exasperated to argue.

"O'Driscol is a good fellow," O'Grady said, turning to

Terence, "but it is a misfortune that he is so prejudiced. Now, what is your own opinion?"

"I have no opinion about it, Captain O'Grady. I have a very strong opinion that I am not going to enjoy my breakfast, and that this motion does not agree with me at all. I have been ill half the night. Dick Ryan is awfully bad, and by the sounds I heard I should say a good many of the others are the same way. On the main deck it is awful; they have got the hatches battened down. I just took a peep in and bolted, for it seemed to me that everyone was ill."

"The best plan, lad, is to make up your mind that you are quite well. If you once do that you will be all right directly."

Terence could not for the moment reply, having made a sudden rush to the side.

"I don't see how I can persuade myself that I am quite well," he said, when he returned, "when I feel terribly ill."

"Yes, it wants resolution, Terence, and I am afraid that you are deficient in that. It must not be half-and-half. You have got to say to yourself, 'This is glorious; I never enjoyed myself so well in my life,' and when you have said that and feel that it is quite true, the whole thing will be over."

"I don't doubt it in the least," Terence said; "but I can't say it without telling a prodigious lie, and worse still, I could not believe the lie when I had told it."

"Then I am afraid that you must submit to be ill, Terence. I know once that I had a drame, and the drame was that I was at sea and horribly sea-sick, and I woke up and said to myself, 'This is all nonsense, I am as well as ever I was;' and, faith, so I was."

Ill as Terence was, he burst into a fit of laughter.

"That was just a dream, Captain O'Grady; but mine is a

reality, you know. I don't think that you are looking quite well yourself."

"I am perfectly well as far as the sea goes, Terence; never was better in my life; but that pork we had for dinner yesterday was worse than usual, and I think perhaps I ought to have taken another glass or two to correct it."

"It must have been the pork," Terence said, as seriously as O'Grady himself; "and it is unfortunate that you are such an abstemious man, or, as you say, its effects might have been corrected."

"It's me opinion, Terence, my boy, that you are a humbug."

"Then, Captain O'Grady, it is clear that evil communications must have corrupted my good manners."

"It must have been in your infancy then, Terence, for divil a bit of manners good or bad have I ever seen in you; you have not even the good manners to take a glass of the cratur when you are asked."

"That is true enough," Terence laughed. "Having been brought up in the regiment, I have learned, at least, that the best thing to do with whisky is to leave it alone."

"I am afraid you will never be a credit to us, Terence."

"Not in the way of being able to make a heavy night of it and then turn out as fresh as paint in the morning," Terence retorted; "but you see, Captain O'Grady, even my abstinence has its advantages, for at least there will always be one officer in the corps able to go the round of the sentries at night."

At this moment the vessel gave such a heavy lurch that they were both thrown off their feet and rolled into the lee-scuppers, while, at the same moment, a rush of water swept over them. Amidst shouts of laughter from the other officers the two scrambled to their feet.

"Holy Moses!" O'Grady exclaimed, "I am drowned en-

TWO FRENCH PRIVATEERS BEAR DOWN UPON THE SEA-HORSE.

tirely, and I sha'n't get the taste of the salt water out of me mouth for a week."

"There is one comfort," Terence said; "it might have been worse."

"How could it have been worse?" O'Grady asked, angrily.

"Why, if we hadn't been in the steadiest ship in the whole fleet we might have been washed overboard."

There was another shout of laughter. O'Grady made a dash at Terence, but the latter easily avoided him and went down below to change his clothes.

The gale increased in strength, and the whole vessel strained so heavily that her seams began to open, and by one o'clock the captain requested Major Harrison, who was in command, to put some of the soldiers at the pumps. For three days and nights relays of men kept the pumps going. Had it not been for the 400 troops on board, the *Sea-horse* would long before have gone to the bottom; but with such powerful aid the water was kept under, and on the morning of the fourth day the storm began to abate, and by evening more canvas was got on her. The next morning two vessels were seen astern at a distance of four or five miles. After examining them through his glass, the captain sent down a message to Major Harrison asking him to come up. In three or four minutes that officer appeared.

"There are two strange craft over there, Major; from their appearance I have not the least doubt that they are French privateers. I thought I should like your advice as to what had best be done."

"I don't know. You see, your guns might just as well be thrown overboard for any good they would be," the major said. "The things would not be safe to fire a salute with blank cartridge."

"No, they can hardly be called serviceable," the master

agreed. "I spoke to the owner about it, but he said that as we were going to sail with a convoy it did not matter, and that we should have some others for the next voyage."

"I should like to see your owner dangling from the yard-arm," the major said, wrathfully. "However, just at present the question is what had best be done. Of course they could not take the ship from us, but they would have very little difficulty in sinking her."

"The first thing is to put on every stitch of sail."

"That would avail us nothing; they can sail two feet to our one."

"Quite so, Major; I should not hope to get away, but they would think that I was trying to do so. My idea is that we should press on as fast as we can till they open fire at us; we could hold on for a bit, and then haul up into the wind and lower our top-sails, which they will take for a proof of surrender."

"You won't strike the flag, Captain; we cannot do anything treacherous."

"No, no, I am not thinking of doing that. You see, the flag is not hoisted yet, and we won't hoist it at all till they get close alongside, then we can haul it up, and sweep their decks with musketry. Of course your men will keep below until the last moment."

"That plan will do very well," the major agreed, "that is, if they venture to come boldly alongside."

"One is pretty sure to do so, though the other may lay herself ahead or astern of us, with her guns pointed to rake us in case we make any resistance; but seeing what we are, and that we carry only four small guns each side, they are hardly likely to suspect anything wrong. I am not at all afraid of beating them off; my only fear is that after they have sheared away they will open upon us from a distance."

"Yes, that would be awkward. However, if they do, we must keep the men below, and in the meantime you had better get your carpenter to cut up some spars and make a lot of plugs in readiness to stop up any holes they make near the water-line. I don't think they are likely to make very ragged holes, the wood is so rotten the shot would go through the side as if it were brown paper; still, you might get a lot of squares of canvas ready, with hammers and nails."

The strange craft were already heading towards the *Seahorse*. No time was lost in setting every stitch of canvas that she could carry; the wind was light now, but the vessel was rolling heavily in a long swell. The major examined the guns closely and found that they were even worse than he had anticipated, the rust holes eaten in the iron having been filled up with putty, and the whole painted. He was turning away, with an exclamation of disgust, when Terence, who was standing near, said to him:

"I beg your pardon, Major, but don't you think that if we were to wind some thin rope very tightly round them three or four inches thick, they might stand a charge or two of grape to give them at close quarters; we needn't put in a very heavy charge of powder. Even if they did burst, I should think that the rope would prevent the splinters from flying about."

"The idea is not a bad one at all, Terence. I will see if the captain has got a coil or two of thin rope on board."

Fortunately the ship was fairly well supplied in this respect, and a few of the sailors who were accustomed to serving rope, with a dozen soldiers to help them, were told off to the work. The rope was wound round as tightly as the strength of a dozen men could pull it, the process being repeated five or six times, until each gun was surrounded by as many layers of rope. A thin rod had been inserted in the touch-hole. The cannon was then loaded with half the usual charge of powder, and filled to the muzzle with bullets. The rod was then drawn out, and powder poured in until it reached the surface.

While this was being done, all the soldiers not engaged in the work went below, and the officers sat down under shelter of the bulwarks. The two privateers, a large lugger and a brig, had been coming up rapidly, and by the time the guns were ready for action they were but a mile away. Presently a puff of smoke burst out from the bows of the lugger, and a round shot struck the water a short distance ahead of the *Seahorse*. She held on her course without taking any notice of it, and for a few minutes the privateer was silent; then, when they were but half a mile away the brig opened fire, and two or three shots hulled the vessel.

"That will do, Captain," the major said. "You may as well lay-to now."

The *Sea-horse* rapidly flew up into the wind, the sheets were thrown off, and the upper sails were lowered, one after the other, the job being executed slowly, as if by a weak crew. The two privateers, which had been sailing within a short distance of each other, now exchanged signals, and the lugger ran on, straight towards the *Sea-horse*, while the brig took a course which would lay her across the stern of the barque, and enable them to rake her with her broadside. Word was passed below, and the soldiers poured up on deck, stooping as they reached it, and taking their places under the bulwarks. The major had already asked for volunteers among the officers, to fire the guns. All had at once offered to do so.

"As it was your proposal, Terence," the major said, "you shall have the honour of firing one; Ryan, you take another; Lieutenant Marks and Mr. Haines, you take the other two, and then England and Ireland will be equally represented."

The deck of the lugger was crowded with men, and the

course she was steering brought her within a length of the *Sea-horse*. Some of the men were preparing to lower her boats, when suddenly a thick line of red coats appeared above the bulwarks, two hundred muskets poured in their fire, while the contents of the four guns swept her deck. The effect of the fire was tremendous. The deck was in a moment covered with dead and dying men; half a minute later another volley, fired by the remaining companies, completed the work of destruction. The halliards of one of the lugger's sails had been cut by the grape, and the sail now came down with a run to the deck.

"Down below, all of you," the major shouted, "the fellow behind will rake us in a minute."

The soldiers ran down to the hold again. A minute later the brig, sailing across the stern, poured in the fire of her guns one by one. Standing much lower in the water than her opponent, none of her shot traversed the deck of the *Sea-horse*, but they carried destruction among the cabins and fittings of the deck below. As this, however, was entirely deserted, no one was injured by the shot or flying fragments. The brig then took up her position three or four hundred yards away, on the quarter of the *Sea-horse*, and opened a steady fire against her.

To this the barque could make no reply, the fire of the muskets being wholly ineffective at that distance. The lugger lay helpless alongside the *Sea-horse*; the survivors of her crew had run below, and dared not return on deck to work their guns, as they would have been swept by the musketry of the *Sea-horse*.

Half an hour later Terence was ordered to go below to see how they were getting on in the hold.

Terence did so. Some lanterns had been lighted there, and he found that four men had been killed and a dozen or so wounded by the enemy's shot, the greater portion of which, however, had gone over their heads. The carpenter, assisted by some of the non-commissioned officers, was busy plugging holes that had been made in her between wind and water, and had fairly succeeded, as but four or five shots had struck so low, the enemy's object being not to sink, but to capture the vessel. As he passed up through the main deck to report, Terence saw that the destruction here was great indeed. The woodwork of the cabins had been knocked into fragments, there was a great gaping hole in the stern, and it seemed to him that before long the vessel would be knocked to pieces. He returned to the deck, and reported the state of things.

"It looks bad," the major said to O'Driscol. "This is but half an hour's work, and when the fellows come to the conclusion that they cannot make us strike, they will aim lower, and there will be nothing to do but to choose between sinking and hauling down our flag."

After delivering his report, Terence went to the side of the ship and looked down on the lugger. The attraction of the ship had drawn her closer to it, and she was but a few feet away. A thought struck him, and he went to O'Grady.

"Look here, O'Grady," he said, "that fellow will smash us up altogether if we don't do something."

"You must be a bright boy to see that, Terence; faith, I have been thinking so for the last ten minutes. But what are we to do? The muskets won't carry so far, at least not to do any good. The cannon are next to useless. Two of that lot you fired burst, though the ropes prevented any damage being done."

"Quite so, but there are plenty of guns alongside. Now, if you go to the major and volunteer to take your company and gain possession of the lugger, with one of the mates and half a dozen sailors to work her, we can get up the main-sail and engage the brig."

"By the powers, Terence, you are a broth of a boy," and he hurried away to the major.

"Major," he said, "if you will give me leave, I will have up my company and take possession of the lugger; we shall want one of the ship's officers and half a dozen men to work the sails, and then we will go out and give that brig pepper."

"It is a splendid idea, O'Grady."

"It is not my idea at all, at all; it is Terence O'Connor who suggested it to me. I suppose I can take the lad with me?"

"By all means, get your company up at once."

O'Grady hurried away, and in a minute the men of his company poured up onto the deck.

"You can come with me, Terence; I have the major's leave," he said to the lad.

At this moment there was a slight shock, as the lugger came in contact with the ship.

"Come on, lads," O'Grady said, as he set the example of clambering down onto the deck of the lugger. He was followed by his men, the first mate and six sailors also springing on board. The hatches were first put on to keep the remnant of the crew below. The sailors knotted the halliards of the main-sail, the soldiers tailed on to the rope, and the sail was rapidly run up. The mate put two of his men at the tiller, and the soldiers ran to the guns, which were already loaded.

"Haul that sheet to windward," the mate shouted, and the four sailors, aided by some of the soldiers, did so. Her head soon payed off, and amid a cheer from the officers on deck the lugger swept round. She mounted twelve guns. O'Grady divided the officers and non-commissioned officers among them, himself taking charge of a long pivot-gun in the bow.

"Take stiddy aim, boys, and fire as your guns bear on her; you ought not to throw away a shot at this distance."

As the lugger came out from behind the *Sea-horse*, gun after gun was fired, and the white splinters on the side of the brig showed that most, if not all, of the shots had taken effect. O'Grady's gun was the last to speak out, and the shot struck the brig just above the water-line.

"Take her round," he shouted to the mate; "give the boys on the other side a chance." The lugger put about and her starboard guns poured in their contents.

"That is the way," he shouted, as he laboured away with the men with him to load the pivot-gun again; "we will give him two or three more rounds, and then we will get alongside and ask for his health."

The brig, however, showed no inclination to await the attack. Some shots had been hastily fired when the lugger's first gun told them that she was now an enemy, and she at once put down her helm and made off before the wind, which was now very light.

"Load your guns and then out with the oars," Captain O'Grady shouted. "Be jabers, we will have that fellow. Let no man attend to the *Sea-horse;* it's from me that you are to take your orders. Besides," he said to Terence, "there is no signal-book on board, and they may hoist as many flags as they like."

The twelve sweeps on board the lugger were at once got out, and each manned by three soldiers. O'Grady himself continued to direct the fire of the pivot-gun, and sent shot after shot into the brig's stern. The latter had but some four hundred yards' start, and although she also hurriedly got out some sweeps, the lugger gained upon her. Her crew clustered on their taffrail, and kept up a musketry fire upon the party working the pivot-gun. Two of these had been killed and four wounded, when O'Grady said to the others:

"Lave the gun alone, boys; we shall be alongside of her in

a few minutes; it is no use throwing away lives by working it. Run all the guns over to the other side; we will give them a warming, and then go at her."

The *Sea-horse* had hoisted signals directly those on board perceived that the lugger was starting in pursuit of the brig. Terence had informed his commanding officer of this, but O'Grady replied:

"I know nothing about them, Terence; most likely they mane 'Good-luck to you! Chase the blackguard, and capture him.' Don't let Woods come near me, whatever you do; I don't want to hear his idea of what the signals may mane."

Terence had just time to stop the mate as he was coming forward.

"The ship is signalling," he said.

"I have told Captain O'Grady, sir," Terence replied. "He does not know what the signal means, but has no doubt that it is instructions to capture the brig, and he means to do so."

The officer laughed.

"I think myself that it would be a pity not to," he said; "we shall be alongside in ten minutes. But I think it my duty to tell you what the signal is."

"You can tell me what it is," Terence said, "and it is possible that in the heat of action I may forget to report it to Captain O'Grady."

"That is right enough, sir. I think it is the recall."

"Well, I will attend to it presently," Terence laughed.

When within a hundred yards of the brig the troops opened a heavy musketry fire, many of the men making their way up the ratlines and so commanding the brig's deck. They were answered with a brisk fire, but the French shooting was wild, and by the shouting of orders and the confusion that prevailed on board it was evident that the privateersmen were disorganized by the sight of the troops and the capture of their consort. The brig's guns were hastily fired, as they could be brought to bear on the lugger, as she forged alongside. The sweeps had already been got in, and the lugger's eight guns poured their contents simultaneously into the brig, then a withering volley was fired, and, headed by O'Grady, the soldiers sprang on board the brig.

As they did so, however, the French flag fluttered down from the peak, and the privateersmen threw down their arms. The English broadside and volley fired at close quarters had taken terrible effect. Of the crew of eighty men thirty were killed and a large proportion of the rest wounded. The soldiers gave three hearty cheers as the flag came down.

The privateersmen were at once ordered below.

"Lieutenant Hunter," O'Grady said, "do you go on board the lugger with the left wing of the company. Mr. Woods, I think you had better stay here, there are a good many more sails to manage than there are in the lugger. One man here will be enough to steer her; we will pull at the ropes for you. Put the others on board the lugger."

"By the by, Mr. Woods," he said, "I see that the ship has hoisted a signal; what does it mean?"

"I believe that to be the recall, sir; I told Mr. O'Connor."

"You ought to have reported that same to me," O'Grady said, severely; "however, we will obey it at once."

The *Sea-horse* was lying head to wind a mile and a half away, and the two prizes ran rapidly up to her. They were received with a tremendous cheer from the men closely packed along her bulwarks. O'Grady at once lowered a boat and was rowed to the *Sea-horse*, taking Terence with him.

"You have done extremely well, Captain O'Grady,"

Major Harrison said, as he reached the deck, "and I congratulate you heartily. You should, however, have obeyed the order of recall; the brig might have proved too strong for you, and, bound on service as we are, we have no right to risk valuable lives except in self-defence."

"Sure I knew nothing about the signal," O'Grady said, with an air of innocence; "I thought it just meant 'More power to ye! give it 'em hot!' or something of that kind. It was not until after I had taken the brig that I was told that it was an order of recall. As soon as I learned that, we came along as fast as we could to you."

"But Mr. Woods must surely have known."

"Mr. Woods did tell me, Major," Terence put in, "but somehow I forgot to mention it to Captain O'Grady."

There was a laugh among the officers standing round.

"You ought to have informed him at once, Mr. O'Connor," the major said, with an attempt at gravity. "However," he went on, with a change of voice, "we all owe so much to you that I must overlook it, as there can be very little doubt that had it not been for your happy idea of taking possession of the lugger we should have been obliged to surrender, for I should not have been justified in holding out until the ship sank under us. I shall not fail, in reporting the matter, to do you full credit for your share in it. Now, what is your loss, Captain O'Grady?"

"Three men killed and eleven wounded, sir."

"And what is that of the enemy?"

"Thirty-two killed and about the same number of wounded, more or less. We had not time to count them before we sent them down, and I had not time afterwards, for I was occupied in obeying the order of recall. I am sorry that we have killed so many of the poor beggars, but if they had hauled down their flag when we got up with them there would have been no occasion for it. I should have told their captain that I looked upon him as an obstinate pig, but as he and his first officer were both killed, there was no use in my spaking to him."

"Well, it has been a very satisfactory operation," the major said, "and we are very well out of a very nasty fix. Now, you will go back to the brig, Captain O'Grady, and prepare to send the prisoners on board. We will send our boats for them. Doctor Daly and Doctor O'Flaherty will go on board with you and see to the wounded French and English. Doctor Daly will bring the worst cases on board here, and will leave O'Flaherty on the brig to look after the others. They will be better there than in this crowded ship. The first officer will remain there with you with five men, and you will retain fifty men of your own company. The second officer, with five men, will take charge of the lugger. He will have with him fifty men of Captain O'Driscol's company, under that officer. That will give us a little more room on board here. How many prisoners are there?"

"Counting the wounded, Major, there are about fifty of them; her crew was eighty strong to begin with. There are only some thirty, including the slightly wounded, to look after."

"If the brig's hold is clear, I think that you had better take charge of them. At present you will both lie-to beside us here till we have completed our repairs, and when we make sail you are both to follow us, and keep as close as possible; and on no account, Captain O'Grady, are you to undertake any cruises on your own account."

"I will bear it in mind, Major; and we will do all we can to keep up with you."

A laugh ran round the circle of officers at O'Grady's obstinacy in considering the *Sea-horse* to be a fast vessel, in spite of the evidence that they had had to the contrary. The major said, gravely:

"You will have to go under the easiest sail possible. The brig can go two feet to this craft's one, and you will only want your lower sails. If you put on more you will be running ahead and losing us at night. We shall show a light over our stern, and on no account are you to allow yourselves to lose sight of it."

A party of men were already at work nailing battens over the shattered stern of the *Sea-horse*. When this was done, sail-cloth was nailed over them, and a coat of pitch given to it. The operation took four hours, by which time all the other arrangements had been completed. The holds of the two privateers were found to be empty, and they learned from the French crews that the two craft had sailed from Bordeaux in company but four days previously, and that the *Sea-horse* was the first English ship that they had come across.

"You will remember, Captain O'Grady," the major said, as that officer prepared to go on board, "that Mr. Woods is in command of the vessel, and that he is not to be interfered with in any way with regard to making or taking in sail. He has received precise instructions as to keeping near us, and your duties will be confined to keeping guard over the prisoners, and rendering such assistance to the sailors as they may require."

"I understand, Major; but I suppose that in case you are attacked we may take a share in any divarsion that is going on?"

"I don't think that there is much chance of our being attacked, O'Grady; but if we are, instructions will be signalled to you. French privateers are not likely to interfere with us, seeing that we are together, and if by any ill-luck a French frigate should fall in with us, you will have instructions to sheer off at once, and for each of you to make your way to Lisbon as quickly as you can. You see, we have transferred four guns from each of your craft to take the place of the rotten cannon on board here, but our united forces would be of no avail at all against a frigate, which would send us to the bottom with a single broadside. We can neither run nor fight in this wretched old tub. If we do see a French frigate coming, I shall transfer the rest of the troops to the prizes and send them off at once, and leave the *Sea-horse* to her fate. Of course we should be very crowded on board the privateers, but that would not matter for a few days. So you see the importance of keeping quite close to us, in readiness to come alongside at once if signalled to. We shall separate as soon as we leave the ship, so as to ensure at least half our force reaching its destination."

Captain O'Driscol took Terence with him on board the lugger, leaving his lieutenant in charge of the wing that remained on board the ship.

"You have done credit to the company, and to my choice of you, Terence," he said, warmly, as they stood together on the deck of the lugger. "I did not see anything for it but a French prison, and it would have broken my heart to be tied up there while the rest of our lads were fighting the French in Portugal. I thought that you would make a good officer some day in spite of your love of devilment, but I did not think that before you had been three weeks in the service you would have saved half the regiment from a French prison."

CHAPTER III

DISEMBARKED

AS soon as the vessels were under way again it was found that the lugger was obliged to lower her main-sail to keep in her position astern of the *Sea-horse*, while the brig was forced to take in sail after sail until the whole of the upper sails had been furled.

"It is tedious work going along like this," O'Driscol said; "but it does not so much matter, because as yet we do not know where we are going to land. Sir Arthur has gone on in a fast ship to Corunna to see the Spanish Junta there, and find out what assistance we are likely to get from Northern Spain. That will be little enough. I expect they will take our money and arms and give us plenty of fine promises in return, and do nothing; that is the game they have been playing in the south, and if there were a grain of sense among our ministers they would see that it is not of the slightest use to reckon on Spain. As to Portugal, we know very little at present, but I expect there is not a pin to choose between them and the Spaniards."

"Then we are not going to Lisbon?" Terence said, in surprise.

"I expect not. Sir Arthur won't determine anything until he joins us after his visit to Corunna, but I don't think that it will be at Lisbon, anyhow. There are strong forts guarding the mouth of the river, and ten or twelve thousand troops in the city, and a Russian fleet anchored in the port. I don't know where it will be, but I don't think that it will be Lisbon. I expect that we shall slip into some little port, land, and wait for Junot to attack us; we shall be joined, I expect, by Stewart's force, that have been fooling about for two or three months waiting for the Spaniards to make up their minds whether they will admit them into Cadiz or not. You see, at present there are only 9,000 of us, and they say that Junot has at least 50,000 in Portugal; but of course they are scattered about, and it is hardly likely that he would venture to withdraw all his garrisons from the large towns, so that the odds may not be as heavy as they look, when we meet him in the field. And I suppose that at any rate some of the Portuguese will join us. From what I hear, the peasantry are brave enough, only they have never had a chance yet of making a fight for it, owing to their miserable government, which never can make up its mind to do anything. I hope that Sir Arthur has orders, as soon as he takes Lisbon, to assume the entire control of the country and ignore the native government altogether. Even if they are worth anything, which they are sure not to be, it is better to have one head than two, and as we shall have to do all the fighting, it's just as well that we should have the whole control of things too."

For four days they sailed along quietly. On the morning of the fifth the signal was run up from the *Sea-horse* for the prizes to close up to her. Mr. Woods, the mate on board the brig, at once sent a sailor up to the mast-head.

"There is a large ship away to the south-west, sir," he shouted down.

"What does she look like?"

"I can only see her royals and top-sails yet, but by their square cut I think that she is a ship-of-war."

"Do you think she is French or English?"

"I cannot say for certain yet, sir, but it looks to me as if she is French. I don't think that the sails are English cut anyhow."

Such was evidently the opinion on board the *Sea-horse*, for as the prizes came up within a hundred yards of her they were hailed by the major through a speaking-trumpet, and ordered to keep at a distance for the present, but to be in readiness to come up alongside directly orders were given to that effect.

In another half-hour the look-out reported that he could now see the lower sails of the stranger, and had very little doubt but that it was a large French frigate. Scarcely had he done so before the two prizes were ordered to close up to the *Sea-horse*. The sea was very calm and they were able to lie alongside, and as soon as they did so the troops began to be transferred to them. In a quarter of an hour the operation was completed, Major Harrison taking his place on board the lugger; half the men were ordered below, and the prize sheered off from the *Sea-horse*.

"The Frenchman is bearing down straight for us," he said to O'Driscol; "she is bringing a breeze down with her, and in an hour she will be alongside. I shall wait another half-hour, and then we must leave the *Sea-horse* to her fate; except for our stores she is worthless. Well, Terence, have you any suggestion to offer? You got us out of the last scrape, and though this is not quite so bad as that, it is unpleasant enough. The frigate when she comes near will see that the *Sea-horse* is a slow sailer, and will probably leave her to be picked up at her leisure, and will go off in chase either of the brig or us. The brig is to make for the north-west and we shall steer south-east, so that she will have to make a choice between us. When we get the breeze we shall either of us give her a good dance before she catches us—that is, if the breeze is not too strong; if it is, her weight would soon bring her up to us."

"Yes, Major, but perhaps she may not trouble about us at all. She would see at once that the lugger and brig are

French, and if they were both to hoist French colours, and the *Sea-horse* were to fly French colours over English, she would naturally suppose that she had been captured by us, and would go straight on her course without troubling herself further about it."

"So she might, Terence. At any rate the scheme is worth trying. If they have anything like good glasses on board they could make out our colours miles away. If she held on towards us after that, there would be plenty of time for us to run, but if we saw her change her course we should know that we were safe. Your head is good for other things besides mischief, lad."

The lugger sailed up near the ship again, and the major gave the captain instructions to hoist a French ensign over an English one, and then, sailing near the brig, told them to hoist French colours.

"Keep all your men down below the line of the bulwarks, O'Grady. Mr. Woods, you had better get your boat down and row alongside of the ship, and ask the captain to get the slings at work and hoist some of our stores into her; we will do the same on the other side. Tell the captain to lower a couple of his boats; also take twenty soldiers on board with you without their jackets; we will do the same, so that it may be seen that we have a strong party on board getting out the cargo."

In a few minutes the orders were carried out, and forty soldiers were at work on the deck of the *Sea-horse*, slinging up tents from below, and lowering them into the boats alongside. The approach of the frigate was anxiously watched from the decks of the prizes. The upper sails of the *Sea-horse* had been furled, and the privateers, under the smallest possible canvas, kept abreast of her at a distance of a couple of lengths. The hull of the French frigate was now visible.

"She is very fast," the mate said to the major, "and she is safe to catch one of us if the breeze she has got holds."

As she came nearer the feeling of anxiety heightened.

"They ought to make out our colours now, sir."

Almost immediately afterwards the frigate was seen to change her course. Her head was turned more to the east. A suppressed cheer broke from the troops.

"It is all right now, sir," the mate said; "she is making for Brest. We have fooled her nicely."

The boats passed and repassed between the *Sea-horse* and the prizes, and the frigate crossed a little more than a mile ahead.

"Five-and-twenty guns a-side," the major said. "By Jove! she would have made short work of us."

As it was not advisable to make any change in the position until the frigate was far on her way, the boats continued to pass to and fro, carrying back to the *Sea-horse* the stores that had just been removed, until the Frenchman was five or six miles away.

"Don't you think that we might make sail again, Captain?" the major then hailed.

"I think that we had better give him another hour, sir. Were she to see us making sail with the prize to the south it would excite suspicion at once, and the captain might take it into his head to come back again to inquire into it."

"Half an hour will surely be sufficient," the major said. "She is travelling at eight or nine knots an hour, and she is evidently bound for port. It would be unlikely in the extreme that her commander would beat back ten miles on what, after all, might be a fool's errand."

"That is true enough, sir. Then in half an hour we shall be ready to sail again."

The major was rowed to the *Sea-horse*. "We may as well

transfer the men at once," he said. "We have had a very narrow escape of it, Captain, and there is no doubt that we owe our safety entirely to the sharpness of that young ensign. We should have been sunk or taken if he had not suggested our manning the lugger in the first place, and of pretending that the ship had been captured by French privateers in the second."

"You are right, Major. Another half-hour and the craft would have foundered under us; and the frigate would certainly have captured the *Sea-horse* and one of the prizes if the Frenchman had not, as he thought, seen two privateers at work emptying our hold. He is a sharp young fellow, that."

"That he is," the major agreed. "He has been brought up with the regiment, and has always been up to pranks of all kinds; but he has used his wits to good purpose this time, and I have no doubt will turn out an excellent officer."

Before sail was made the major summoned the officers on board the *Sea-horse*. The troops from the lugger and brig were drawn up on deck, and the major, standing on the poop, said in a voice that could be heard from end to end of the ship:

"Officers and men, we have had a narrow escape from a French prison, and as it is possible that before we arrive at our destination we may fall in with an enemy again and not be so lucky, I think it right to take this occasion at once of thanking Mr. O'Connor, before you all, in my own name, and in yours, for to his intelligence and quickness of wit it is entirely due that we escaped being captured when the brig was pounding us with its shot, without our being able to make any return, and it was certain that in a short time we should have had to haul down our flag or be sunk. It was he who suggested that we should take possession of the lugger, and with her guns drive off the brig. As the result of that suggestion this craft was saved from being sunk, and the brig was also captured.

"In the second place, when that French frigate was bearing down upon us and our capture seemed certain, it was he who suggested to me, that by hoisting the French flag and appearing to be engaged in transferring the cargo of the ship to the privateers, we might throw dust into the eyes of the Frenchmen. As you saw, the ruse succeeded perfectly. I therefore, Mr. O'Connor, thank you most heartily in my own name, and in that of your fellow-officers, also in the name of the four hundred men of the regiment, and of the ship's company, for the manner in which you have, by your quickness and good sense, saved us all from a French prison, and saved his Majesty from the loss of the wing of a fine regiment."

As he concluded the men broke into loud cheering, and the officers gathered around Terence and thanked and congratulated him most heartily on the service that he had rendered them.

"You are a broth of a boy, Terence," Captain O'Grady said. "I knew that it was in you all along. I would not give a brass farthing for a lad who had not a spice of divilment in him. It shows that he has got his wits about him, and that when he steddys down he will be hard to bate."

Terence was so much overpowered at the praise he had received that, beyond protesting that it was quite undeserved, he had no reply to make to the congratulations that he received from the captain. O'Driscol, seeing that he was on the verge of breaking down, at once called upon him to take his place in the boat, and rowed with him to the lugger.

A few minutes later all sail was set on the *Sea-horse*, and with her yards braced tautly aft she laid her course south, close-hauled; a fresh breeze was now blowing, and she ploughed her way through the water at a rate that almost justified O'Grady's panegyrics upon her. In another three days she entered the port of Vigo, where the convoy was to rendezvous, and all were glad to find that the whole fleet were still there. On anchoring, the major went on board the *Dauphin*, which had brought the head-quarters, and the other wing of the regiment. He was heartily greeted by the colonel.

"We were getting very uneasy about you, Harrison," he said. "The last ship of the convoy came in three days ago, and we began to fear that you must have been either dismasted or sunk in the gale. I saw the senior naval officer this morning, and he said that if you did not come in during the day he would send a frigate out in search of you; but I could see by his manner that he thought it most likely that you had gone down. So you may imagine how pleased we were when we made out your number, though we could not for the life of us make out what those two craft flying the English colours over the French, that came in after you, were. But of course they had nothing to do with you. I suppose they were two privateers that had been captured by one of our frigates, and sent in here with prize crews to refit before going home. They have both of them been knocked about a bit."

"I will tell you about them directly, Colonel; it is rather a long story. We have had a narrow squeak of it. We got through the storm pretty well, but we had a bad time of it afterwards, and we owe it entirely to young O'Connor that we are not, all of us, in a prison at Brest at present."

"You don't say so! Wait a moment, I will call his father here; he will be glad to hear that the young scamp has behaved well. I may as well call them all up; they will like to hear the story."

Turning to the group of officers who were standing on the quarter-deck a short distance away, waiting to hear the news when the major had given his report, he said: "You may as well come now and hear Major Harrison's story; it will save his telling it twice. You will be glad to hear, O'Connor, that

Terence has been distinguishing himself in some way, though I know not yet in what; the major says that if it had not been for him the whole wing of the regiment would have now been in a French prison."

"Terence was always good at getting out of scrapes, Colonel, though I don't say he was not equally good in getting into them; but I am glad to hear that this time he has done something useful."

The major then gave a full account of their adventure with the privateers, and of the subsequent escape from the French frigate.

"Faith, O'Connor," the colonel said, warmly, holding out his hand to him, "I congratulate you most heartily, which is more than I ever thought to do on Terence's account. I had some misgivings when I recommended him for a commission, but I may congratulate myself as well as you that I did so. I was sure the lad had plenty in him, but I was afraid that it was more likely to come out the wrong way than the right; and now it turns out that he has saved half the regiment, for there is no doubt from what Harrison says that he has done so."

"Thank you, Colonel; I am glad indeed that the boy has done credit to your kindness. It was a mighty bad scrape this time, and he got out of it well."

"Of course, Major, you will give a full report in writing of this, and will send it in to Sir Arthur; he arrived this morning. I will go on board the flag-ship at once and report as to the prizes. Who they belong to I have not the least idea. I never heard of a transport capturing a couple of privateers before; but, I suppose, as she is taken up for the king's service and the prizes were captured by his Majesty's troops, they will rank as if taken by the navy, that is, a certain amount of their value will go to the admiral. Anyhow, the bulk of it will go, I should think, to the troops—the crew and officers of the ship, of course, sharing."

"It won't come to much a head, Colonel, anyhow. You see, they were both empty, and there is simply the value of the ships themselves, which I don't suppose would fetch above five or six hundred apiece."

"Still, the thing must be done in a regular way, and I must leave it in the admiral's hands. I will take your boat, Major, and go to him at once. You will find pen and ink in my cabin, and I should be glad if you would write your report by the time that I return; then I will go off at once to Sir Arthur."

"I have it already written, Colonel," the major said, producing the document.

"That looks to me rather long, Harrison, and busy as Sir Arthur must be, he might not take the trouble to read it. I wish you would write out another, as concise as you can make it, of the actual affair, saying at the end that you beg to report especially the conduct of Ensign O'Connor, to whose suggestions the escape of the ship both from the privateers and French frigate were due. I will hand that in as the official report, and with it the other, saying that it gives further details of the affair. Of course, with them I must give in an official letter from myself, inclosing your two reports. But first I will go and see the admiral."

In a little over half an hour he returned. "The admiral knows no more than I do whether the navy have anything to do with the prizes or not. Being so small in value he does not want to trouble himself about it. He says that the matter would entail no end of correspondence and bother, and that the crafts might rot at their anchors before the matter was decided. He thinks the best thing that I can do will be to sell the two vessels for what they will fetch, and divide the money according to prize rules, and say nothing about it. In that way there is not likely ever to be any question about it, while if the Admiralty and Horse Guards once get into a correspondence over the matter, there is no saying what bother I might have; and that he should advise me, if I do not adopt that plan, to simply scuttle them both, and report that they have sunk. Now I will just write my official letter and take it to head-quarters."

In two hours he was back again.

"I have not seen the chief," he said, "but I gave the reports to his adjutant-general. General Fane was with him; he is an old friend of mine, and I told him the story of your voyage, and the adjutant-general joined in the conversation. Fane was waiting to go in to Sir Arthur, who was dictating some despatches to England, and he said that if he had a chance he would mention the affair to Sir Arthur; and, at any rate, the other officer said that he would lay the reports before him, with such mention that Sir Arthur would doubtless look through them both. I find that there is a bit of insurrection going on in Portugal, but that no one thinks much will come of it, as bands of unarmed peasants can have no chance with the French. Nothing is determined as yet about our landing. Lisbon and the Tagus are completely in the hands of the French.

"Sir Arthur is going down to Oporto to-morrow, where it is likely that he will learn more about the situation than he did at Corunna. Fane says that he hopes we shall soon be ashore, as the general is not the man to let the grass grow under his feet."

After holding counsel with his officers the colonel determined to adopt the advice he had received, and to sell the two craft for what they would fetch, the officers all agreeing to refund their shares if any questions were ever asked on the subject. The captain of the *Sea-horse* agreed to accept the share of a captain in the line, and his mates those of first and second lieutenant. The colonel put himself in communication with some merchants on shore, and the two craft were sold for twelve hundred pounds.

"This gave something over a pound a head to the 400 soldiers and the crew, twice that amount to the non-commissioned officers, and sums varying from ten pounds apiece to the ensigns to fifty pounds to the major. The admiral was asked to approve of the transaction, and said, 'I have no right formally to sanction it, since, so far as I know, it is not a strictly naval matter; but I will give you a letter, Colonel, saying that you have informed me of the course that you have adopted, and that I consider that under the peculiar circumstances of the capture, and the fact that there are no men available for sending the prizes to England, the course was the best and most convenient that could possibly be adopted, though, had the craft been of any great value, it would, of course, have been necessary to refer the matter home.'"

A week passed without movement. The expedition had left England on the 12th of July, 1808, and Sir Arthur rejoined it towards the end of the month. He had learned at Oporto from Colonel Brown, our agent there, that, contrary to what he had been told at Corunna, there were no Spanish troops in the north of Portugal, but that a body of some 8,000 Portuguese irregulars and militia, half-armed and but slightly disciplined, were assembled on the river Mondego. After a consultation with Admiral Sir Charles Cotton, Sir Arthur had concluded that an attack at the mouth of the Tagus was impracticable, owing to the strength of the French there, the position of the forts that commanded the entrance of the river, and the heavy surf that broke in all the undefended creeks and bays near. There was then the choice of landing far enough north of Lisbon to ensure a disembarkation undisputed by the French, or else to sail south, join Spencer, and act against the French army under Dupont.

Sir Arthur finally determined that the Mondego River was the most practicable for the enterprise. The fort of Figuéira at its mouth was already occupied by British marines, and the Portuguese force was at least sufficient to deter any small body of troops approaching the neighbourhood. Therefore, to the great joy of the troops, the order was given that the fleet should sail on the following morning; two days later they anchored off the mouth of the Mondego. Just before starting a vessel arrived with despatches from Spencer, saying that he was at St. Mary's and was free to act with Sir Arthur, and a fast vessel was despatched with orders to him to sail to the Mondego.

On arriving there Sir Arthur received the mortifying intelligence that Sir Hew Dalrymple had been appointed over his head, nevertheless he continued to push on his own plans with vigour, pending the arrival of that general. With this bad news came the information that the French general, Dupont, had been defeated. This set free a small force under General Anstruther, and some fast-sailing craft were at once despatched to find his command, and order it to sail at once to the Mondego. Without further delay, however, the landing of the troops began on the 1st of August, and the 9,000 men, their guns and stores, were ashore by the 5th.

On that day Spencer fortunately arrived with 3,300 men. He had not received Sir Arthur's orders, but the moment that Dupont surrendered he had sailed for the Tagus, and had learned from Sir C. Cotton, who commanded the fleet at the entrance to the river, where Sir Arthur was, and at once sailed to join him. While the troops were disembarking Sir Arthur had gone over to the Portuguese head-quarters, two miles distant, to confer with Bernardin Friere, the Portuguese commander-in-chief. The visit was a disappointing one. He found that the Portuguese troops were almost unarmed, and that their commander was full of inflated ideas. He proposed that the forces should unite, that they should relinquish the coast, and march into the interior and commence an offensive campaign, and was lavish in his promises to provide ample stores of provisions. The English general saw, however, that no effectual assistance could be hoped for from the Portuguese troops, and as little from the promises of their commander. He gave Friere 5,000 muskets for his troops, but absolutely declined to adopt the proposed plan, his own intention being to keep near the coast, where he could receive his supplies from the ships and be joined by reinforcements.

As soon as they had landed the Mayo regiment was marched to a village two miles inland, and, with two others of the same brigade, encamped near it. All idea of keeping up a regimental officers' mess had been abandoned, and as soon as the tents were pitched and the troops had settled down in them, O'Grady said to Terence:

"We will go into the village and see if we can find a suitable place for taking our meals. It may be that in time our fellows will learn how to cook for us, but, by jabers! we will live dacent as long as we can. My servant, Tim Hoolan, has gone on ahead to look for such a place, and he is the boy to find one if there is one anyhow to be got. As our companies are number 1 and 2, it is reasonable that we should stick together, and though O'Driscol's a quare stick, with all sorts of ridiculous notions, he is a good fellow at heart, and I will put up with him for the sake of having you with me."

As they entered the village the servant came up. "I have managed it, Captain; we have got hold of the best quarters in the village; it is a room over the only shebeen here. The ould scoundrel of a landlord wanted to keep it as a general room, but I brought the Church to bear on him, and I managed it finally."

"How did you work it, Tim?"

"Sure, your honour, I went to the praste, and by good luck his house is in front of the church. I went into the church, and I crossed myself before the altar and said a prayer or two. As I did so who should come out of the vestry but the father himself. He waited until I had done and then came up to me, and to my surprise said in good Irish:

"'So it's a Catholic you are, my man?'

"'That am I, your riverence,' said I, 'and most all of the rigiment are; sure, we were raised in the ould country, and belong, most of us, to County Mayo, and glad we were to come out here to fight for those of the true religion against these Frenchmen, who they say have no religion at all, at all. And how is it you spake the language, your riverence, if I may be so bold as to ask?'"

"Then he told me that he had been at college at Lisbon, where the sons of many Catholic Irish gentlemen were sent to be educated, and that he had learned it from them.

"'And how is it that you are not with your regiment, my man?'

"'I am here to hire rooms for the officers, your riverence, just a place where they can ate a dacent meal in peace and quietness. I have been to the inn, but I cannot for the life of me make the landlord understand. He has got a room that would be just suitable, so I thought I would come to your riverence to explain to you that the rigiment are not heretics, but true sons of the Church. I thought that, being a learned man, I might make shift to make you understand, and that you would maybe go wid me and explain the matter to him.'

"'That will I,' says he; and he wint and jabbered away

with the innkeeper, and at last turned to me and said: ' He will let you have a room, seeing that it is for the service of good Catholics and not heretics.' "

" But, you rascal, you know that we are not Catholics."

" Sure, your honour, didn't I say that most all the rigiment were Catholics; I did not say all of them."

" I must go and explain the matter to him, Hoolan. If he calls upon us, as like he may do, he would find out at once that you have desaved him."

" Sure, your honour, if you think that it is necessary, of course it must be done; but would it not be as well to go to the shebeen first and to take possession of the room, and to get comfortably settled down in it before ye gives me away?"

" I think it might be worth while, Tim," O'Grady said, gravely. " What do you say, Terence?"

" I think the matter will keep for a few hours," Terence said, laughing, " and when we are once settled there it will be very hard to turn us out."

The room was found to be larger than they had expected, and O'Grady proposed that they should admit the whole officers of their wing to share it with them, to which Terence at once agreed heartily. " I think that with a little squeezing the place would hold the officers of the five companies, and the major and O'Flaherty. The more of us there are, the merrier, and the less fear of our being turned out."

" That is so. We had better put the names up on the door. You go down and try and make that black-browed landlord understand that you want some paper and pen and ink."

With some difficulty and much gesticulation Terence succeeded. The names of the officers were written down on a paper and it was then fastened on the door.

" Now, Terence, I will go and fetch the boys; you and

Hoolan make the landlord understand that we want food and wine for fifteen or sixteen officers. Of course they won't all be able to get away at once. We must contint ourselves with anything we can get now; afterwards we will send up our rations, and with plenty of good wine and a ham (there are lots of them hanging from the ceiling down below), we shall do pretty well, with what you can forage outside."

Terence left this part of the work to Hoolan, who, by bringing up a number of plates and ranging them on the table, getting down a ham and cutting it into slices, and by pointing to the wine-skins, managed to acquaint the landlord with what was required. In this he was a good deal aided by the man's two nieces, who acted as his assistants, and who were much quicker in catching his meaning than was the landlord himself. Very soon the room below was crowded with officers from other regiments, and Hoolan went up to Terence:

"I think, Mr. O'Connor, that it would be a good job if you were to go down and buy a dozen of them hams. A lot of them have been sold already, and it won't be long before the last has gone, though I reckon that there are three or four dozen of them still there."

"That is a very good idea, Tim. You come down with me and bring them straight up here, and we will drive some nails into those rafters. I expect before nightfall the place will be cleared out of everything that is eatable."

The bargain was speedily concluded. The landlord was now in a better temper. At first he had been very doubtful of the intentions of the new-comers. Now that he saw that they were ready to pay for everything, and that at prices much higher than he could before have obtained, his face shone with good-humour. He and the two girls were already busy drawing wine and selling it to the customers.

"I will get some wood, your honour, and light a fire here, or it is mighty little dinner that you will be getting. The soldiers will soon be dropping in, that is, if they don't keep this place for officers only, for there are two other places where they sell wine in the village. When I came up two officers had a slice of ham each on the points of their swords over the fire."

"That will be a very good plan, Tim; you had better set to work about it at once, and at the same time I will try and get some bread."

By the time that O'Grady returned with seven or eight other officers the fire was blazing. Terence had managed to get a sufficient number of knives and forks; there was, however, no table-cloth in the house. He and Terence were cooking slices of ham on a gridiron over the fire.

"This is first-rate, O'Grady," Major Harrison said; "the place is crowded down below, and we should have fared very badly if you had not managed to get hold of this room."

"If some of the boys will see to the cooking, Major, I will go down with Hoolan and get a barrel of wine and bring it up here; then we shall do first-rate."

"How about the rations, Major?" Terence asked.

"They have just been served out. I sent my man down to draw the rations for the whole wing at once, and told him to bring them up here."

"And I have told mine," Captain O'Driscol said, "to go round the village and buy up two or three dozen chickens, if he can find them, and as many eggs as he can collect. I think that we had better tell off two of the men as cooks. I don't think it is likely that they will be able to get much done that way below. Hoolan and another will do."

"I should think it best to keep Hoolan as forager; he is rather a genius in that capacity. I think he has got round those two girls, whether by his red hair or his insinuating manners I cannot say, but they seem ready to do anything for him, and we shall want lots of things in the way of pots and pans and so on."

"Very well, Terence, then we will leave him free and put two others on."

CHAPTER IV

UNDER CANVAS

IN a short time O'Grady returned, followed by Hoolan, carrying a small barrel of wine.

"It is good, I hope," the major said, as the barrel was set down in one corner of the room.

"I think that it is the best they have; one of the girls went down with Tim into the cellar and pointed it out to him. I told him to ask her for *bueno vino*. I don't know whether it was right or not, but I think she understood."

"How much does it hold, O'Grady?"

"I cannot say; five or six gallons, I should think; anyhow, I paid three dollars for it."

"You must put down all the outgoings, O'Grady, and we will square up when we leave here."

"I will put them down, Major. How long do you think we shall stop here?"

"That is more than anyone can say; we have to wait for Anstruther and Spencer. It may be three or four days; it may be a fortnight."

Dick Ryan assisted Terence in the cooking, while Tim went down to get something to drink out of. He returned with three mugs and two horns.

"Divil a thing else is there that can be found, yer honour," he said, as he placed them on the table; "every mortial thing is in use."

"That will do to begin with," the major said; "we will get our own things up this afternoon. We must manage as best we can for this meal; it is better than I expected by a long way."

Tim now relieved the two young officers at the gridiron, and sitting down at the benches along the table the meal was eaten with much laughter and fun.

"After all, there is nothing like getting things straight from the gridiron," the major said.

O'Grady had got the bung out of the barrel and filled the five drinking vessels, and the wine was pronounced to be very fair. One by one the other officers dropped in, and Hoolan was for an hour kept busy. The major, who spoke a little Spanish, went down and returned with a dozen bottles of spirits, two or three of which were opened and the contents consumed.

"It is poor stuff by the side of whisky," O'Grady said, as he swallowed a stiff glass of it; "still, I will not be denying that it is warming and comforting, and if we can get enough of it we can hold on till we get home again. Here is success to the campaign. I will trouble you for that bottle, O'Driscol."

"Here it is. I shall stick to wine; I don't care for that fiery stuff. Here is success to the campaign, and may we meet the French before long!

"We are pretty sure to do that," he went on, as he set his horn down on the table. "If Junot knows his business he won't lose a day before marching against us directly he hears of our landing. He will know well enough that unless he crushes us at once he will have all Portugal up in arms. Here, Terence, you can have this horn."

The difficulty of drinking had to some extent been solved by Hoolan, who had gone downstairs, and returned with a tin pot capable of holding about a couple of quarts. This he had cleaned by rubbing it with sand and water, and it went round as a loving-cup among those unprovided with mugs or horns. When all had finished, the two soldier servants, who had now arrived with the rations, were left in charge. O'Driscol's servant had brought in a dozen fowls and a large basket full of eggs, and, ordering supper to be ready at eight, the officers returned to their camp. They found that their comrades had done fairly well. Several rooms had been obtained in the village, and hams, black sausages, and other provisions purchased, and cooked in a rough way on a gridiron.

"I am afraid that it is too good to last," the colonel said, as the officers gathered around him as the bugle sounded for parade; "a week of this and the last scrap of provisions here will have been eaten, and we shall have nothing but our rations to fall back upon. There is one thing, however, that is not likely to give out, that is wine. They grow it about here, and I hear that the commissariat have bought up large quantities without difficulty to serve out to the troops."

The regiment had a long afternoon's drill to get them out of the slackness occasioned by their enforced idleness on the voyage. When it was over they were formed up, and the colonel addressed a few words to the men.

"Men of the Mayo regiment," he said, "I trust that, now we are fairly embarked upon the campaign, you will so behave as to do credit to yourselves and to Ireland. Perhaps some of you think that, now that you are on a campaign, you can do just as you like. Those who think so are wrong; it is just the other way. When you were at home I did not think it necessary that I should be severe with you; and as long as a man was able, when he came into barracks, to walk to his quarters, I did not trouble about him. But it is different here; any breach of duty will be most severely punished, and any man who is found drunk will be flogged. Any man plundering or ill-treating the people of the country will be handed over to the provost-marshal, and, unless I am mistaken, he is likely to be shot.

"Sir Arthur Wellesley is not the man to stand nonsense. There must be no straggling; you must keep within the bounds of the camps, and no one must go into the village without a permit from the captain of his company. As to your fighting — well, I have no fear of that; we will say nothing about it. Before the enemy I know that you will all do your duty, and it is just as necessary that you should do your duty and be a credit to your regiment at other times. There are blackguards in the regiment, as there are in every other, but I tell them that a sharp eye will be kept upon them, and that no mercy will be shown them if they misbehave while they are in Portugal. That is all I have to say to you."

"That was the sort of thing, I think, Major," he said, as, after the men were dismissed, he walked back to his tent with Major Harrison.

"Just the sort of thing, Colonel," the other said, smiling; "and said in the sort of way that they will understand. I am afraid that we shall have trouble with some of them. Wine and spirits are cheap, and it will be very difficult to keep them from it altogether. Still, if we make an example of the first fellow who is caught drunk it will be a useful lesson to the whole. A few floggings at the start may save some hangings afterwards. I know you are averse to flogging—there have only been four men flogged in the last six months—but this is a case where punishment must be dealt out sharply if discipline is to be maintained, and the credit of the regiment be kept up."

O'Grady and one of the other officers called upon the priest to thank him for his good offices in obtaining the room for them.

"I am afraid from what my man tells me that he did not state the case quite fairly to you. Our regiment was, as he said, raised in Ireland, and the greater portion of the men are naturally of your faith, Father, but we really have no claim to your services whatever."

The priest smiled.

"I am, nevertheless, glad to have been of service to you, gentlemen," he said, courteously; "at least you are Irishmen, and I have many good friends countrymen of yours. And you have still another claim upon us all, for are you not here to aid us to shake off this French domination? I hope that you are comfortable, but judging from what I see and hear when passing I fear that your lodging is a somewhat noisy one."

"You may well say that, Father; and we do our full share towards making it so; but having the room makes all the difference to us. They have no time to cook downstairs, and it is done by our own servants; but it is handy to have the wine and other things within call, and if we always do as well, we shall have good cause to feel mighty contented; for barring that we are rather crowded, we are just as well off here as we were at home, saving only in the quality of the spirits. Now, Father, we cannot ask you up there, seeing that it is your own village, but if you would like to take a walk through the camps we should be glad to show you what there is to be seen, and can give you a little of the real cratur. It is not much of it that we have been able to bring ashore, for the general is mighty stiff in the matter of baggage, but I doubt whether there is one of us who did not manage to smuggle a bottle or two of the real stuff hidden in his kit."

The priest accepted the invitation, and was taken through the brigade camp, staying some time in that of the Mayos, and astonishing some of the soldiers by chatting to them in English, and with a brogue almost as strong as their own. He then spent half an hour in O'Grady's tent, and sampled the whisky, which he pronounced excellent, and of which his entertainer insisted upon his taking a bottle away with him.

Three days later it was known in camp that two French divisions had been set in motion against them, the one from Abrantes to the east under Loison, the other from the south under Laborde. Junot himself remained at Lisbon. The rising in the south, and the news of the British landing caused an intense feeling among the population, and the French general feared that at any moment an insurrection might break out. The natural point of junction of these two columns would be at Leirya. That night orders were issued for the tents of the division to which the Mayo regiment belonged to be struck before daylight, and the troops were to be under arms and ready to march at six o'clock.

"Good news!" O'Grady said, as he entered the mess-room at four o'clock in the afternoon, after having learned from the colonel the orders for the next morning; "our brigade is to form the advanced guard, and we are to march at six to-morrow."

A general exclamation of pleasure broke from the five or six officers present. "We shall have the first of the fun, boys; hand me that horn, Terence. Here is to Sir Arthur; good-luck to him, and bad cess to the French!"

The toast was drunk with some laughter. "Now we are going to campaign in earnest," he went on; "no more wine swilling, no more devilled ham——"

"No more spirits, O'Grady," one of the group cut in; "and as for the wine, you have drunk your share, besides twice your share of the spirits."

"Whin there is nothing to do, Debenham, I can take me liquor in moderation."

"I have never remarked that, O'Grady," one of the others put in.

"In great moderation," O'Grady said, gravely, but he was again interrupted by a shout of laughter.

"Ye had to be helped home last night, O'Grady, and it took Hoolan a quarter of an hour to wake you this morning. I heard him say, 'Now, master dear, the bugle will sound in a minute or two; it's wake you must, or there will be a divil of botheration over it.' I looked in, and there you were. Hoolan was standing by the side of you shaking his head gravely, as if it was a hopeless job that he had in hand, and if I had not emptied a water-bottle over you, you would never have been on parade in time."

"Oh! it was you, was it?" O'Grady said, wrathfully. "Hoolan swore by all the saints that he had not seen who it was. Never mind, me boy, I will be even wid ye yet; the O'Grady is not to be waked in that fashion; mind I owe you one, though I am not saying that I should have been on parade in time if you had not done it; I only just saved my bacon."

"And hardly that," Terence laughed, "for the adjutant was down upon you pretty sharply; your coatee was all buttoned up wrong; your hair had not been brushed, and stuck up all ways below your shako; your sword-belt was all awry, and you looked worse than you did when I brought you home."

"Well, it is a poor heart that never rejoices, Terence. We must make a night of it, boys; if the tents are to be struck before daylight it will be mighty little use your turning in."

"You won't catch me sitting up all night," Terence said, "with perhaps a twenty-mile march in the morning, and maybe a fight at the end of it. If it is to Leirya we are going it will be nearer thirty miles than twenty, and even you, seasoned vessel as you are, will find it a long walk after being up all night, and having had pretty hard work to-day."

"I cannot hold wid the general there," O'Grady said, gravely; "he has been kapeing us all at it from daybreak till night, ivery day since we landed, and marching the men's feet off. It is all very well to march when we have got to march, but to keep us tramping fifteen or twenty miles a day when there is no occasion for it is out of all reason."

"We shall march all the better for it to-morrow, O'Grady. It has been hard work, certainly, but not harder than it was marching down to Cork; and we should have a good many stragglers to-morrow if it had not been for the last week's work. We have got half a dozen footsore men in my company alone, and you would have fifty to-morrow night if the men had not had all this marching to get them fit."

"It is all very well for you, Terence, who have been tramping all over the hills round Athlone since you were a gossoon; but I am sure that if I had not had that day off duty when I showed the priest round the camp I should have been kilt."

"Here is the general order of the day," the adjutant said, as he came in with Captain O'Connor. "The general says that now the army is about to take the field he shall expect the strictest discipline to be maintained, and that all stragglers from the ranks will at once be handed over to the provost-marshal, and all offences against the peasantry or their property will be severely punished. Then there are two or three orders that do not concern us particularly, and then there is one that concerns you, Terence. The general has received a report from Colonel Corcoran of the Mayo Fusiliers stating that 'the transport carrying the left wing of that regiment was attacked by two French privateers, and would have been compelled to surrender, she being practically unarmed, had it not been for the coolness and quick wit of Ensign Terence O'Connor. Having read the report the general commanding fully concurs, and expresses his high satisfaction at the conduct of Ensign O'Connor, which undoubtedly saved from capture the wing of the regiment.'

"There, Terence, that is a feather in your cap. Sir Arthur is not given to praise unduly, and it is seldom that an ensign gets into general orders. It will do you good some day, perhaps when you least expect it."

"I am heartily pleased, my lad," Captain O'Connor said, as he laid his hand upon Terence's shoulder. "I am proud of you. I have never seen my own name in general orders, but I am heartily glad to see yours. Bedad, when I think that a couple of months ago you were running wild and getting into all sorts of mischief, it seems hard to believe that you should not only be one of us, but have got your name into general orders."

"And all for nothing, father," Terence said. "I call it a beastly shame that just because I thought of using that lugger I should be cracked up more than the others."

"It was not only that, though, Terence; those guns that crippled the lugger could not have been fired if you had not thought of putting rope round them, and that French frigate would never have left you alone had not you suggested to the major how to throw dust into their eyes. No, my lad, you thoroughly deserve the credit that you have got, and I am sure that there is not a man in the regiment who would not say the same."

"Gintlemen," Captain O'Grady said, solemnly, "we will drink to the health of Ensign Terence O'Connor; more power to his elbow!" And the toast was duly honoured.

"It is mighty good of me to propose it," O'Grady went on, after Terence had said a few words of thanks, "because I have a strong idea that in another two or three minutes I should have made just the same suggestion that you did, me lad. I knew at the time that there was a plan I wanted to propose, but sorra a word came to me lips. I was just brimful with it when you came up and took the words out of me mouth. If I had spoken first it is a brevet majority I had got, sure enough."

"You must be quicker next time, O'Grady," the adjutant said, when the laughter had subsided; "as you say, you have missed a good thing by your slowness. I am afraid your brain was still a little muddled by your indulgence the night before."

"Just the contrary, me boy; I feel that if I had taken just one glass more of the cratur me brain would have been clearer and I should have been to the fore. But I bear you no malice, Terence. Maybe the ideas would not have managed to straighten themselves out until after we had had to haul down the flag, and then it would have been too late to have been any good. It has happened to me more than once before that I have just thought of a good thing when it was too late."

"It has occurred to most of us, O'Grady," Captain O'Connor said, laughing. "Terence, you see, doesn't care for whisky, and perhaps that has something to do with his ideas coming faster than ours. Well, so we are off to-morrow; though, of course, no one knows which way we are going to march, it must be either to Leirya or along the coast road. It is a good thing Spencer has come up in time, for there is no saying how strong the French may be; though I fancy they are all so scattered about that, after leaving a garrison to keep Lisbon in order, and holding other points, Junot will hardly be able at such short notice to gather a force much superior to ours. But from what I hear there are some mighty strong positions between this and Lisbon, and if he sticks himself up on the top of a hill we shall have all our work to turn him off again."

"I fancy it will be to Leirya," the adjutant said; "the Portuguese report that one French division is at Candieros and another coming from Abrantes, and Sir Arthur is likely to endeavour to prevent them from uniting."

That evening there was a grand feast at the mess-room. The colonel had been specially invited, and every effort was made to do honour to the occasion. Tim Hoolan had been very successful in a foraging expedition, and had brought in a goose and four ducks, and had persuaded the landlord's nieces to let him and the cook have sole possession of the kitchen. The banquet was a great success, but the majority of those present did not sit very long afterwards. The colonel set the example of rising early.

"I should advise you, gentlemen, to turn in soon," he said. "I do not say where we are to march to-morrow, but I can tell you at least that the march is a very long one, and that it were best to get as much sleep as possible, for I can assure you that it will be no child's play; and I think that it is quite probable we shall smell powder before the day is over."

Accordingly, all the young officers and several of the seniors left with him, but O'Grady and several of the hard drinkers kept it up until midnight, observing, however, more moderation than usual in their potations.

There was none of the grumbling common when men are turned out of their beds before dawn; all were in high spirits that the time for action had arrived; the men were as eager to meet the enemy as were their officers; and the tents were all down and placed in the waggons before daylight. The regimental cooks had already been at work, and the officers went round and saw that all had had breakfast before they fell in. At six o'clock the whole were under arms and in their place as the central regiment in the brigade. They tramped on without a halt until eleven; then the bugle sounded, and they fell out for half an hour.

The men made a meal from bread and the meat that had been cooked the night before, each man carrying three days' rations in his haversack. There was another halt, and a longer one, at two o'clock, when the brigade rested for an hour in the shade of a grove.

"It is mighty pleasant to rest," O'Grady said, as the officers threw themselves down on the grass, "but it is the starting that bates one. I feel that my feet have swollen so that every step I take I expect my boots to burst with an explosion. Faith, if it comes to fighting I shall take them off altogether, and swing them at my belt. How can I run after the French when I am a cripple?"

"You had better take your boots off now, O'Grady," one of the others suggested.

"It is not aisy to get them off, and how should I get them on again? No; they have got there, and there they have got to stop, bad cess to them! I told Hoolan to rub grease into them for an hour last night, but the rascal was as drunk as an owl."

There was no more talking, for every man felt that an hour's sleep would do wonders for him; soon absolute quiet reigned in the grove, and continued until the bugle again called them to their feet. All knew now that it was Leirya they were making for, and that another ten miles still remained to be accomplished. A small body of cavalry which accompanied them now pushed on ahead, and when half the distance had been traversed a trooper brought back the news that the enemy had not yet reached the town. It was just six o'clock when the brigade marched in amid the cheers and wild excitement of the inhabitants. The waggons were not yet up, and the troops were quartered in the town, tired, and many of them foot-sore, but proud of the march they had accomplished, and that it had enabled them to forestall the French.

Laborde, indeed, arrived the same night at Batalha, eight miles distant, but on receiving the news in the morning that the British had already occupied Leirya, he advanced no farther. His position was an exceedingly difficult one; his orders were to cover the march of Loison from Abrantes, and to form a junction with that general; but to do so now would be to leave open the road through Alcobaca and Obidos to the commanding position at Torres Vedras. Batalha offered no position that he could hope to defend until the arrival of Loison; therefore, sending word to that general to move from Torras Novas, as soon as he reached that town, to Santarem, and then to march to join him at Rolica, he fell back to Alcobaca and then to Obidos, a town with a Moorish castle, built on a gentle eminence in the middle of a valley.

Leaving a detachment here, he retired to Rolica, six miles to the south of it. At this point several roads met, and he at once covered all the approaches to Torres Vedras, and the important port of Peniche, and could be joined by Loison marching down from Santarem.

The advanced brigade of the British force remained in quiet possession of Leirya during the next day, and on the following, the 11th of August, the main body of the army arrived, having taken two days on the march. The Portuguese force also came in under Friere. That general at once took possession of the magazines there, and although he had promised the English general that their contents should be entirely devoted to the maintenance of the English army, he divided them among his own force.

Disgusted as the British commander was at this barefaced dishonesty, he was not in a position to quarrel with the Portuguese. It was essential to him that they should accompany him, not for the sake of the assistance that they would give, for he knew that none was to be expected from them, but from a political point of view. It was most important that the people at large should feel that their own troops were acting with the British, and that no feelings of jealousy or suspicion of the latter should arise. Friere was acting under the orders of the Bishop and Junta of Oporto, whose great object was to keep the Portuguese army together and not to risk a defeat, as they desired to keep this body intact in order that, if the British were defeated, they should be able to make favourable terms for themselves. Consequently, even after appropriating the whole of the stores and provisions found at Leirya, Friere continued to make exorbitant demands, and to offer a vigorous opposition to any further advance.

So far did he carry this that the British general, finding that in no other way could he get the Portuguese to advance with him, proposed that they should follow behind him and wait the result of the battle, to which Friere at last consented. The Portuguese, in fact, had no belief whatever that the British troops would be able to withstand the onslaught of the French, whom they regarded as invincible. Colonel Trant, however, one of our military agents, succeeded in inducing Friere to place 1,400 infantry and 250 cavalry under the command of Sir Arthur.

The addition of the cavalry was a very useful one, for the English had with them only 180 mounted men; the country was entirely new to them, scarcely an officer could speak the language, and there was no means, therefore, of obtaining information as to the movements of the enemy. Moving forward through Batalha, and regaining the coast road at Alcobaca, the British forces arrived at Caldas on the 15th; and on the same day Junot quitted Lisbon with a force of 2,000 infantry, 2,000 cavalry, and ten pieces of artillery, leaving 7,000 to garrison the forts and keep down the population of the city. His force was conveyed to Villa Franca by water, and the general then pushed forward to Santarem, where he found Loison, and took command of his division.

The British advanced guard, after arriving at Caldas, pushed forward, drove the French pickets out of Brilos, and then from Obidos. Here, however, a slight reverse took place. Some companies of the 95th and 60th Rifles pressed forward three miles farther in pursuit, when they were suddenly attacked in flank by a greatly superior force, and had it not been that General Spencer, whose division was but a short distance behind, pressed forward to their assistance, they would have suffered heavily; as it was they escaped with the loss of two officers and twenty-seven men killed and wounded. Their rashness, however, led to the discovery that Laborde's force had taken up a strong position in front of the village of Rolica, and that he apparently intended to give battle there.

The next day was spent in reconnoitring the French position. It was a very strong one. Rolica stood on a table-land rising in a valley, affording a view of the road as far as Obidos. The various points of defence there, and on the flank, were held by strong parties of the enemy. A mile in the rear was a steep and lofty ridge that afforded a strong second line of defence. By the side of this ridge the road passed through a deep defile, and then mounted over a pass through the range of hills extending from the sea to the Tagus, and occupying the intermediate ground until close to Lisbon. Laborde's position was an embarrassing one. If he retired upon Torres Vedras his line of communication with Loison would be lost, if he moved to meet Loison he would leave open the direct road to Lisbon, while if he remained at Rolica he had to encounter a force almost three times his own strength.

Trusting in the advantages of his position, and confident in the valour of his troops, he chose the last alternative. Very anxiously, during the day, the British officers watched the French line of defence, fearful lest the enemy would again retreat. By sunset they came to the conclusion that Laborde intended to stay where he was, and to meet them. The French, indeed, had been so accustomed to beat the Spanish and Portuguese, that they had not woke up to the fact that they had troops of a very different material facing them.

"We ought to have easy work," Major Harrison said, as the officers gathered round the fire that had been built in front of the colonel's tent; "the people here all declare that Laborde has not above 5,000 troops with him, while, counting Trant's Portuguese, we have nearly 14,000."

"There will be no credit in thrashing them with such odds as that," Dick Ryan grumbled.

"I suppose, Ryan," Major Harrison said, "if you had been in Sir Arthur's place you would have preferred remaining at Leirya until Junot could have gathered all his forces, and obtained a reinforcement of some fifty thousand or so from Spain, then you would have issued a general order saying, that as the enemy had now a hundred thousand troops ready, the army would advance and smite them."

"Not so bad as that, Major," the young ensign said, colouring, as there was a general laugh from the rest; "but there does not seem much satisfaction in thrashing an enemy when we are three to one against him."

"But that is just the art of war, Ryan. Of course, it is

glorious to defeat a greatly superior army and to lose half your own in doing so; that may be heroic, but it is not modern war. The object of a general is, if possible, to defeat an enemy in detail, and to so manœuvre that he is always superior in strength to the force that is immediately in front of him, and so to ensure victory after victory until the enemy are destroyed. That is what the general is doing by his skilful manœuvring; he has prevented Junot from massing the whole of the army of Portugal against us.

"To-morrow we shall defeat Laborde, and doubtless a day or two later we shall fight Loison; then I suppose we shall advance against Lisbon, Junot will collect his beaten troops and his garrison, there will be another battle, and then we shall capture Lisbon, and the French will have to evacuate Portugal. Whereas, if all the French were at Rolica they would probably smash us into a cocked hat, in spite of any valour we might show; and as we have no cavalry to cover a retreat, as the miserable horses can scarcely drag the few guns that we have got, and the carriages are so rickety that the artillery officers are afraid that as soon as they fire them they will shake to pieces, it is not probable that a single man would regain our ships."

"Please say no more, Major; I see I was a fool."

"Still," Captain O'Connor said, "you must own, Major, that one does like to win against odds."

"Quite so, O'Connor; individuals who may survive such a battle no doubt would be glad that it was a superior force that they had beaten, but then you see battles are not fought for the satisfaction of individuals. Moreover, you must remember that the proportion of loss is much heavier when the numbers are pretty equally matched, for in that case they must meet to a certain extent face to face. Skill on the part of the general may do a great deal, but in the end it must come to sheer hard fighting. Now, I expect that to-morrow, although there may be hard fighting, it is not upon that that Sir Arthur will principally rely for turning the French out of those strong positions.

"He will, no doubt, advance directly against them with perhaps half his force, but the rest will move along on the top of the heights, and so threaten to cut the French line of retreat altogether. Laborde is, they say, a good general, and therefore won't wait until he is caught in a trap, but will fall back as soon as he sees that the line of retreat is seriously menaced. I fancy, too, that he must expect Loison up some time to-morrow, or he would hardly make a stand, and if Loison does come up, Ryan's wish will be gratified and we shall be having the odds against us.

"Then you must remember that our army is a very raw one. A large proportion of it is newly raised, and though there may be a few men here who fought in Egypt, the great bulk have never seen a shot fired in earnest; while, on the other hand, the French have been fighting all over Europe. They are accustomed to victory, and are confident in their own valour and discipline. Our officers are as raw as our men, and we must expect that all sorts of blunders will be made at first. I can tell you that I am very well satisfied that our first battle is going to be fought with the odds greatly on our side. In six months I should feel pretty confident, even if the French had the same odds on their side."

"The major gave it you rather hotly, Dick," Terence said to his friend, as they sauntered off together from the group. "I am glad that you spoke first, for I had it on the tip of my tongue to say just what you did, and I expect that a good many of the others felt just the same."

"Yes, I put my foot in it badly, Terence. I have no doubt the major was right; anyhow, I have nothing to say against it. But for all that I wish that either we were not so strong or that they were stronger. What credit is there, I should like to know, in thrashing them when we are three to one? Anyhow, I hope that we shall have some share in the scrimmage. We shall get an idea when the orders are published to-night, and shall see where Fane's brigade is to be put."

CHAPTER V

ROLICA AND VIMIERA

AT nine o'clock in the evening it became known that the general plan of attack predicted by Major Harrison was to be carried out. Some five thousand men under General Ferguson were to ascend the hills on the left of the valley, while Trant, with a thousand Portuguese infantry and some Portuguese horse, were to move on the hills on the right; the centre, nine thousand strong, and commanded by Sir Arthur himself, were to march straight up the valley.

Early in the morning the British troops marched out from Obidos. Ferguson's command at once turned to the left and ascended the hills, while Trant's moved to the west.

After proceeding a short distance, Fane's brigade moved off from the road and marched along the valley, equidistant from the main body and from Ferguson, forming a connecting link between them; and on reaching the village of St. Mamed, three-quarters of a mile from the French position, Hill's brigade turned off to the right. From their elevated position the French opened fire with their artillery, and this was answered by the twelve guns in the valley and from Ferguson's six guns on the heights. Fane's brigade, extended to its left, was the first in action, and drove back the French skirmishers and connected Ferguson with the centre. They then turned to attack the right of the French position; while Ferguson, seeing no signs of Loison's force, descended from the high ground to the rear of Fane, while the Portuguese pressed forward at the foot of the hills on the other side of the valley and threatened the enemy's left flank.

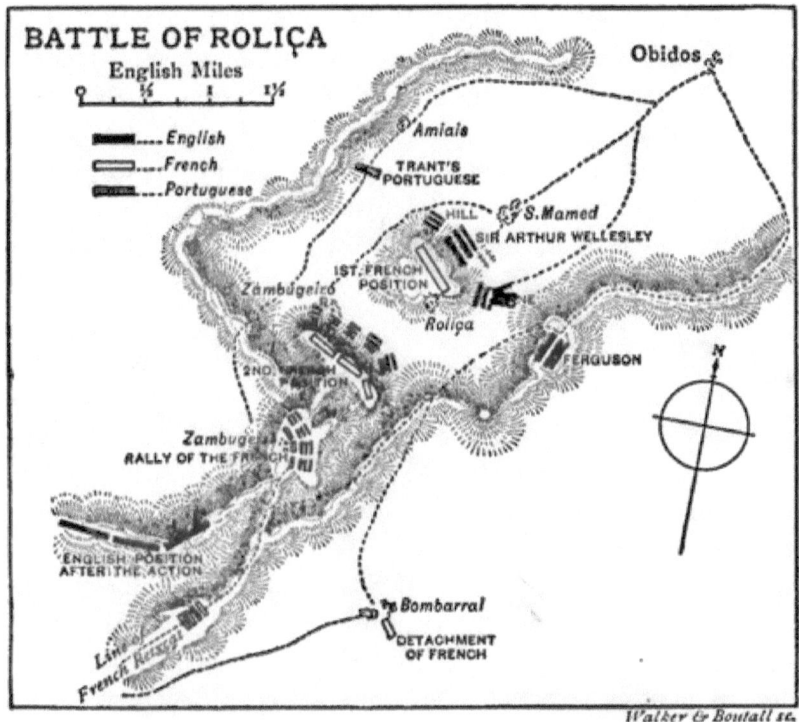

Seeing that his position was absolutely untenable, Laborde did not wait the assault, but fell back, covered by his cavalry, to the far stronger position in his rear. A momentary pause ensued before the British continued their advance. The new position of the French was of great natural strength, and could be approached only by narrow paths winding up through deep ravines on its face. Ferguson and Fane received orders to keep to the left, and so turn the enemy's right. Trant similarly was to push forward and threaten his left flank, while Hill and Nightingale advanced against the front.

The battle commenced by a storm of skirmishers from these brigades running forward. These soon reached the foot of the precipitous hill and plunged into the passes. Neither the fire of the enemy nor the difficulties of the ascent checked them. Spreading right and left from the paths they made their way up, and taking advantage of the shelter afforded by great boulders, broken masses of rock, and the stumps of trees, climbed up wherever they could find a foothold. The supporting columns experienced much greater difficulty; the paths were too narrow, and the ground too broken for them to retain their formation, and they made their way forward as best they could in necessary disorder.

The din of battle was prodigious, for the rattle of musketry was echoed and re-echoed from the rocks. The progress of the skirmishers could only be noted by the light smoke rising through the foliage and by the shouts of the soldiers, which were echoed by the still louder ones of the French, gathered strongly on the hill above them. As the British made their way up, Laborde, who was still anxiously looking for the expected coming of Loison, withdrew a portion of his troops from the left and strengthened his right, in order to hold on as long as possible on the side from which aid was expected. The ardour of the British to get to close quarters favoured this movement.

It had been intended that the 9th and 29th Regiments should take the right-hand path where the track they were following up the pass forked, and so join Trant's Portuguese at the top of the hill and fall upon the French left. The left-hand path, however, was the one that would take them direct to the enemy, and the 29th, which was leading, took this, and the 9th followed them. So rapidly did they press up the hill that they arrived at the crest before Ferguson and Fane, on the left, and Trant on the right, had got far enough to menace the line of retreat, and so shake the enemy's position. The consequence was, that as the right wing of the 29th arrived at the top of the path it was met by a very heavy fire before it could form, and some companies of a French regiment, who had been cut off from the main body by its sudden appearance, charged through the disordered troops and carried with them a major and fifty or sixty other prisoners.

The rest of the wing, thus exposed to the full fire of the French, fell back over the crest, and there rallied on the left wing; and being joined by the 9th, pushed forward again and obtained a footing on the plateau. Laborde in vain endeavoured to hurl them back again. They maintained their footing, but suffered heavily, both the colonels being killed, with many officers and men. But the 5th Regiment were now up, and at other points the British were gathering thickly at the edge of the plateau. Ferguson and Trant were pushing on fast past the French flanks, and Laborde, seeing that further resistance would lead to great disaster, gave the order to retire to a third position, still farther in the rear. The movement was conducted in splendid order. The French steadily fell back by alternate masses, their guns thundering on their flanks, while their cavalry covered the rear by repeated charges.

Gaining the third position, Laborde held it for a time, and so enabled isolated bodies of his force to join him. Then, finding himself unable to resist the impetuosity of the British attack, he retired, still disputing every foot of ground, and took to the narrow pass of Runa. He then marched all night to the strong position of Montechique, thereby securing his junction with Loison, but leaving the road to Torres Vedras open to the British. The loss of the French in this fight was

600 killed and wounded, and three guns. Laborde himself was among the wounded. The British lost nearly 500 killed, wounded, or taken prisoners. The number of the combatants actually engaged on either side was about 4,000, and the loss sustained showed the obstinacy of the fighting. Sir Arthur believed that the French had, as they retreated, been joined by Loison, and therefore prepared to march at once by the coast-line to seize the heights of Torres Vedras before the French could throw themselves in his way.

Great was the disappointment among officers and men of the Mayo Fusiliers that they had taken no part whatever in the actual fighting, beyond driving in the French skirmishers at the beginning of the operations.

"Divil a man killed or wounded!" Captain O'Grady remarked, mournfully, as the regiment halted at the conclusion of the fight. "Faith, it is too bad, entirely; there we are left out in the cold, and scarce a shot has been fired!"

"There are plenty of others in the same case," Captain O'Driscol said. "None of our three brigades on the left have had anything to do with the matter, as far as fighting went. I don't think more than four thousand of our troops were in action; but you see if it had not been for our advance, Hill and Nightingale might not have succeeded in driving Laborde off the hill. There is no doubt that the French fought well, but it's our advance that forced him to retire, not the troops in front of him; so that, even if we have not had any killed or wounded, O'Grady, we have at least the satisfaction of having contributed to the victory."

"Oh, bother your tactics! We have come here to fight, and no fighting have we had at all, at all. When we marched out this morning it looked as if we were going to have our share in the divarshon, and we have been fairly chated out of it."

"Well, O'Grady, you should not grumble," Terence said, "for we had some fighting on the way out, which is more than any of the other troops had."

"That was a mere skirmish, Terence. First of all we were shot at, and could not shoot back again; and thin we shot at the enemy, and they could not shoot back at us. And as for the boarding affair, faith, it did not last a minute. The others have had two hours of steady fighting, clambering up the hill, and banging away at the enemy, and shouting and cheering, and all sorts of fun; and there were we, tramping along among those bastely stones and rocks, and no one as much as took the trouble to fire a shot at us!"

"Well, if we had been there, O'Grady, we should have lost about a hundred and twenty men and officers—if we had suffered in the same proportion as the others—and we should now be mourning their loss—perhaps you among them. We might have been saying: 'There is O'Grady gone; he was a beggar to talk, but he meant well. Faith, the drink bill of the regiment will fall off.'"

"Well, it might have been so," O'Grady said, in a more contented voice; "and if I had been killed going up the hill, without even as much as catching a glimpse of the Frenchies, I would niver have forgiven them—niver!"

There was a roar of laughter at the bull.

"Phwat is it have I said?" he asked, in surprise.

"Nothing, O'Grady; but it would be an awful thing for the French to know that after your death you would have gone on hating them for ever."

"Did I say that? But you know my maneing, and as long as you know that, what does it matter which way I put it? Well, now, I suppose Sir Arthur is going to take us tramping along again. Ah, it is a weary thing being a soldier!"

"Why, you were saying yesterday, O'Grady, that your feet were getting all right," Terence said.

"All right in a manner, Terence. And it is a bad habit that you have got of picking up your supayrior officer's words and throwing them into his teeth. You will come to a bad end if you don't break yourself of it; and the worst of it is, you are corrupting the other lads, and the young officers are losing all respect for their seniors. I am surprised, Major, that you and the colonel don't take the matter in hand before the discipline of the regiment is destroyed entirely."

"You draw it upon yourself, O'Grady, and it is good for us all to have a laugh sometimes. We should all have missed you sorely had you gone down on that hill over there—as many a good fellow has done. I hear that both the 9th and 29th have lost their colonels."

"The Lord presarve us from such a misfortune, Major! It would give us a step all through the regiment; but then, you see——" And he stopped.

"You mean I should be colonel, O'Grady," the major said, with a laugh; "and you know I should not take things as quietly as he does. Well, you see, there are consolations all round."

The firing had ceased at four o'clock, and until late that night a large portion of the force were occupied in searching the ground that had been traversed, burying the dead, and carrying the wounded of both nationalities down into the hospital that had been established at Rolica. Sir Arthur determined to march at daybreak, so as to secure the passes through Torres Vedras; but in the evening a messenger arrived with the news that Anstruther and Acland's division, with a large fleet of store-ships, were off the coast. The dangerous nature of the coast, and the certainty that, should a gale spring up, a large proportion of the ships would be wrecked, rendered it absolutely necessary to secure the disembarkation of the troops at once. The next morning, therefore, he only marched ten miles to Lourinha, and thence advanced to Vimiera, eight miles farther, where he covered the disembarkation of the troops.

The next day Anstruther's brigade were with difficulty, and some loss, landed on an open sandy beach, and on the night of the 20th Acland's brigade were disembarked at Maciera Bay. The reinforcements were most opportune, for already the British had proof that Junot was preparing a heavy blow. That general had, indeed, lost no time in taking steps to bring on a decisive battle. While the British were marching to Lourinha, he had, with Loison's division, crossed the line of Laborde's retreat, and on the same evening reached Torres Vedras, where the next day he was joined by Laborde, and on the 20th by his reserve. In the meantime he sent forward his cavalry, which scoured the country round the rear of the British camp, and prevented the general from obtaining any information whatever as to his position or intentions.

The arrival of Acland's brigade on the night of the 20th increased the fighting strength of the army to 16,000 men, with eighteen guns, exclusive of Trant's Portuguese, while Sir Arthur judged that Junot could not put more than 14,000 in the field. Previous to leaving Mondego he had sent to Sir Harry Burrard notice of his plan of campaign, advising him to let Sir John Moore, on his arrival with 5,000 men, disembark there and march on Santarem, where he would protect the left of the army in its advance, block the line of the Tagus, and menace the French line of communication between Lisbon and the important fortress of Elvas. The ground at Santarem was suited for defence, and Moore could be joined with Friere, who was still, with his 5,000 men, at Leirya.

The general intended to make a forced march, keeping by the sea-road. A strong advance guard would press forward and occupy the formidable position of Mathia in the rear of the hills. With the main body he intended to seize some heights a few miles behind Torres Vedras, and to cut the road between that place and Montechique, on the direct road to Lisbon, and so interpose between Junot and the capital. At twelve o'clock that night Sir Arthur was roused by a messenger, who reported that Junot, with 20,000 men, was advancing to attack him, and was but an hour's march distant. He disbelieved the account of the force of the enemy, and had no doubt but that the messenger's fears had exaggerated the closeness of his approach. He therefore contented himself with sending orders to the pickets to use redoubled vigilance, and at daylight the whole British force was, as usual, under arms.

Nothing could have suited the British commander better than that Junot should attack him, for the position of Vimiera was strong. The town was situated in a valley, through which the little river Maciera flows. In this were placed the commissariat stores, while the cavalry and Portuguese were on a small plain behind the village. In front of Vimiera was a steep hill with a flat top, commanding the ground to the south and east for a considerable distance. Fane's and Anstruther's infantry, with six guns, were posted here. Fane's left rested on a churchyard, blocking a road which led round the declivity of the hill to the town. Behind this position, and separated by the river and road, was a hill extending in a half-moon to the sea.

Five brigades of infantry, forming the British right, occupied this mountain. On the other side of the ravine formed by the river, just beyond Vimiera, was another strong and narrow range of heights. There was no water to be found on this ridge, and only the 40th Regiment and some pickets were stationed here. It was vastly better to be attacked in such a position than to be compelled to storm the heights of Torres Vedras, held by a strong French army. The advance of the French was fortunate in another respect. On the 20th Sir Harry Burrard arrived in the bay on board

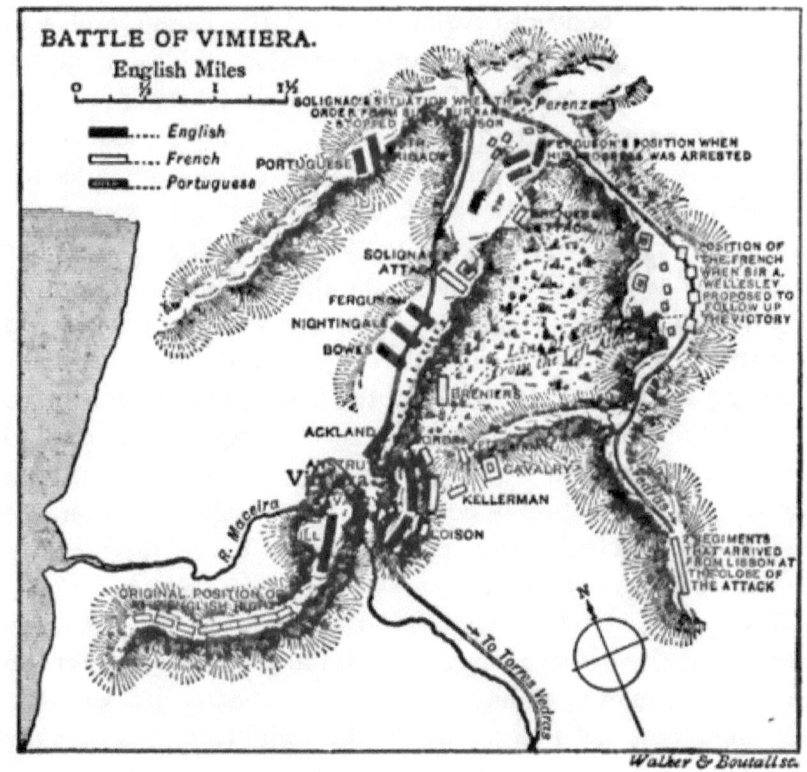

a frigate, and Sir Arthur, thus superseded, went on board to report the position of affairs, renewing his recommendation that Sir John Moore should land at Mondego and march to Santarem. Sir Harry Burrard, however, had already determined that his force should land at Maciera, and he refused to permit Sir Arthur's plan of advance to be carried out, and ordered that no offensive step should be undertaken until Sir John Moore had landed.

The advance of Junot, happily, left Wellesley at liberty to act; and disposing his force in order of battle, he awaited the appearance of the enemy. It was not until seven o'clock that a cloud of dust was seen rising above the opposite ridge, and an hour later a body of cavalry crowned the height and sent out a swarm of scouts in every direction. Almost immediately afterwards a body of cavalry and infantry were seen marching along the road from Torres Vedras to Lourinha, threatening to turn the left of the British position. As the British right was not menaced, four of the brigades on the hill on that flank were ordered to cross the valley and to take post with the 40th Regiment for the defence of the ridge.

This movement, being covered by the Vimiera heights, was unseen by the enemy; the 5th brigade and the Portuguese were on a second ridge behind the other, and thus assisted to cover the English left and protect its rear. The ground between the crest on which the French were first seen and our position was so thickly covered with wood, that after the enemy had descended into it no correct view of their movements could be obtained.

Junot had intended to fall upon the English army at daybreak, but the defiles through which the force had to pass had delayed the march, as had the fatigue of the troops, who had been marching all night. From the height from which he obtained a view of the British position it seemed to him that the British centre and right were held in great strength, and that the left was almost unguarded. He therefore determined to attack upon that flank, which, indeed, was in any case the most favourable, as, were he successful there, he would cut the line of the British retreat and pen them up on the sea-shore.

The march of the four brigades through Vimiera to take post on the British left was hidden from him, and he divided his force into two heavy columns, one of which was to attack the British left, and having mounted the height to sweep all before it into the town; the other was to attack Vimiera Hill, held by Anstruther and Fane.

Brennier commanded the attack against the left, Laborde against the centre, Loison followed at a short distance. Kellermann commanded the reserve of Grenadiers. Unfortunately for the success of Junot's plan, he was unaware of the fact that along the foot of the ridge on the British left ran a deep ravine, that rendered it very difficult to attack except at the extreme end of the position.

"We are going to have our share of the fun to-day," O'Grady said, as he stood with a group of officers, watching the wooded plain and the head of Laborde's column debouching from among the trees, and moving towards the hill.

There was a general murmur of satisfaction from the officers, for although they had all laughed at O'Grady's exaggerated regrets at their not being engaged at Rolica, all were somewhat sore at the regiment having had no opportunity of distinguishing itself on that occasion. No sooner had the column cleared the wood than the six guns posted with Fane's and Anstruther's brigade at once opened fire upon it. It had been intended that Brennier's attack should begin at the same time as Laborde's, but that advance had been stopped by the defile, which was so steep and so encumbered with rocks, brushwood, and trees, that his troops had the most extreme difficulty in making their way across. This enabled Acland, whose brigade was in the act of mounting the heights from the town, to turn his battery against Laborde's column, which was thus smitten with a shower of grape both in front and flank, and to this was added a heavy musketry fire from the three brigades.

"Take it easy, lads, take it easy," the colonel said, as he walked up and down the ranks. "They are hardly in range yet, and you had better keep your ammunition until they get to the foot of the hill, then you can blaze away as hard as you like."

Junot, receiving news of the arrest of Brennier's column and the obstacles that he had encountered, and seeing that the whole British fire was now directed against Laborde, ordered Loison to support that general with one brigade, and directed Solignac to turn the ravine in which Brennier was entangled and to fall upon the left extremity of the enemy's line.

Fane had been given discretionary power to call up the reserve artillery posted in the village behind him, and seeing so strong an attack against his position about to be made called it up to the top of the hill.

Loison and Laborde now formed their troops into three columns of attack. One advanced against that part of the hill held by Anstruther's brigade, another endeavoured to penetrate by the road past the church on Fane's extreme left, while the main column, represented by a large number of the best troops, advanced against the centre of the position. The reserve artillery, and the battery originally there, opened a terrible fire, which was aided by the musketry of the infantry. But with loud shouts the French pressed forward, and although already shaken by the terrible fire of the artillery, and breathless from their exertions, they gained the crest of the hill. Before they could re-form a tremendous volley was poured into them, and with a wild yell the Mayo Fusiliers and the 50th charged them in front and flank and hurled them down the hill.

In the meantime, Anstruther, having repulsed the less serious attack made on him, detached the 43d to check the enemy's column moving through the churchyard, and prevented their advance until Kellermann brought up a force of Grenadiers, who, running forward with loud shouts, drove back the advanced companies of the 43d. The guns on the heights were turned upon them with great effect, and those of Acland's and Bowe's brigades on the left of the ridge took them in flank and brought them almost to a stand-still; then the 43d, in one mass, charged furiously down on the column, and after a fierce struggle drove them back in confusion.

The French attacks on this side had now completely failed, and Colonel Taylor, riding out with his little body of cavalry, dashed out into the confused mass, slaying and scattering it. Margaron, who commanded a superior force of French cavalry, led them down through their infantry, and falling upon the British force killed Taylor and cut half his squadron to pieces. Kellermann took post with his reserve of Grenadiers in a pinewood in advance of the wooded country through which they had advanced, while Margaron's horsemen maintained a position covering the retreat of the fugitives into the wood. At this moment Solignac reached his assigned position and encountered Ferguson's brigade, which was on the extreme left of the division, and was taken by surprise on finding a force equal to his own where he had expected to find the hill untenanted. Ferguson was drawn up in three lines on a steep declivity. A heavy artillery fire opened upon the French as soon as they were seen, while the 5th brigade and the Portuguese marched along the next ridge and threatened the enemy's rear.

Ferguson did not wait to be attacked, but marched his brigade against the French, who, falling fast under the musketry and artillery fire which had swept their lines, fell back fighting to the farthest edge of the ridge. Solignac was carried off severely wounded, and his brigade was cut off from its line of retreat and driven into a low valley, in which stood the village of Peranza, leaving six guns behind them. Ferguson left two regiments to guard these guns, and with the rest of his force pressed hard upon the French; but at this moment Brennier, who had at last surmounted the difficulties that had detained him, fell upon the two regiments suddenly, and retook the guns.

The 82d and 71st, speedily recovered from their surprise, rallied on some higher ground, and then, after pouring in a tremendous volley of musketry, charged with a mighty shout and overthrew the French brigade and recovered the guns. Brennier himself was wounded and taken prisoner, and Ferguson having completely broken up the brigade opposed to him would have forced the greater part of Solignac's troops to surrender, if he had not been required to halt by an unexpected order. The French veterans speedily rallied, and in admirable order, protected by their cavalry, marched off to join their comrades who had been defeated in their attack upon the British centre.

It was now twelve o'clock; the victory was complete; thirteen guns had been captured. Neither the 1st, 5th, nor Portuguese brigades had fired a shot, and the 4th and 8th had suffered very little, therefore Sir Arthur resolved with these five brigades to push Junot closely, while Hill, Anstruther, and Fane were to march forward as far as Torres Vedras, and, pushing on to Montechique, cut him off from Lisbon. Had this operation been executed Junot would probably have lost all his artillery, and seven thousand stragglers would have been driven to seek shelter under the guns of Elvas, from which fortress, however, he would have been cut off had Moore landed as Sir Arthur wished at Mondego. Unhappily, however, the latter was no longer commander-in-chief. Sir Harry Burrard, who had been present at the action, had not interfered with the arrangements, but as soon as victory was won he assumed command, sent an order arresting Ferguson's career of victory, and forbade all further offensive operations until the arrival of Sir John Moore.

The adjutant-general and quartermaster supported his views, and Sir Arthur's earnest representations were disregarded. Sir Arthur's plan would probably have been crowned with success, but it was not without peril. The French had rallied with extraordinary rapidity under the protection of their cavalry. The British artillery-carriages were so shaken as to be almost unfit for service, the horses insufficient in number and wretched in quality, the commissariat waggons in the greatest confusion, and the hired Portuguese vehicles had made off in every direction. The British cavalry were totally destroyed, and two French regiments had just made their appearance on the ridge behind the wood where Junot's troops were re-forming.

Sir Harry Burrard, with a caution characteristic of age, refused to adopt Wellesley's bold plan. A great success had been gained, and that would have been imperilled by Junot's falling with all his force upon one or other of the British columns. Sir Arthur himself, at a later period, when a commission was appointed by Parliament to inquire into the circumstances, admitted that, though he still believed that success would have attended his own plan, he considered that Sir Harry Burrard's decision was fully justified on military grounds.

Junot took full advantage of the unexpected cessation of hostilities. He re-formed his broken army on the arrival of the two regiments, which brought it up to its original strength; and then, covered by his cavalry, marched in good order until darkness fell. He had regained the command of the passes of Torres Vedras, and the two armies occupied precisely the same positions that they had done on the previous evening.

One general, thirteen guns, and several hundred prisoners fell into the hands of the British, and Junot's total loss far exceeded that of the British, which was comparatively small. At the commencement of the fight the British force was more than two thousand larger than that of the French, but of these only a half had taken an active part in the battle, while every man in Junot's army had been sent forward to the attack.

Sir Harry Burrard's command was a short one, for on the following morning Sir Hew Dalrymple superseded him. Thus in twenty-four hours a battle had been fought and the command of the army had been three times changed, a striking proof of the abject folly and incapacity of the British ministry of the day.

Two of these three commanders arrived fresh on the scene without any previous knowledge of the situation, and all three differed from each other in their views regarding the general plan of the campaign; the last two were men without any previous experience in the handling of large bodies of troops, and without any high military reputation; while the man displaced had already shown the most brilliant capacity in India, and was universally regarded as the best general in the British service. Dalrymple adopted neither the energetic action advised by Sir Arthur nor the inactivity supported by Burrard, but, taking a middle course, decided to advance on the following morning, but not to go far until Sir John Moore landed at Maciera.

Sir Arthur was strongly opposed to this policy. He pointed out that there were at present on shore but seven or eight days' provisions for the force at Vimiera. No further supplies could be obtained in the country, and at any moment a gale might arise and scatter or destroy the fleet, from which alone they could draw supplies during their advance. The debate on the subject was continuing when the French general, Kellermann, bearing a flag of truce and escorted by a strong body of cavalry, arrived at the outposts and desired a conference. The news was surprising, indeed. Junot's force was practically unshaken. He possessed all the strong places in Portugal, and could have received support in a short time from the French forces in Spain.

Upon the other hand, the position of the British, even after winning a victory, was by no means a satisfactory one; they had already learnt that it was useless to rely in the slightest degree upon Portuguese promises or Portuguese assistance, and that, even in the matter of provisions and carriage, their commander-in-chief expected to be maintained by those who had come to aid in freeing the country of the French, instead of these receiving any help from him. In carriage the British army was wholly deficient; of cavalry they had none. When Sir John Moore landed there would be but four days' provisions on shore for the army, and were the fleet driven off by a gale, starvation would at once threaten them.

The gallantry with which the French had fought in both engagements, the skill with which they had been handled, and above all, the quickness and steadiness with which, after defeat, they had closed up their ranks and drawn off in excellent order, showed that the task of expelling such troops from the country would, even if all went well in other respects, be a very formidable one, and the offer of a conference was therefore at once embraced by Sir Hew Dalrymple.

Kellermann was admitted to the camp. His mission was to demand a cessation of arms in order that Junot might, under certain conditions, evacuate Portugal. The advantage of freeing the country from the French without further fighting was so evident that Sir Hew at once agreed to discuss the terms, and took Sir Arthur Wellesley into his counsels. The latter quite agreed with the policy by which a strong French army would be quietly got out of the country, in which it held all the military posts and strong positions. A great moral effect would be produced, and the whole resources of Portugal would then be available for operations in Spain.

By the afternoon the main points of the convention had been generally agreed upon. The French were to evacuate Portugal, and were to be conveyed in the English vessels to France with their property, public or private. There was to be no persecution of persons who had been the adherents of France during the occupation; the only serious difference that arose was as to the Russian fleet in the Tagus. Kellermann proposed to have it guaranteed from capture, with leave to return to the Baltic. This, however, was refused, and the question was referred to Admiral Cotton, who, as chief representative of England, would have to approve of the treaty before it could be signed.

Kellermann returned to Lisbon with Colonel Murray, the quartermaster-general, and after three days' negotiations the treaty was finally concluded, the Russian difficulty being settled by their vessels being handed over to the British, and the crew transported in English ships to the Baltic. The convention was, under the circumstances, unquestionably a most advantageous one. It would have cost long and severe fighting and the siege of several very strong fortresses before the French could have been turned out of Portugal. Heavy siege-guns would have been necessary for these operations. At the very shortest calculation a year would have been wasted, very heavy loss of life incurred, and an immense expenditure of money before the result, now obtained so suddenly and unexpectedly, had been arrived at.

Nevertheless, the news of the convention was received with a burst of popular indignation in England, where the public, wholly ignorant of the difficulty of the situation, had formed the most extravagant hopes, founded on the two successes obtained by their troops. The result was that a commission was appointed to investigate the whole matter. The three English generals were summoned to England to attend before it, and so gross were the misrepresentations and lies by which the public had been deceived by the agents of the unscrupulous and ambitious Bishop of Oporto and his confederates, that it was even proposed to bring the generals to trial who had in so short a time and with such insufficient means freed Portugal from the French. Sir John Moore remained in command of the troops in Portugal.

CHAPTER VI

A PAUSE

THE Mayo Fusiliers had suffered their full proportion of losses at the battle of Vimiera. Major Harrison had been killed, Captain O'Connor had been severely wounded, as his company had been thrown forward as skirmishers on the face of the hill, and a third of their number had fallen when Laborde's great column had driven them in as it charged up the ascent. Terence's father had been brought to the ground by a ball that struck him near the hip; had been trampled on by the French as they passed up over him, and again on their retreat; and he was insensible when, as soon as the enemy retired, a party was sent down to bring up the wounded. By the death of the major, O'Connor, as senior captain, now attained that rank, but the doctor pronounced that it would be a long time before he would be able to take up his duties. Another captain and three subalterns had been killed, and several other officers had been wounded. Among these was O'Grady, whose left arm had been carried away below the elbow by a round

"I SHOULD NOT HAVE MINDED BEING HIT, FATHER, IF YOU HAD ESCAPED."

shot. As Terence was in the other wing of the regiment he did not hear of his father's wounds until after the battle was over, and on the order being given that there was to be no pursuit the regiment fell out of its ranks. As soon as the news reached him he obtained permission to go down to Vimiera, where the church and other buildings had been turned into temporary hospitals, to which the seriously wounded had been carried as soon as the French retired. Hurrying down, he soon learned where the wounded of General Fane's brigade had been taken. He found the two regimental doctors hard at work. O'Flaherty came up to Terence as soon as he saw him enter the barn that had been hastily converted into a hospital by covering the floor deeply with straw.

"I think your father will do, Terence, my boy," he said, cheeringly; "we have just got the bullet out of his leg, and we hope that it has not touched the bone, though we cannot be altogether sure. We shall know more about that when we have got through the rough of our work. Still, we have every hope that he will do well. He is next the door at the further end; we put him there to let him get as much fresh air as possible, for, by the powers, this place is like a furnace!"

Captain O'Connor was lying on his back, the straw having been arranged so as to raise his shoulders and head. He smiled when Terence came up to him.

"Thank God you have got safely through it, lad!"

"I should not have minded being hit, father, if you had escaped," Terence said, with difficulty suppressing a sob, while in spite of his efforts the tears rolled down his cheeks.

"The doctors say I shall pull through all right. I hear poor Harrison is killed; he was a good fellow. Though it has given me my step, I am heartily sorry. So we have thrashed them, lad; that is a comfort. I was afraid when they went up the hill that they might be too much for us, and I was delighted when I heard them coming tearing down again, though I had not much time to think about it. They had stepped over me pretty much as they went up, but they had no time to pick their way as they came back again, and after one or two had jumped on me, I remembered no more about it until I found myself here with O'Flaherty probing the wound and hurting me horribly. I am bruised all over, and I wonder some of my ribs are not broken; at present they hurt me a good deal more than this wound in the hip. Still, that is only an affair of a day or two. Who have been killed besides the major?"

"Dorman, Phillips, and Henderson are killed. O'Grady is wounded, I hear, and so are Saunders, Byrne, and Sullivan; there have been some others hit, but not seriously; they did not have to fall out."

"O'Grady is over on the other side somewhere, Terence; I heard his voice just now. Go and see where he is hurt."

O'Grady was sitting up with his back to the wall; the sleeves of his jacket and shirt had been cut off, and a tourniquet was on his arm just above the elbow.

"Well, Terence," he said, cheerfully, "I am in luck, you see."

"I can't see any luck about it, O'Grady."

"Why, man, it might have been my right arm, and where should I have been then? As to the left arm, one can do without it very well. Then, again, it is lucky that the ball hit me below the elbow and not above it. O'Flaherty says they will be able to make a dacent job of it, and that after a bit they will be able to fit a wooden arm on, so that I can screw a fork into it. The worst of it at present is, that I have a terrible thirst on me, and nothing but water have they given me, a thing that I have not drunk for years. They have tied up the arteries, and they are going presently to touch up the loose ends with hot pitch to stop the bleeding altogether. It is not a pleasant job; they have done it to three or four of the men already. One of them stood it well, but the others cried a thousand murders. O'Flaherty has promised me a drink of whisky and water before they do it, and just at present I feel as if I would let them burn all my limbs at the same price. It is sorry I am, Terence, to hear that your father is hit so hard, but O'Flaherty says he will get through it all right. Well, he will get his majority, though I am mightily sorry that Harrison is killed; he was a good boy, though he was an Englishman. Ah, Terence, my heart's sore when I think what I said that evening after the fight at Rolica! I did not mean it altogether, but the words come home to me now. It is not for meself but for the poor boys that have gone. It was just thoughtlessness, but I would give me other arm not to have said those words."

"I know that you did not mean it, O'Grady, and we were all feeling sorry that the regiment had not had a chance to be in the thick of it."

"Here they are, coming this way with the pitch kettle. You had better get away, lad, before they begin."

Terence was glad to follow the advice, and hurried out of the barn and walked three or four hundred yards away. He was very fond of O'Grady, who had always been very kind to him, and who was thoroughly warm-hearted and a good fellow, in spite of his eccentricities. In a quarter of an hour he returned. Just as he was entering, O'Flaherty came out of the door.

"I must have a breath of fresh air, Terence," he said. "The heat is stifling in there, and though we are working in our shirt-sleeves we are just as damp as if we had been thrown into a pond."

"Has O'Grady's arm been seared?"

"Yes, and he stood it well; not a word did he say until it was over. Then he said, 'Give me another drink, O'Flaherty; it's wake-like I feel.' Before I could get the cup to his lips he went off in a faint. He has come round now and has had a drink of weak whisky and water, and is lying quiet and composed. It is better that you should not go near him at present. I hope that he will drop off to sleep presently. I have just given a glance at your father, and he is nearly, if not quite, asleep too, so you had better leave them now and look in again this evening. Now that the affair is over, and there is time to go round, they will clear out some houses and get things more comfortable. The principal medical officer was round here half an hour ago. He said they would fit up rooms for the officers at once, and I will have your father, O'Grady, and Saunders carried up on stretchers and put into a room together. If they can bear the moving it will be all in their favour, for it will be cooler there than in this oven of a place. I hear the church has been requisitioned, and that the worst cases among our men will be taken there."

In comparison with the loss of the French that of the British had been very small. From their position on commanding heights they had suffered but little from the fire of the French artillery, and the casualties were almost confined to Fane's brigade, the 43d Regiment, Anstruther's, and the two regiments of Ferguson's brigade that had been attacked by Brennier, and before nightfall the whole of the wounded had been brought in and attended to, the hospitals arranged, and the men far more comfortably bestowed than in the temporary quarters taken up during the heat of the conflict. As there was no prospect of an immediate movement, the soldier servants of the wounded officers had been excused from military duty and told off to attend to them, and when

Terence went down in the evening he found his father, O'Grady, and Saunders—the latter a young lieutenant—comfortably lodged in a large room in which three hospital beds had been placed. O'Grady had quite recovered his usual good spirits.

"Don't draw such a long face, Terence," he said, as the lad entered; "we are all going on well. Your father has been bandaged all over the chest and body, and is able to breathe more comfortably; as for me, except that I feel as if somebody were twisting a red-hot needle about in my arm, I am as right as possible, and Saunders is doing first-rate. The doctors thought at first that he had got a ball through his body; after they got him here they had time to examine him carefully, and they find that it has just run along the ribs and gone out behind, and that he will soon be about again. If it wasn't that the doctors say I must drink nothing but water with lemon-juice squeezed into it, I would have nothing to complain of. We have got our servants. Hoolan came in blubbering like a calf, the omadhoun, and I had to threaten to send him back to the regiment before he would be sensible. He has sworn off spirits until I am well enough to take to them, which is a comfort, for I am sorry to say he is one of those men who never know when they have had enough."

"Like master, like man, O'Grady."

"Terence, when I get well you will repint of your impudence to your supayrior officer, when he is not able to defend himself."

Terence went across to his father's bed.

"Do you really feel easier, father?"

"A great deal, lad. I was so bruised that every breath I took hurt me; since I have been tightly bandaged I am better, ever so much. Daly says that in a few days I shall be all right again as to that, but that the other business will keep me on my back for a long time. He has examined my wound again, and says he won't touch it for a few days; but I can see that he is rather afraid that the bone has been grazed if not splintered. You have not heard what is going to be done, have you?"

"No, father; the talk is that no move will be made anyhow until Sir John Moore lands with his troops; after that I suppose we shall go forward."

"It is a pity we did not push forward to-day, lad, if, as I hear, half the force were never engaged at all. Junot would not have carried off a gun if our fellows had been launched against them while they were in disorder. As it is, I hear they have marched away over that ridge in as good order as they came, and so we shall have all the work of thrashing them to do over again."

"They say that is what Sir Arthur wanted to do, father, but Burrard overruled him."

"Did any man ever hear of such nonsense as a general who knows nothing at all about the matter coming and taking over the command from a general who has just won a battle, and who has all the ins and outs of the matter at his finger-ends!"

"Now, my dear O'Connor," O'Grady broke in, "you know what Daly said, the quieter you lie and the less you talk the better. He did not say so to meself; in the first place, because he knew it would be of no use, and in the second, because there is no raison on earth why, because a man has lost a bit of his arm, his tongue should not wag. And what does the colonel say, Terence; is he not delighted with the regiment?"

"He *is* that, and he has a right to be," Terence said. "The way they went at the French, and tumbled them over the crest and down the hill was splendid. The tears rolled down his cheeks when he heard that the major and the others were killed, but he said that a man could not die more gloriously. He shook hands with all the officers after it was over, and sent a party down to the town to buy and bring up some barrels of wine, and served out a good allowance to each man. As soon as the firing ceased I heard him tell O'Driscol that he was proud to have commanded the regiment."

"That is good, Terence; and now, do you think that you could bring me up just a taste of the cratur?"

"The divil a drop, O'Grady; if Daly and O'Flaherty both say that you are not to have it, it is certain that it is bad for you. But I'll tell you what I will do; I have one bottle of whisky left, and I will promise you that it sha'n't be touched till you are well enough to drink it, and if we are marched away, as I suppose we shall be, I will hand it over to O'Flaherty to give you when you are fit to take it. He tells me that he will be left to look after the wounded when we move."

"I could not trust him, Terence; I would hand over a bag of gold uncounted to him, but as for whisky, the temptation would be too great for an Irishman to resist. Look here, you put it into a wooden box and nail it up securely, and write on it 'O'Grady's arm,' and hand it over to him solemnly, and tell him that I have a fancy for burying the contents myself, which will be true enough, though it is me throat I mean to bury it in."

Knowing that it was best they should be left in quiet, Terence soon left them and returned to the regiment.

"Well, Dick, what did you think of a battle?" he asked his chum.

"I don't quite know what I did think. It does not seem to me that I thought much about it at all, what with the noise of the firing and the shouting of the men, and the whistle overhead of the French round shot, and the men cheering, the French shouting, and the excitement, there was no time for thinking at all. From the time the skirmishers came running up the hill to the time when we rolled the French down it, I seem to have been in a dream. It's lucky that I had no words of command to give, for I am sure I should not have given them. I don't think l was frightened at all; somehow I did not seem to think of the danger. It was just a horrible confusion."

"I felt very much like that, too. It was not a bit like what it was when we took that brig; I felt cool enough when we jumped on to her deck. But then there was no noise to speak of, while the row this morning was tremendous. I tried to cheer when the men did, but I could not hear my own voice, and I don't know whether I made any sound or not."

A delay of some weeks took place after the battle of Vimiera. The Mayo Fusiliers were not among the troops who entered Lisbon in order to overawe the populace and prevent attacks both upon French soldiers and officers, and Portuguese suspected of leaning towards the French cause. Throughout the country everything was in confusion. A strong party, at whose head were the Bishop of Oporto and Friere, denounced the convention with the French—against whom they themselves had done nothing—as gross treachery on the part of the English to Portugal. They endeavoured in every way to excite the feelings of the population, both in the country and the capital, against the British; but in this they failed altogether, for the people were too thankful to get rid of the oppression and exactions of the invaders to feel aught but satisfaction at their being compelled to leave the country.

The Junta at Oporto, at whose head was the bishop, desired to grasp the entire power throughout the country, and were furious at being thwarted in their endeavours to prevent a central Junta being established at Lisbon. Throughout Spain also chaos reigned. Each provincial Junta refused co-operation with others, and instead of concerting measures for resistance against the great force that Napoleon was assembling on the frontier, thought only of satisfying the ambitions and greed of its members. The generals disregarded alike the orders from the central Junta at Madrid and those of the provincial Juntas, quarrelled among themselves to a point that sometimes approached open hostility, and each acted only for his private ends. Arms had been sent in vast numbers from England; yet, while the money so lavishly bestowed by British agents went into the pockets of individuals, the arms were retained by the Juntas of Seville, Cadiz, and the maritime ports, and the armies of Spain were left almost unarmed.

The term army is indeed absurd, as applied to the gatherings of peasants without an idea of discipline, with scarcely any instruction in drill, and in the majority of cases, as the result proved, altogether deficient in courage; and yet, while neglecting all military precautions and ready to crumble to pieces at the first approach of the French, the arrogance and insolence of the authorities, civil and military alike, were absolutely unbounded. They disregarded wholly the advice of the British officers and agents, and treated the men who alone could save them from the consequences of their folly with open contempt.

After a fortnight's halt at Vimiera the Mayo Fusiliers were marched, with four other regiments, to Torres Vedras, where they took up their quarters. In the middle of October O'Grady and Saunders rejoined, and Terence obtained a few days' leave to visit his father.

The latter's progress had been slow; the wound was unhealed, pieces of bone working their way out, and the doctors had decided that he must be invalided home, as it was desirable to clear out the hospitals altogether before the army marched into Spain.

"They think the change of air will do me good," Major O'Connor said to Terence, as they were chatting together after the latter arrived, "and I think so myself. It is evident that I cannot take part in the next campaign, but I hope to rejoin again in the spring. Of course it is hard, but I must not grumble; if the bullet had been half an inch more to the right it would have smashed the bone altogether, then I should have had small chance indeed, for taking off the leg at the hip is an operation that not one man in twenty survives. O'Flaherty says he thinks that all the bits of bone have worked out now, and that I may not be permanently lame; but if it is to be so, lad, it is of no use kicking against fate. I have got my majority, and if permanently disabled by my wounds, can retire on a pension on which I can live comfortably.

"So I hear that Sir John Moore is going to march into Spain. By the way, you have got some cousins in Oporto or the neighbourhood, though I don't suppose you are likely to run against them."

"I never heard you say anything about them before, father."

"No; I don't think that I ever did mention it. A first cousin of mine went over, just about the time that I was married, to Oporto, and established himself there as a wine merchant. He had been out there before for a firm in Dublin, and when Clancy's father died, and he came into some money he went out, as I said, and started for himself. He was a sharp fellow and did well, and married the daughter of a big land-owner. We used to hear from him occasionally. He died about a year ago, and left a girl behind him; she had been brought up in her mother's religion. He never said much about his wife, but I fancy she was a very strong Roman Catholic, and that they did not quite agree about the girl, who, as I gathered, had a hankering after her father's religion.

However, after Clancy died we never heard any more of them.

"There was a letter from their man of business announcing the death, and stating that Clancy had left his own property, that is to say, the money he had made in business, to the girl. What has become of her since I do not know. It was no business of mine, though I believe that I was his nearest relation—at least my uncle had no other children, and there were neither brothers nor sisters except him and my father. Still, as he left a widow who had a good big property on her own account, and was connected with a lot of grandee families, there was no occasion for me to mix myself up in the affair; and, indeed, it never entered my head to do so. Yet, Clancy and I were great friends, and I should be glad to know what has become of his girl. I fancy that she is about your age, and if Moore should take you up north you might make some inquiries there. The mother's family name was Montarlies, and I fancy, from what Clancy said, her father's property was somewhere to the north of Oporto, so I expect that at that town you would be likely to hear something of them."

"All right, father; if we go there I will be sure to make some inquiries."

On the fourth day after Terence's arrival the hospital was broken up, the convalescents marched for Torres Vedras, and Major O'Connor, with four other officers and forty men, were put on board a ship to be taken to England.

"Your visit has done your father good, Terence," O'Flaherty said, as, after seeing the party safely on board ship, he returned to the town whence they were to march with the convalescents, sixty in number, among whom were five officers. "He has brightened up a deal the last four days, and his wound looks distinctly more healthy. I have a strong hope that all those splinters have worked out now, and your being here has given him a fillip, so that he is altogether better and more cheerful. I hope by the spring he will be able to rejoin us. I can tell you I am mighty glad to be off again myself. It has been pretty hard work here, for I have had, for the last fortnight, a hundred and twenty men on my hands. At first there were three of us here, but two went off with the last batch of convalescents, and I have been alone since. Luckily Major Peters has been well enough to look after things in general, and help the commissariat man; still, with forty bad cases, I have not had much time on my hands. Of course I knew him and all the other officers, but they all belonged to other regiments, and it was not like being among the Mayos. And when do you think we will be starting again?"

"I have no idea. I have heard that Moore is doing everything he can to hurry on things, but that he is awfully hampered for want of money. It is scandalous. Here are our agents supplied with immense sums for the use of these blackguard Spaniards, yet they keep their own army without funds."

"If the general has no funds, Terence, he had better be stopping where he is. There is no getting anything in Portugal without paying ten times the proper price for it, and from what I hear of the Spaniards they will charge twenty times, put the money in their pockets, and then not even give you what you paid for. As to their being any good to us as allies, it is not to be hoped for; they will take our arms and our money, expect us to feed their troops, and will then run away at the sight of a French soldier; you will see if they don't."

"I hear that the Junta of Corunna says that all the north will rise as soon as we enter their country."

"They may rise and flock round us until they have got arms and money, and then they will go off to their homes again. That is the sort of assistance that is to be had from them. We should do a deal better if there was not a Spaniard in the country, and it was left to us to fight it out with the French."

"In that case, O'Flaherty, we should never cross the frontier at all. They say that Napoleon is gathering a great army, and against such a force, with the French troops already in Spain, our twenty or twenty-five thousand men would fare very badly, especially as they say that the emperor is coming himself."

"That is worse news than the other, Terence. It is only because the French generals have always been quarrelling among themselves that the whole Peninsula has not been conquered; but with Napoleon at the head of affairs it would be a different matter altogether, and my humble opinion is that we had better stay where we are until he has wiped out the Spaniards altogether."

Terence laughed.

"You don't take a sanguine view of things."

"You have been with the regiment, Terence, and have had very little to do with the natives. I have not seen very much of them either, thank goodness; but I have seen quite enough to know that though perhaps the peasants would make good soldiers, if officered by Englishmen, there is mighty little feeling of patriotism among the classes above them. Reading and writing may be good for some countries, but as far as I see here, reading and writing spoil them here, for every man one comes across who can sign his name is intent either on filling his pocket, or on working some scheme or other for his own advantage. If I were Sir John Moore I would send up a division to Oporto, hang the bishop and every member of the Junta, shoot Friere and a dozen of his principal officers, and if the people of Oporto gave them the chance clear the streets with grape-shot. Why, if it hadn't been for a small guard of our fellows with the French garrisons that were marched down there to embark, the Portuguese would have murdered every man-jack of them.

"They did murder a good many, and robbed them all of their baggage; and if it had not been that our men loaded and would have fired on them if they had gone further, not a Frenchman would have got off alive. If this had been done in Lisbon, where the French had been masters, there might have been some sort of excuse for it; but they had never been near Oporto at all, and therefore the people there had no scores to settle with them."

"I am afraid, O'Flaherty, that an army worked on your principles would never get far from the coast, for we should have the whole country against us."

"So much the better if we never got far from the coast. How much help have we had from them? There is not a single horse or waggon for transport except those we have hired at exorbitant prices; not a single ounce of food. They would not even divide with us the magazines at Leirya, which they had no share in capturing. The rabble they call an army has never fired a shot or marched a yard with us, except Trant's small command, and they were kept so far out of it in both fights, that I doubt whether they fired a shot; and yet they take upon themselves to throw every obstacle in our way, to dictate to our generals, and to upset every plan as soon as it is formed.

"Well, I shall be glad to be back with the regiment again, Terence. There is some fun going on there anyhow, and I have not had a hearty laugh since O'Grady went off ten days ago."

"We were all heartily glad to see him back again," Terence said. "He does not seem a bit the worse for having lost his hand."

"No, he has got through it a deal better than I had expected, considering that he is not what might be called a very temperate man."

"Not by any means. It is not very often that he takes more liquor than he can carry, but he generally goes very close to the mark."

"I kept him very short here," O'Flaherty laughed, "and told him that if he did not obey orders I would have him invalided home; I have got him to promise that he will draw in a bit in future, and have good hopes of his keeping it, seeing that when the army starts again you won't get much chance of indulging."

"It will be a good thing for others as well as O'Grady," Terence said, quietly. "I suppose in Ireland the whisky does not do much harm, seeing that it is a wet country; but here I notice that they cannot drink half as much as they were accustomed to without feeling it."

"That is true for you, Terence. Half a bottle here goes as far as a bottle in the old country; and I find with the wounded, spirits have a very bad effect, even in very small quantities. There is one thing, when the troops are on the march they not only get small chance of getting drink, but mighty little time to think of it. When you have been doing your twenty miles a day, with halts and stoppages on these beastly roads and defiles, and are on your feet from daylight until late in the evening, and then, perhaps, a turn at the outposts, a man hasn't got much time for divarshun; and even if there is liquor to be had, he is glad enough when he has had a glass or so to wrap himself in his cloak and lie down to sleep. I have nearly sworn off myself, for I found that my head troubled me in the morning after a glass or two, more than it did after an all-night's sitting at Athlone. Ah, Terence, it is lucky for you that you have no fancy for it!"

"I hope I never shall have, O'Flaherty. If one has got thoroughly wet through in a long day's fishing, it may be that a glass of punch may keep away a cold, though even that I doubt. But I am sure that I am better without it at any other time; and I hope some day the fashion will change, and instead of it being considered almost as a matter of course after a dinner that half the men should be under the table, it will then be looked upon as disgraceful for a man to get drunk, as it is now for a woman to do so."

O'Flaherty looked at his companion with amused surprise. "Faith, Terence, that would be a change indeed, and you might as well say that you hope the time will come when you can whip off a fellow's leg without his feeling pain."

"Perhaps that may come too," Terence laughed; "there is no saying."

The next morning the detachment started at daybreak and marched to Torres Vedras, where they heard that a general movement was expected to begin. The regiment had now a comfortable mess, and the situation was freely discussed as scraps of news arrived from Lisbon. Could the English ministry have heard the comments on their imbecility passed by the officers of the British army, even they might have doubted the perfect wisdom of their plan. On the 6th of October, Moore had received a despatch stating that 30,000 infantry and 5,000 cavalry were to be employed in the north of Spain. Ten thousand of these were to be sent out direct from England, the remainder were to be composed of regiments from the army in Portugal. Moore had the choice of taking the troops round in ships or of marching them direct. He decided upon the latter course, for arrangements had been made by Sir Hew Dalrymple to enter Spain by Almeida, and, moreover, he thought that the resources of the sea-coast of Galicia would not be more than sufficient to supply transport and food for the 10,000 men who were to land there under the command of Sir David Baird.

The English general's difficulties were indeed overwhelming. He had soldiers who, although but recently raised, had shown themselves good fighters; but he was altogether without even transport sufficient for the officers. With an ample supply of money, an experienced staff, and a well-organized commissariat, the difficulties might have been overcome, but Sir John Moore was practically without money. His staff had no experience whatever, and the commissariat and transport officers were alike ignorant of the work they were called upon to perform. He was unacquainted with the views of the Spanish government, and uninformed as to the numbers, composition, and situation of the Spanish armies with whom he was to act, or with those of the enemy. He had a winter march of 300 miles before he could join Sir David Baird, who would have 200 miles to march from Corunna to join him, and there was then a distance of another 300 miles to be traversed before he reached the Ebro, which was designated as the centre of his operations.

And all this had to be done while a great French army was already pouring in through the passes of the Pyrenees. No more tremendous, or, it may be said, impossible, task was ever assigned to an English commander; and to add to the absurdity of their scheme, the British government sent off Sir David Baird without instructions, and even without money. The Duke of York had vainly protested against the plan of the ministry, and had pointed out that nothing short of an army of 60,000 men, fully equipped with all necessaries for war—money, transport, and artillery—could achieve success of any kind.

Upon the day Terence rejoined, news came from the engineers in advance that the assurances Sir John Moore had received that the road by which the army was to travel was perfectly practicable for artillery and baggage-waggons, were wholly false, and it was probable that the artillery and cavalry would have to make a long circuit to the south.

It was too late now to change the route for the rest of the army. Nearly half the force had already started on the road to Almeida, and the supplies for their subsistence had been collected at that town. Therefore it was necessary that the main body of the infantry should travel by that road, while three thousand were to act as a guard for the artillery and cavalry on the other route.

CHAPTER VII

THE ADVANCE

"IT is enough to drive Sir John out of his senses," the colonel said, as the news was discussed after mess. "These people must be the champion liars of the world. Not content with doing nothing themselves, they seem to delight in inventing lies to prevent our doing anything for them. Who ever heard of an army marching, without artillery and cavalry, one way, while these arms travelled by a different road entirely, and that not for a march of twenty miles, but for a march of three hundred? One battery is to go with us. But what will be the use of six guns against an enemy with sixty? Every day the baggage is being cut down owing to these blackguard Portuguese breaking their engagements to furnish waggons, and we shall have to march pretty nearly as we stand, and to take with us nothing beyond one change of clothes."

Loud exclamations of discontent ran round the table. It

was bad enough that in the midst of a campaign waggons should break down and baggage be left behind, but that troops should start upon a campaign with scarcely the necessaries of life had caused general anger in the army; and no order would have been more willingly obeyed than one to march upon Lisbon, shoot every public official, establish a state of siege, and rule by martial law, seizing for the use of the army every draught animal, waggon, and carriage that could be found in the city, or swept in from the country round. The colonel had not exaggerated matters. The number of tents to be taken were altogether insufficient for the regiment, even with the utmost crowding possible. The officers' baggage had been cut down to twenty pounds a head—an amount scarcely sufficient for a single change of clothes and boots. Even the amount of ammunition to be taken would be insufficient to refill the soldiers' pouches after the supply they carried was exhausted.

The paucity of baggage would not have mattered so much had the march begun at the commencement of summer, instead of just as winter was setting in. In the former case, men could have slept in the open air, and a solitary blanket and one change of clothes would have sufficed; but with the wet season at hand, to be followed by winter cold, the grievance was a very serious one. Terence had already learned that the brigade was to march in two days, and that the great bulk of the baggage was to be stored at Torres Vedras, which was to be occupied on their leaving by some of the troops that would remain in Portugal.

"Faith, it is an evil look-out, Terence," O'Grady, who was sitting next to him, said, pathetically. "Sorra a drop of whisky is there in the camp, and now we sha'n't be able to have even a drink of their bastely spirits, onless we can buy it at the towns; and as Anstruther's division has gone on ahead of us, it is likely that every drop has been drunk up."

"It will be all the better for you, O'Grady. Daly tells me that your arm is not fully healed yet. I know that you would not like to be left behind when we have once started."

"That is true enough, but a drop of the cratur hurts no one."

"I beg your pardon, O'Grady, it is very bad for anything like a wound. The doctor told me, when I was chatting with him before dinner, that he really did not think that you could go, for you would not obey his orders to give up spirits altogether."

"Well, I own that it has been smarting a good deal the last few days," O'Grady admitted, reluctantly, "though I have not said as much to the doctor. I don't know that you are not about right, Terence; but faith, after being kept upon bastely slops by O'Flaherty, it was not in human nature to drink nothing but water when one gets a chance. At any rate, I am not likely to find any great temptation after we have started."

"Well, you had better begin to-night, O'Grady. I am going to get away as soon as I can, and if you will take my advice you will come too."

"What! and us to march in two days? It is not to be thought of. You mane well, Terence, but a lad like you must not take to lecturing your supayrior officer. Shure, and don't I know what to do for meself better than any other?"

Terence saw that it was useless to endeavour to persuade him to move, and presently went round to Dr. Daly and said, quietly:

"Doctor, O'Grady tells me that his arm has been hurting him a good deal more during the last two days. I expect they will make a night of it this evening, and again to-morrow, and if he once begins, nothing will stop him until they break up. Could not you do anything?"

"I will talk to him like a father, Terence. You are a good boy to have told me; I might have gone away without thinking of it."

"Don't mention my name, Doctor."

The doctor nodded, and Terence went away and took a vacant seat at some distance from him. Presently the doctor got up and went round to O'Grady. The supply of claret had just been finished, and bottles of spirits had been placed upon the table. O'Grady stretched out his hand to one near him, but the doctor quietly removed it.

"Not for you, O'Grady," he said; "you have had more than sufficient wine already. I have been doubting whether you are fit to go on with the regiment; and, by the powers, if you touch spirits to-night or to-morrow, I will put your name down in the list of those who are to be left behind as unfit for service!"

"Sure you are joking, Doctor?"

"Never was more earnest in my life, O'Grady. You don't want to be left behind, I suppose, in some filthy Portuguese town, while we march on, and that is what it will come to if your wound inflames. I told you this morning that it was not doing as well as it ought to, and that you must cut off liquor altogether. I have had my eye upon you, and you have taken down more than a bottle of wine already. I don't think I ought to let you go with us, even as it is; but, by the piper that played before Moses, if you don't go off to your quarters, without touching a drop more, I will have you left behind!"

"You are mighty hard on a poor fellow, and must have a heart of stone to treat a man, who has lost his arm and wants a bit of comfort, in such fashion. Faith, I would not do it to a dog."

"There would be no occasion, O'Grady; a dog has got sense."

"And I haven't? Thank ye for the compliment. I will appeal to the colonel. Colonel, the doctor says if I drink a drop of spirits to-night or to-morrow he will put me down in the black list. Now, I ask you, do the regulations justify his using such a threat as that?"

"I think they do," the colonel said, with a laugh. "I think that his order is good and sensible, and I endorse it. You know yourself that spirits are bad for you, with an arm only just healed up. Now, behave like a raisonable fellow, and go off to your quarters. You know well enough that if you stop here you won't be able to keep from it."

"Faith, if the two of you are against me I have nothing more to say. It is mighty hard that after having lost an arm in the service of my country I should be treated like a child and sent off to bed."

"I am going, too, O'Grady," Terence, who had gone back to his original place, now said. "There is no occasion to go to bed. I have a box of good cigars in my tent, and we can sit there and chat as long as you like."

But O'Grady's dignity was ruffled.

"Thank you, Mr. O'Connor," he said, stiffly; "but with your lave I will do as I said."

"That is the best thing," the doctor said. "You have not had a long night's rest since you rejoined. I am going myself, and I see that some of the others are getting up, too, and it would be a good thing if all would do so, for, with such work as we have got before us, the more sleep we get, while we can, the better."

As nearly half the officers now rose from their seats, O'Grady was mollified, and as we went out he said:

"I think, after all, Terence, I will try one of those cigars of yours."

On the 14th of October Fane's brigade left Torres Vedras.

"I AM TOLD THAT YOU WISH TO SPEAK TO ME, GENERAL."

A number of the troops had been stationed along the line of route to be followed, and these had started simultaneously with the departure of Fane's brigade from Torres Vedras. The discontent as to the reduction of baggage ceased as soon as the troops were in motion. They were going to invade Spain, and ignorant as the soldiers were of the real state of affairs, none doubted but that success would attend them there. Among the officers better acquainted with the state of things there was no such feeling of confidence, but they hoped that they should at least give as good an account of themselves as before, against any French force of anything like equal strength they might encounter. O'Grady, influenced by the doctor's threats, which he knew the latter would be firm enough to carry out, had obeyed his orders, and had confided to Terence, when the regiment formed up at daybreak for the march, that his arm felt much better.

"I don't say that the doctor may not have been right, Terence, but he need not have threatened me in that way, at all, at all."

"I don't know," Terence replied. "I feel pretty sure that if he hadn't, you would not have knocked off spirits. Well, it is a glorious morning for starting, but I am afraid the fine weather won't last long. Everyone says that the rains generally begin about this time."

As Terence fell in with his company the adjutant rode up.

"Mr. O'Connor, you are to report yourself to the brigadier."

Wondering much at the message, Terence hurried to the house occupied by General Fane. He and several officers were standing in front of it.

"I am told that you wish to speak to me, General," he said, saluting.

"Oh, you are Mr. O'Connor! Can you ride?"

"Yes, sir," Terence replied; for he had often had a scamper across the hills around Athlone on half-broken ponies, and occasionally on the horses of some of his friends in the regiment.

"I have a vacancy on my staff. Lieutenant Andrews was thrown when riding out from Lisbon with a despatch last night, and broke a leg. I was on board the flag-ship when your colonel brought his report about the fight between the transport and the two privateers. I read it, and was so much struck with the quickness and intelligence you displayed, that I made a note at the time that if I should have a vacancy on my staff I would appoint you."

"I am very much obliged, General," Terence said, "but I have no horse."

"I have arranged that. Lieutenant Andrews will not be fit for service for a long time. It is a compound fracture, and he will, the doctor says, probably be sent back to England by the first ship that arrives after he reaches Lisbon. His horse is therefore useless to him, and as it is only a native animal and would not fetch a ten-pound note, he agreed at once to hand it over to his successor, and in fact was rather glad to get it off his hands. He has an English saddle, bridle, and holsters; he will take five pounds for them. If you happen to be short of cash the paymaster will settle it for you."

"Thank you, sir; I have the money about me, and I am very much obliged to you for making the arrangement."

Terence was indeed in funds, for in addition to the ten pounds that had fallen to him as his share of the prize money, his pay had been almost untouched from the day he left England, and his father had, on embarking, added ten pounds to his store.

"I won't want it, Terence," he said; "I have got another twenty pounds by me, and by the time I get to England I shall have another month's pay to draw, and shall no doubt be put in a military hospital, where I shall have no occasion for money till I am out again."

"But I sha'n't want it either, father."

"There is never any saying, lad; it is always useful to have money on a campaign. You may be in places where the commissariat breaks down altogether, and you have to depend on what you buy; you may be left behind wounded, or may be taken prisoner, one never can tell. I shall feel more comfortable about you if I know that you are well provided with cash, whatever may happen. My advice is, Terence, get fifteen or twenty pounds in gold sewn up in your boot; have an extra sole put on, and the money sewn inside. If it is your bad luck to be taken prisoner, you will find the money mighty useful in a great many ways."

Terence had followed this advice and had fifteen pounds hidden away, besides ten that he carried in his pockets; he therefore hurried to the hut where Lieutenant Andrews was lying. He was slightly acquainted with him, as he had been Fane's aide-de-camp from the time of landing. The young lieutenant's servant was standing at the door with a horse ready saddled and bridled.

"I am very sorry to hear of your injury," he said to the young officer.

"Yes, it is a horrible nuisance," the other replied; "and just as we were starting, too. There is an end of my campaigning for the present. I should not have minded if it had been a French ball, but to be merely thrown from a horse is disgusting."

"I am extremely obliged to you for the horse, Andrews, but I would rather pay you for it; it is not fair that I should get it for nothing."

"Oh, that is all right! It would be a bother taking it

down, and I should not know what to do with it when I got to Lisbon; it would be a nuisance altogether, and I am glad to get rid of it. The money is of no consequence to me one way or the other. I wish you better luck with it than I have had."

"At any rate here are five pounds for the saddle and bridle," and he put the money down on the table by the bed.

"That is all right," the other said, without looking at it; "they are well off my hands, too. I hope the authorities will send me straight on board ship when I get to Lisbon; my servant will go down with me. If I am kept there, he will of course stay with me until I sail; if not, he will rejoin as soon as he has seen me on board. He is a good servant, and I can recommend him to you; he is rather fond of the bottle, but that is his only fault as far as I know. He is a countryman of yours, and you will be able to make allowances for his failing," he added, with a laugh.

There was no time to be lost—the bugles were sounding—so, with a brief adieu, Terence went out, mounted the horse and rode after the general, who had just left with his staff, and taken his place at the head of the column. As he passed his regiment, he stopped for a moment to speak to the colonel.

"I heard that you were wanted by the general, Terence," the latter said, "and I congratulate you on your appointment. I am sorry that you are leaving us, but, as you will be with the brigade, we shall often see you. O'Driscol is as savage as a bull at the loss of one of his subalterns. Well, it is your own luck that you have and another's; drop in this evening, if you can, and tell us how it was that Fane came to pick you out."

"It was thanks to you, Colonel. If you remember, you told us at Vigo that Fane was on board when you went to make your report, and that he and Sir Arthur's adjutant-general read it over together, and asked you a good many questions. It was owing to that affair that he thought of me."

"That is good, lad. I thought at the time that more might come of it than just being mentioned in orders, and I am very glad that it was for that you got it. At any rate, come in this evening; I want to hear where you have stolen that horse from, and all about it."

Terence rode off and took his place with his fellow aide-de-camp behind the two other officers of the staff. He scarcely knew whether to be glad or sorry, at present, at the change that had so suddenly taken place. It was gratifying to have been selected as he had been. It was certainly more pleasant to ride through a campaign than to march; and there would be a good many more chances of distinguishing himself than there could be as a regimental officer; while, on the other hand, he would be away from the circle of his friends and comrades, and should greatly miss the fun and jollity of the life with them.

"An unfortunate affair this of Andrews," Lieutenant Trevor, his fellow aide-de-camp, said.

"Most unfortunate. I little thought when you and he lunched with us two days since that to-day he would be down with a broken leg and I riding in his place. Just at present I certainly do not feel very delighted at the change. You see, from my father being a captain in the regiment, I have been brought up with it, and to be taken so suddenly away from them seems a tremendous wrench."

"Yes, I can understand that," the other said. "In my case it is different. My regiment was not coming out, and of course I was greatly pleased when the general gave me a chance of going with him. Still, you see, as your regiment is in the brigade you will still be able to be with it when off duty, and when the end of the campaign comes you will return to it. Besides, there are compensations—you will at least get a roof to sleep under, at any rate nine times out of ten. I don't know how you feel it, but to me it is no small comfort being on horseback instead of tramping along these heavy roads on foot. The brigadier is a capital fellow; and though he does keep us hard at work, at any rate he works hard himself, and does not send us galloping about with all sorts of trivial messages that might as well be unsent. Besides, he is always thoughtful and considerate. Is he related to you in any way?"

"Not at all."

"Then I suppose you had good interest in some way, or else how did he come to pick you out?"

"It was just a piece of luck," Terence said; "it was because he had heard my name in connection with a fight the transport I came over in had with two French privateers."

"Oh, yes, I remember now," the other said; "I had forgotten that the name was O'Connor. I remember all about it now. He told us the story at Vigo, and you were put in general orders by Sir Arthur. I know the chief spoke very highly about your conduct in that affair. It is just like him to remember it, and to pick you out to take Andrews' place. Well, you fairly won it, which is more than one can say for most staff appointments, which are in ninety-nine cases out of a hundred the result of pure favouritism or interest.

"Well, O'Connor, I am very glad to have you on the staff. You see, it makes a lot of difference, when there are only two of us, that we should like each other. I own I have not done anything as yet to get any credit, for at Vimiera it was just stand up and beat them back, and I had not a single message to carry, and, of course, at Rolica our brigade was not in it; but I hope I shall get a turn some day. Then it was your father who was badly wounded?"

"Yes; I saw him off to England four days ago. I hope that he will be able to rejoin before long, but it is not certain yet that the wound won't bring on permanent lameness. I am very anxious about it, especially as he has now got his step, and it would be awfully hard on him to leave the service just as he has got field-officer's rank."

"Yes, it would be hard. However, I hope that the sea-voyage and English air will set him up again."

Presently one of the officers who were in front turned and said: "The general wishes you to ride back along the line, Mr. Trevor, and report whether the intervals between the regiments are properly kept, and also as to how the baggage-waggons are going on."

As Trevor turned to ride back the general cantered on, followed by the three officers and the four troopers who served as orderlies. Two miles ahead they came to a bridge across a torrent. The road, always a bad one, had been completely cut up by the passage of the provision and ammunition carts going to the front, and was now almost impassable.

"Will you please to ride back, Mr. O'Connor, and request the colonel of the leading regiment to send on the pioneers and a company of men at the double to clear the road and make it passable for the waggons."

The work was quickly done. While some men filled up the deep ruts, others cut down shrubs and bushes growing by the river bank, tied them into bundles, and put them across the narrow road, and threw earth and stones upon them, and in half an hour from the order being given the bugle sounded the advance. The head of the column had been halted just before it reached the bridge, and the men fell out, many of them running down to the stream to refill their water-bottles. As the bugle sounded they at once fell in again, and the column got into motion. General Fane and his staff remained at the bridge until the waggons had all crossed it.

"It is not much of a job," Fane said. "Of course the four regiments passing over it flattened the earth well down, but the waggons have cut it all up again. The first heavy shower will wash all the earth away, and in a couple of days it will be as bad as before. There are plenty of stones down in the river, but we have no means of breaking up the large ones, or of carrying any quantity of small ones. A few hundred sappers and engineers, with proper tools, would soon go a long way towards making the road fairly fit for traffic, but nothing can be done without tools and wheel-barrows, or at least hand-barrows for carrying stones. You see, the men wanted to use their blankets, but the poor fellows will want them badly enough before long, and those contractors' goods would go all to pieces by the time they had carried half a dozen loads of stones. At any rate, we will content ourselves with making the road passable for our own waggons, and the troops who come after us must do the same. By the way, Mr. O'Connor, you have not got your kit yet."

"No, sir; but I have no doubt that it is with the regimental baggage, and I will get it when we halt to-night."

"Do so," the general said. "Of course it can be carried with ours, but I should advise you always to take a change of clothes in your valise, and a blanket strapped on with your greatcoat."

"I have Mr. Andrews' blanket, sir. It was strapped on when I mounted, and I did not notice it."

"That is all right. The store blankets are very little use for keeping off rain, but we all provided ourselves with good thick horse-cloths before leaving England. They are a great deal warmer than blankets, and are practically water-proof. I have no doubt that Mr. Andrews told his servant to strap it on as usual."

Many and many a time during the campaign had Terence good reason for thinking with gratitude of Andrews' kindly thought. His greatcoat, which like those of all the officers of the regiment, had been made at Athlone, of good Irish frieze lined with flannel, would stand almost any amount of rain, but it was not long enough to protect his legs while lying down. But by rolling himself in the horse-cloth he was able to sleep warm and dry, when without it he would have been half-frozen, or soaked through with rain from above and moisture from the ground below. He found that the brigadier and his staff carried the same amount of baggage as other officers, the only difference being that the general had a tent for himself, his assistant-adjutant and quartermaster one between them, while a third was used as an office-tent in the day, and was occupied by the two aides-de-camp at night.

The baggage-waggon allotted to them carried the three tents, their scanty kits, and a box of stationery and official forms, but was mainly laden with musketry ammunition for the use of the brigade. After marching eighteen miles the column halted at a small village. The tents were speedily pitched, rations served out, and fires lighted. The general took possession of the principal house in the village for the use of himself and his staff, and the quartermaster-general apportioned the rest of the houses between the officers of the four battalions. The two aides-de-camp accompanied the general in his tour of inspection through the camp.

"It will be an hour before dinner is ready," Trevor said, as they returned to the house, "and you won't be wanted before that. I shall be about if the chief has any orders to send out. I don't think it is likely that he will have; he is not given, as some brigadiers are, to worrying; and, besides, there are the orderlies here to take any routine orders out, so you can be off if you like."

Terence at once went down to the camp of the Mayo Fusiliers. The officers were all there, their quartermaster having gone into the village to fix their respective quarters.

"Hooray, Terence, me boy!" O'Grady shouted, as he came up, "we all congratulate you. Faith, it is a comfort to see that for once merit has been recognized. I am sure that there is not a man in the regiment but would have liked to have given you a cheer as you rode along this morning just before we started. We shall miss you, but as you will be up and down all day and can look in of an evening, it won't be as if you had been put on the staff of another brigade. As to Dicky Ryan, he is altogether down in the mouth, whether it is regret for your loss or whether it is from jealousy at seeing you capering about on horseback, while he is tramping along on foot, is more than I know."

"If you were not my superior officer, Captain O'Grady, I should make a personal onslaught on you," Ryan laughed. "You will have to mind how you behave now, Terence; the brigadier is an awfully good fellow, but he is pretty strict in matters of discipline."

"I will take care of meself, Dicky, and now that you will have nobody to help you out of your scrapes, you will have to mind yourself too."

"I am glad that you have got a lift, Terence," Captain O'Driscol said; "but it is rather hard on me losing a subaltern just as the campaign is beginning in earnest."

"Menzies likes doing all the work," Terence said, "so it won't make so much difference to you."

"It would not matter if I was always with my company, Terence, but now, you see, that I am acting as field-officer to the left wing till your father rejoins, it makes it awkward."

"I intend to attach Parsons to your company, O'Driscol," the colonel said. "Terence went off so suddenly this morning that I had no time to think of it before we marched, but he shall march with your company to-morrow. You will not mind, I hope, Captain Holland?"

"I shall mind, of course, Colonel; but, as O'Driscol's company has now really only one officer, of course it cannot be helped, and as Menzies is the senior lieutenant, I have no doubt that he can manage very well with Parsons, who is very well up in his work."

"Thank you, Captain Holland; it is the first compliment that you ever paid me; it is abuse that I am most accustomed to."

"It is thanks to that that you are a decent officer, Parsons," Captain Holland laughed. "You were the awkwardest young beggar I ever saw when you first joined, and you have given me no end of trouble in licking you into shape. How do you think you will like your work, Terence?"

"I think I shall like it very much," the lad replied. "The other aide-de-camp, Trevor, is a very nice fellow, and every one likes Fane; as to Major Dowdeswell and Major Errington, I haven't exchanged a word with either of them, and you know as much about them as I do."

"Errington is a very good fellow, but the other man is very unpopular. He is always talking about the regulations, as if anyone cared a hang about the regulations when one is on service."

"I expect that if Fane were not such a good fellow Dowdeswell would make himself a baste of a nuisance, and be bothering us about pipe-clay and buttons, and all sorts of rigmarole," O'Grady said; "as if a man would fight any the better for having his belt white as snow!"

"He would not fight any the better, O'Grady, but the regiment would do so," the colonel put in. "All these little matters are nothing in themselves, but still they have a good deal to do with the discipline of the regiment; there is no doubt that we are not as smart in appearance as we ought to be, and that the other regiments in the brigade show up better than we do. It is a matter that must be seen to. I shall inspect the regiment very carefully before we march to-morrow."

There was a little silence among the group, but a smile stole over several of the faces. As a rule, the colonel was very lax in small matters of this kind, but occasionally he thought it necessary to put on an air of severity, and to insist upon the most rigid accuracy in this respect; but the fit seldom lasted beyond twenty-four hours, after which things went on pleasantly again. Some of the officers presently sauntered off to warn the colour-sergeants that the colonel himself intended to inspect the regiment closely before marching the next morning, and that the men must be warned to have their uniforms, belts, and firearms in perfect order.

Terence remained for some little time longer chatting, and then got possession of his kit, which was carried by Tim Hoolan across to his quarters.

"We are all sorry you've left us, yer honour," that worthy said, as he walked a short distance behind Terence; "the rigiment won't be like itself widout you. Not that it has been quite the same since you joined us reg'lar, and have taken to behaving yourself."

"What do you mean, you impudent rascal?" Terence said, with a pretence at indignation.

"No offence, yer honour, but faith the games that you and Mr. Ryan and some of the others used to play, kept the boys alive, and gave mighty contintment to the regiment."

"I was only a lad then, Hoolan."

"That was so, yer honour, and now you are a man and an officer, it is natural it should be different."

"Tim Hoolan, you are a humbug," Terence said, laughing.

"Sorra a bit of one, yer honour. I am not saying that you won't grow a bit more; everyone says what a fine man you will make. But sure ye saved our wing from being captured, and you would not have us admit that, if it had not been for a boy, a wing of the Mayo Fusiliers would have been captured by the French. No, your honour, when we tell that story we spake of one of our officers who had the idea that saved the *Sea-horse*, and brought thim two privateer vessels into Vigo."

"Well, Tim, it is only three months since I joined, and I don't suppose I have changed much in that time; but of course I cannot play tricks now as I used to do, before I got my commission."

"That is so, yer honour; the rigiment misses your tricks, though they did bother us a bit. Three times were we turned out at night, under arms, when we were at Athlone, once on a wet night too, and stood there for two hours till the colonel found out it was a false alarm, and there was me and Mr. Ryan, and two or three others as was in the secret, nigh choking ourselves with laughter, to hear the men cursing and swearing at being called out of bed. That was a foine time, yer honour."

"Attention, Tim!" Terence said, sharply.

They had now entered the village, and the burst of laughter in which Hoolan indulged at the thought of the regiment being turned out on a false alarm was unseemly, as he was accompanying an officer. So Tim straightened himself up, and then followed in Terence's footsteps with military precision and stiffness.

"There is a time for all things, Tim," the latter said, as he took the little portmanteau from him. "It won't do to be laughing like that in sight of head-quarters. I can't ask you to have a drink now; there is no drink to be had, but the first time we get a chance I will make it up to you."

"All right, yer honour! I was wrong entirely, but I could not have helped it if the commander-in-chief had been standing there.

Terence went up to the attic that he and Trevor shared. There was no changing for dinner, but after a wash he went below again.

"You are just in time," Trevor said, "and we are in luck. The head man of the village sent the general a couple of ducks, and they will help out our rations. I have been foraging, and have got hold of half a dozen bottles of good wine from the priest.

"We always try to get the best of things in the village, if they will but part with them. That is an essential part of our duties. To-morrow it will be your turn."

"But our servants always did that sort of thing," Terence said, in some surprise.

"I dare say, O'Connor, but it would not do for the general's servant to be going about picking up things. No matter what he paid, we should have tales going about in no time of the shameful extortion practised by our servants, who under threats compelled the peasantry to sell provisions for the use of their masters at nominal prices."

"I did not think of that," Terence laughed. "Yes, as the Portuguese have circulated scores of calumnious lies on less foundation, one cannot be too particular. I will see what I can do to-morrow."

CHAPTER VIII

A FALSE ALARM

THE march was continued until the brigade arrived at Almeida, which they reached on the 7th of November, and Sir John Moore and the head-quarters staff came up on the following day. All the troops were now assembled at that place; for Anstruther, by some misconception of orders, had halted the leading division, instead of, as intended by the general, continuing his march to Salamanca. The condition of the troops was excellent. Discipline, which had been somewhat relaxed during the period of inactivity, was now thoroughly restored. The weather had continued fine, and the steady exercise had well prepared them for the campaign which was beginning. Things, however, were in other respects going on unfavourably.

The Junta of Corunna had given the most solemn promises that transport and everything necessary for the advance of Sir David Baird's force should be ready by the time that officer arrived. Yet nothing whatever had been done, and so conscious were the Junta of their shortcomings, that when the fleet with the troops arrived off the port they refused to allow them to enter without an order from the central Junta, and fifteen days were wasted before the troops could disembark. Then it was found that neither provisions nor transport had been provided, and that nothing whatever was to be hoped for from the Spanish authorities. Baird was entirely unprovided with money, and was supplied with £8,000 from Moore's scanty military chest, while at the very time the British agent, Mr. Frere, was in Corunna with two millions of dollars for the use of the Spaniards, which he was squandering, like the other British agents, right and left among the men who refused to put themselves to the slightest trouble to further the expedition.

Spain was at this time boasting of the enthusiasm of its armies, and of the immense force that it had in the field, and succeeded in persuading the English cabinet and the English people that with the help of a little money they could alone and unaided drive the French right across the frontier. The emptiness of this braggadocio, and the utter incapacity of the Spanish authorities and generals was now speedily exposed, for Napoleon's newly arrived armies scattered the Spaniards before them like sheep, and it was only on one or two occasions that anything like severe fighting took place. Within the space of three weeks there remained of the great armies of Spain but a few thousand fugitives hanging together without arms or discipline. Madrid, the centre of this pretended enthusiasm and patriotism, surrendered after a day's pretence at resistance, and the whole of the eastern provinces fell, practically without a blow, into the hands of the invaders.

At present, however, Moore still hoped for some assistance from the Spaniards. He, like Baird, was crippled for want of money, but determined not to delay his march, and sent agents to Madrid and other places to make contracts and raise money; thus while the ministers at home squandered huge sums on the Spaniards, they left it to their own military commanders to raise money by means of loans to enable them to march. Never in the course of the military history of England were her operations so crippled and foiled by the utter incapacity of her government as in the opening campaigns of the Peninsular War.

While Baird was vainly trying to obtain transport at Corunna, a reinforcement of some five thousand Spanish troops under General Romana landed at San Andero, and, being equipped from the British stores, joined the Spanish general, Blake, in Biscay. These troops had been raised for the French service at the time Napoleon's brother Joseph was undisputed King of Spain. They were stationed in Holland, and when the insurrection at home broke out, the news of the rising was sent to them, and in pursuance of a plan agreed upon they suddenly rose, marched down to a port and embarked in English ships sent to receive them, and were in these transported to the northern coast of Spain.

Sir David Baird was a man of great energy, and, having succeeded in borrowing a little more money from Mr. Frere, he started on his march to join General Moore. He had with great difficulty hired some country carts at an exorbitant rate, but the number was so small that he was obliged to send up his force in half-battalions, and so was able to proceed but very slowly.

Sir John Moore was still in utter ignorance of the situation in Spain. The jealousy among the generals, and the disinclination of the central Junta to appoint any one person to a post that might enable him to interfere with their intrigues, had combined to prevent the appointment of a commander-in-chief, and there was no one therefore with whom Sir John could open negotiations and learn what plans, if any, had been decided upon for general operations against the advancing enemy.

On the day that Moore arrived at Almeida Blake was in full flight, pursued by a French army 50,000 strong, and Napoleon was at Vittoria with 170,000 troops.

Of these facts he was ignorant, but the letters that he received from Lord William Bentinck and Colonel Graham, exposing the folly of the Spanish generals, reached him. On the 11th he crossed the frontier of Spain, marching to Ciudad-Rodrigo. On that day Blake was finally defeated, and one of the other armies completely crushed and dispersed. These events left a large French army free to act against the British. Sir John Moore, however, did not hear of this until a week later. He knew, however, that the situation was serious; and after all the reports of Spanish enthusiasm, he was astonished to find that complete apathy prevailed, that no effort was made to enroll the population, or even to distribute the vast quantity of British muskets stored up in the magazines of the cities.

The general arrived at Salamanca with 4,000 British infantry. The French cavalry were at Valladolid, but three marches distant. On the 18th more troops had arrived, and on the 23d 12,000 infantry and six guns were at Salamanca. But Moore now knew of the defeat of Blake, and that the French army that had crushed him was free to advance against Salamanca. But he did not yet know of the utter dispersal of the Asturian army, or that the two armies of Castaños and Palafox were also defeated and scattered beyond any attempt at rallying, and that their conquerors were also free to march against him. Although ignorant of the force with which Napoleon had entered Spain, and having no idea of its enormous strength, he knew that it could not be less than 80,000 men, and that it could be joined by at least 30,000 more.

His position was indeed a desperate one. Baird was still twenty marches distant, his cavalry and artillery still far away. It would require another five days to bring the rear of his own army to Salamanca, as only a small portion could come forward each day, owing to want of transport; and yet, while in this position of imminent danger, the Spanish authorities, through Mr. Frere and other agents, were violently urging an advance to Madrid.

General Moore was indeed in a position of imminent danger; but the lying reports as to the strength of the Spanish army induced him for a moment to make preparations for such a movement. When, however, he learned the utter overthrow and dispersal of the whole of the Spanish armies, he saw that nothing remained but to fall back, if possible, upon Portugal.

It was necessary, however, that he should remain at Salamanca until Hope should arrive with the guns, and the army be in a position to show a front to the enemy. Instructions had been previously sent to Hope to march to the Escurial. Hope had endeavoured to find a road across the mountains of Ciudad-Rodrigo, but the road was so bad that he dared not venture upon it, as the number of horses was barely sufficient to drag the guns and ammunition waggons along a good road. He therefore kept on his way until he reached the Escurial; but after advancing three days farther towards Madrid, he heard of the utter defeat of the Spaniards and the flight of their armies. His cavalry outposts brought in word that more than 4,000 cavalry were but twelve miles away, and that other French troops were at Segovia and other places. The prospect of his making his way to join Sir John Moore seemed well-nigh hopeless; but, with admirable skill and resolution, Hope succeeded in eluding some of his foes, in checking others by destroying or defending bridges, and finally joined the main force without the loss of any of the important convoy of guns and ammunition that he was escorting.

The satisfaction of the troops at the arrival of the force that had been regarded as lost was unbounded. Hitherto, unprovided as they were with artillery and cavalry, they could have fought only under such disadvantages as would render defeat almost inevitable, for an enemy could have pounded them with artillery from a distance beyond their musket range, and they could have made no effectual reply whatever. His cavalry could have circled round them, cut their communications, and charged down on their lines in flank and rear while engaged with his infantry. Now every man felt that once again he formed part of an army, and that that army could be relied upon to beat any other of equal numbers.

Terence had enjoyed the march to Salamanca. The fine

weather had broken up, and heavy rains had often fallen, but his thick coat kept him dry except in the steadiest downpours; while on one or two occasions only the general and his staff had failed to find quarters available. As they proceeded they gradually closed up with the troops forming a part of the same division, and at Almeida came under the command of General Fraser, whose division was made complete by their arrival. Up to this point the young aide-de-camp's duties had been confined solely to the work of the brigade—to seeing that the regiments kept their proper distances, that none of the waggons loitered behind, and that the roads were repaired, where absolutely necessary, for the baggage to pass.

In the afternoon he generally rode forward with Major Errington, the quartermaster-general of the brigade, to examine the place fixed upon for the halt, to apportion the ground between the regiments, and ascertain the accommodation to be obtained in the village. Two orderlies accompanied them, each carrying a bundle of light rods. With these the ground was marked off, a card with the name of the regiment being inserted in a slit at the end of the rod; the village was then divided in four quarters for the accommodation of the officers. But beyond fixing the name of each regiment to the part assigned to it, no attempt was made to allot any special quarters to individual officers, this being left for the regimental quartermaster to do on the arrival of the troops.

When the column came up Terence led each regiment to the spot marked off, and directed the baggage-waggons to their respective places. While he was doing this, Trevor, with the orderlies, saw the head-quarters baggage carried to the house chosen for the general's use, and that the place was made as comfortable as might be, and then endeavoured to add to the rations by purchases in the village. Fane himself always remained with the troops until the tents were erected, and they were under cover, the rations distributed, and the fires lighted. The latter operation was often delayed by the necessity of fetching wood from a distance, the wood in the immediate neighbourhood having been cut down and burned either by the French on their advance, or by the British regiments ahead.

He then went to his quarters, where he received the reports of the medical, commissariat, and transport officers, wrote a report of the state of the road and the obstacles that he had encountered, and sent it back by an orderly to the officer commanding the six guns which were following a day's march behind him. These had been brought along with great labour, it being often necessary to take them off their carriages and carry them up or down difficult places, while the men were frequently compelled to harness themselves to ropes and aid the horses to drag the guns and waggons through the deep mud. Between the arrival of the troops and dinner Terence had his time to himself, and generally spent it with his regiment.

"Never did I see such a country, Terence," O'Grady complained to him one day. "Go where you will in ould Oirland, you can always get a jugful of poteen, a potful of 'taties, and a rasher of bacon; and if it is a village, a fowl and eggs. Here there are not even spirits or wine; as for a chicken, I have not seen the feather of one since we started, and I don't believe the peasants would know an egg if they saw it."

"Nonsense, O'Grady! If we were to go off the main road we should be able to buy all these things, barring the poteen, and maybe the potatoes, but you could get plenty of onions instead. You must remember that the French army came along here, and I expect they must have eaten nearly everything up on their way, and you may be sure that Anstruther's brigade gleaned all they left. As we marched from the Mondego we found the villagers well supplied—better a good deal than places of the same size would be in Ireland—except at our first halting-place."

"I own that, although Hoolan sometimes fails to add to our rations, we have not been so badly off, Terence. He goes out with two or three more of the boys directly we halt, laving the other servants to get the tents ready, and he generally brings us half a dozen fish, sometimes a dozen, that he has got out of the stream.

"He is an old hand, is Tim, and if he can't get them for dinner he gets them for breakfast. He catches them with night-lines and snares, and all sorts of poaching tricks. I know he bought a bag with four or five pounds of lime at Torres Vedras, and managed to smuggle it away in the regimental baggage. I asked him what it was for, and the rascal tipped me a wink, as much as to say, Don't ask no questions, master; and I believe that he drops a handful into a likely pool when he comes across one. I have never dared to ask him, for my conscience would not let me countenance such an unsportsmanlike way of getting round the fish."

"I don't think that there is much harm in it under the present circumstances," Terence laughed. "It is not sport, but it is food. I am afraid, Tim, that you must have been poaching a good deal at home or you would never have thought of buying lime before starting on this march."

"I would scorn to take in an Oirish fish, yer honour!" Hoolan said, indignantly. "But it seems to me that as the people here are trating us in just as blackguardly a manner as they can, shure it is the least we can do to catch their fish any way we can, just to pay them off."

"Well, looking at it in that light, Tim, I will say no more against the practice. I don't think I could bring myself to lime even Portuguese water, but my conscience would not trouble me at eating fish that had been caught by somebody else."

"I will bear it in mind, yer honour, and next time we come on a good pool a dish of fine fish shall be left at your quarters, but yer honour must not mintion to the gineral where you got them from. Maybe his conscience in the matter of ateing limed fish would be more tender than your own, and it might get me into trouble."

"I will take care about that, Tim; at any rate, I will try and manufacture two or three hooks, and when we halt for a day will try and do a little fishing on my own account."

"I will make you two or three, Mr. O'Connor. I made a couple for Mr. Ryan, and he caught two beauties yesterday evening."

"Thank you, Hoolan. Fond as I am of fishing, I wonder it did not strike me before. I can make a line by plaiting some office string, with twisted horse-hair instead of gut."

"I expect that that is just what Mr. Ryan did, yer honour. I heard the adjutant using powerful language this morning because he could not find a ball of twine."

After this Terence generally managed to get an hour's fishing before the evening twilight had quite faded away; and by the aid of a long rod cut on the river bank, a line manufactured by himself, and Hoolan's hook baited with worms, he generally contrived to catch enough fish to supplement the ordinary fare at the following morning's breakfast.

"This is a welcome surprise, Trevor," the brigadier said the first time the fish appeared at table. "I thought I smelt fish frying, but I felt sure I must be mistaken. Where on earth did you get them from?"

"It is not my doing, General, but O'Connor's. I was as much surprised as yourself when I saw Burke squatting over the fire frying three fine fish. I asked him where he had stolen them. He told me that Mr. O'Connor brought them in at eight o'clock yesterday evening."

"Where did you get them from, O'Connor?"

"I caught them in the stream that we crossed half a mile back, sir. I found a likely pool a few hundred yards down it, and an hour's work there gave me those three fish. They stopped biting as soon as it got dark."

"What did you catch them with?"

Terence explained the nature of his tackle.

"Capital! You have certainly given us a very pleasant change of food, and I hope that you will continue the practice whenever there is a chance."

"There ought often to be one, General. We cross half a dozen little mountain streams every day, and the villages are generally built close to one. I don't suppose I should have thought of it, if I had not found that some of the men of my regiment have been supplying the mess with them. I hope to do better in future, for going over the ground where some of the troops in front of us have bivouacked I came upon some white feathers blowing about, and I shall try to tie a fly. That ought to be a good deal more killing than a worm when the light begins to fade."

"You have been a fisherman, then, at home?"

"Yes, sir; I did a good deal of fishing round Athlone, and was taught to tie my own flies. I wish I had a packet of hooks—the two one of our fellows made for me are well enough for worms, but they are rather clumsy for flies."

"I used to be fond of fishing myself," Fane said; "but I have always bought my tackle, and I doubt whether I should make much hand at it, if left to my own devices. We are not likely to be able to get any hooks till we get to Almeida, but I should think you would find some there."

"I shall be able to get some wire to make them with, no doubt, sir."

"I fancy after we have left Almeida you won't find many opportunities of fishing, O'Connor. We shall have other work on hand then, and shall, I hope, be able to buy what we want; at any rate, we shall have as good a chance of doing so as others, while along this road there is nothing to be had for love or money, and the peasants would no doubt be glad to sell us anything they have, but they are living on black bread themselves; and, indeed, the greater part have moved away to less-frequented places. No doubt they will come back again as soon as we have all passed, but how long they will be allowed to live in peace and quietness is more than I can say. As long as it is only our troops who come along they have nothing much to complain of, for they can sell everything they have to dispose of at prices they never dreamt of before; but they complain bitterly of the French, who ate their fruit and drank their wine, killed their pigs and fowls, appropriated their cattle and horses, and they thought themselves lucky to escape with their lives. You see there are very few men about here; they have all gone off to join one or other of the Portuguese bands."

"I fancy these Portuguese fellows will turn out useful some day, General," Major Errington said. "They are stout fellows, and though I don't think the townspeople would be of any good, the peasantry ought to make good soldiers if they were well drilled and led."

"That is a very large if," Fane laughed. "I see no signs of any leader, and unless we could lend them a few hundred non-commissioned officers I don't see where their drill instructors are to come from. Still, I have more hope of them than I have of the Spaniards. Those men under Trant were never tried much under fire, but they certainly improved in discipline very much in the short time they were with us. If we could but get rid of all the Portuguese authorities and take the people in hand ourselves, we ought to be able to turn out fifty thousand good fighting troops in the course of a few months, but so long as things go on as they are I see no hope of any efficient aid from them.''

At Almeida Terence managed to procure some hooks. They were clumsily made, but greatly superior to anything that he could turn out himself. He was also able to procure some strong lines, but the use of flies seemed to be altogether unknown. However, during his stay he made half a dozen different patterns, and with these in a small tin box and a coil of line stowed away at the bottom of one of his holsters, he felt that if opportunity should occur he ought to be able to have fair sport. He had suffered a good deal during the heavy rains, which came on occasionally, from the fact that his infantry cloak was not ample enough to cover his legs when riding. He was fortunate enough here to be able to buy a pair of long riding-boots, and with these and a pair of thick canvas trousers, made by one of the regimental tailors, and coming down just below the knee, he felt that in future he could defy the rain.

At Salamanca there were far better opportunities of the officers supplementing their outfits. Landing on the Mondego early in August, they had made provision against the heat, but had brought no outfit at all suited for wear in winter, and all seized the opportunity of providing themselves with warm under-garments, had linings sewn into greatcoats, and otherwise prepared for the cold which would shortly set in. The greater part of the troops were here quartered in the convents and other extensive buildings, and as Fane's brigade was one of the first to arrive they enjoyed a short period of well-earned rest. Terence had by this time picked up a good deal of Portuguese, and was able to make himself pretty well understood by the Spanish shopkeepers. He, as well as the other officers, was astonished and disgusted at the lethargy that prevailed when, as all now knew, the great Spanish armies were scattered to the winds, and large bodies of French troops were advancing in all directions to crush out the last spark of resistance.

The officers of the Mayo Fusiliers had established a mess, and Terence often dined there. He was always eagerly questioned as to what was going to be done.

"I can assure you, O'Grady," he said, one day, "that aides-de-camp are not admitted to the confidence of the officer commanding-in-chief. I know no more as to Sir John's intentions than the youngest drummer-boy. I suppose that everything will depend upon the weather, and whether General Hope, with the artillery and cavalry, manages to join us. If he does, I suppose we shall fight a battle before we fall back. If he does not, I suppose we shall have to fall back without fighting, if the French will let us."

"I wish, Terence, you would give these lazy Spaniards a good fright, just as you gave the people at Athlone. Faith, I would give a couple of months' pay to see them regularly scared."

"If I were not on the staff I might try it, O'Grady, but it would never do for me to try such a thing now."

Dick Ryan, who was standing by, winked significantly, and in a short time he and Terence were talking eagerly together in a corner of the room.

"Who is to know you are a staff-officer, Terence?" the latter urged. "Isn't it an infantry uniform that you are wearing? and ain't there hundreds of infantry officers here? It was good fun at Athlone, but I don't think that many of them believed there was any real danger. It would be altogether different here; they are scared enough as it is, though they walk about with their cloaks wrapped round them and pretend to be mighty confident."

"Let us come and talk it over outside, Dick. It did not much matter before if it had been discovered we had a hand in it. Of course the colonel would have given us a wigging, but at heart he would have been as pleased at the joke as any of us. But it is a different affair here."

Going out, they continued their talk and arranged their plans. Late the following night two English officers rushed suddenly into a drinking-shop close to the gate through which the road to Valladolid passed.

"The French! the French!" one exclaimed. "Run for your lives and give the alarm!"

The men all leapt to their feet, rushed out tumultuously, and scattered through the streets, shouting at the top of their voices: "The French are coming! the French are coming! Get up, or you will all be murdered in your beds!"

The alarm spread like wildfire, and Terence and Ryan made their way back, by the shortest line, to the room where most of the officers were still sitting, smoking and chatting.

"Any news, O'Connor?" the colonel asked.

"Nothing that I have heard of, Colonel. I thought I would drop in for a cigar before turning in."

A few minutes later Tim Hoolan entered.

"There is a shindy in the town, your honour," he said to the colonel. "Meself does not know what it is about; but they are hallooing and bawling fit to kill themselves."

One of the officers went to the window and threw it up.

"Hoolan is right, Colonel; there is something the matter. There—" he broke off as a church bell pealed out with loud and rapid strokes.

"That is the alarm, sure enough!" the colonel exclaimed.

"Be off at once, gentlemen, and get the men up and under arms."

"I must be off to the general's quarters!" Terence exclaimed, hastily putting on his greatcoat again.

"The divil fly away with them," O'Grady grumbled, as he hastily finished the glass before him; "sorrow a bit of peace can I get at all, at all, in this bastely country."

Terence hurried away to his quarters. A score of church bells were now pealing out the alarm. From every house men and women rushed out panic-stricken, and eagerly questioned each other. All sorts of wild reports were circulated.

"The British outposts have been driven in; the Valladolid gate has been captured; Napoleon himself, with his whole army, is pouring into the town."

The shrieks of frightened women added to the din, above which the British bugles calling the troops to arms could be heard in various quarters of the city.

"Oh, here you are, Mr. O'Connor!" General Fane exclaimed, as he hurried in. "Mr. Trevor has just started for the convent; he may be intercepted, and therefore do you carry the same message; the brigade is to get under arms at once, and to remain in readiness for action until I arrive. From what I can gather from these frightened fools, the French have already entered the town. If the convent is attacked, it is to be defended until the last. I am going to head-quarters for orders."

A good deal alarmed at the consequences of the tumult that he and Dick Ryan had excited, Terence made his way through the streets at a run; his progress, however, was impeded by the crowd, many of whom seized him as he passed and implored him to tell them the news. He observed that not a weapon was to be seen among the crowd; evidently resistance was absolutely unthought of. Trevor had reached the convent before him. The four regiments had already gathered there under arms.

"Have you any orders, Mr. O'Connor?" Colonel Corcoran asked, eagerly, for the Mayo Fusiliers happened to be formed up next the gate of the convent.

"No, sir; only to repeat those brought by Mr. Trevor, as the general thought that he might be intercepted on the way. The troops are to remain here in readiness until he arrives. If attacked, they are to hold the convent until the last."

"Have you seen any signs of the French?"

"None, whatever, Colonel."

"Did you hear any firing?"

"No, sir; but there was such an uproar—what with the church bells, everyone shouting, and the women screaming—that I don't suppose I should have heard it unless it had been quite close."

"We thought we heard musketry," the colonel replied, "but it might have been only fancy. There is such a hullabaloo in the city that we might not have heard the fire of small-arms, but I think that we must have heard artillery."

In ten minutes Fane with his staff galloped in. "The brigade will march down towards the Valladolid gate," he said. "If you encounter any enemies, Colonel Corcoran, you will at once occupy the houses on both sides of the street and open fire upon them from the windows and roofs; the other regiments will charge them. At present," he went on, as the colonel gave the order for the regiment to march, "we can obtain no information as to the cause of this uproar. An officer rode in, just as I was starting, from Anstruther's force, encamped outside the walls, asking for orders, and reporting that his outposts have seen no signs of the enemy. I believe it is a false alarm after all, and we are marching rather to reassure the populace than with any idea of meeting the enemy."

The troops marched rapidly through the streets, making their way without ceremony through the terrified crowd. They had gone but a short distance when the bells of the churches one by one ceased their clamour, and a hush succeeded the din that had before prevailed. When the head of the column reached the gate, they saw Sir John Moore and his staff sitting there on horseback. Fane rode up to him for orders.

"It is, as I fancied, wholly a false alarm," the general said. "How it could have started I have no idea. I have had another report from Anstruther; all is quiet at the outposts, and there is no sign whatever of the enemy. There is nothing to do but to march the troops back to barracks. However, I am not sorry, for possibly the scare may wake the authorities up to the necessity of taking some steps for the protection of the town."

Terence rode back with General Fane to his quarters.

"I cannot make out," Trevor said, as they went, "how the scare can have begun; everything was quiet enough. I was just thinking of turning in when we heard a shouting in the streets. In three minutes the whole town seemed to have gone mad, and I made sure that the French must be upon us; but I could not make out how they could have done so without our outposts giving the alarm. Where were you when it began?"

"I was in the mess-room of the Mayos, when one of the servants ran in to say that there was a row. Directly afterwards the alarm-bells began to ring, the colonel at once gave orders for the regiment to be got under arms, and I ran back to the general for orders; and I must have passed you somewhere on the road. Did you ever see such cowards as these Spaniards? Though there are arms enough in the town for every man to bear a musket—and certainly the greater portion of them have weapons of some sort or other—I did not see a man with arms of any kind in his hand."

"I noticed the same thing," Trevor said. "It is disgusting. It was evident that the sole thought that possessed them was as to their own wretched lives. I have no doubt that, if they could have had their willl, they would have disarmed all our troops, in order that no resistance whatever should be offered. And yet only yesterday the fellows were all bragging about their patriotism, and the bravery that would be shown should the French make their appearance. It makes one sick to be fighting for such people."

The following afternoon Terence went up to the convent.

"Well, O'Connor, have you heard how it all began?" the colonel asked, as he went into the mess-room.

"No one seems to know at all, Colonel. The authorities are making inquiries, but, as far as I have heard, nothing has taken place to account for it."

"It reminds me," the colonel said, shutting one eye and looking fixedly at Terence, "of a certain affair that took place at Athlone."

"I was thinking the same myself," Terence replied, quietly, "only the scare was a good deal greater here than it was there; besides, a good many of the townspeople in Athlone did turn out with guns in their hands, whereas here, I believe every man in the town hid his gun in his bed before running out."

"I always suspected you of having a hand in that matter, Terence."

"Did you, Colonel?" Terence said, in a tone of surprise. "Well, as, fortunately, I was sitting here when this row began, you cannot suspect me this time."

"I don't know; you and Ryan came in together, which was suspicious in itself, and it was not two minutes after you had come in that the rumpus began. Just give me a wink, lad, if you had a finger in the matter. You know you are safe with me; besides, ain't you a staff-officer now, and outside my jurisdiction altogether?"

"Well, Colonel, a wink does not cost anything," Terence said, "so here is to ye."

He exchanged a wink with the colonel, who burst into a fit of laughter so loud that he startled all the other officers, who at once came up to hear the joke.

"It is just a little story that Terence has been telling me," the colonel said, when he had recovered his breath, "about the scare last night, and how a young woman, with next to nothing on her, threw her arms round his neck and begged him to save her. The poor young fellow blushed up to his eyelids with the shame of it in the public streets!"

CHAPTER IX

THE RETREAT

O'GRADY asked no questions, but presently whispered to Terence: "Faith, ye did it well, me boy."

"Did what well, O'Grady?"

"You need not tell me about it, Terence. I was expecting it. Didn't I spake to ye the day before about it, and didn't I feel sure that something would come of it? When that row began last night, I looked at you hard and saw you wink at that young spalpeen, Dicky Ryan; and sure all the time that we were standing there, formed up, I well-nigh burst the buttons off me coatee in holding in me laughter, when everyone else was full of excitement.

"'Are you ill, O'Grady?' the colonel said, for I had to

sit meself down on some steps and rock meself to and fro to aise meself. 'Is it sick ye are?' 'A sudden pain has saised me, Colonel,' says I, 'but I will be all right in a minute.' 'Take a dram out of me flask,' says he; 'something must have gone wrong wid ye.' I took a drink—"

"That I may be sure you did," Terence interrupted.

"—And thin told him that I felt better; but as we marched down through the crowd and saw the fright of the men, and the women screaming in their night-gowns at the windows, faith, I well-nigh choked."

"Have you spoken to Ryan about this absurd suspicion, O'Grady?"

"I spoke to him, but I might as well have spoke to a brick wall. Divil a thing could I get out of him. How did you manage it at all, lad?"

"How could I manage it?" Terence said, indignantly. "No, no, O'Grady; I know you did make some remark about that scare at Athlone, and said it would be fun to have one here. I was a little shocked at hearing such a thing from, as you often say, a superior officer, and it certainly appears to me that it was you who first broached the idea. So I have much more right to feel a suspicion that you had a hand in the carrying of it out than for you to suspect me."

"Well, Terence," O'Grady said, in an insinuating way, "I won't ask you any questions now, and maybe some day when you have marched away from this place, you will tell me the ins and outs of the business."

"Maybe, O'Grady, and perhaps you will also confess to me how you managed to bring the scare about."

"Go along wid you, Terence, it is yourself knows better than anyone else that I had nothing to do with it, and I will never forgive you until you make a clean breast of it to me."

"We shall see about it," Terence laughed. "Anyhow,

if you allude to the subject again, I shall feel it my duty to inform the colonel of my reasons for suspecting that you were concerned in spreading those false reports last night."

"It was first-rate, wasn't it?" Dick Ryan said, as he joined Terence, when the latter left the mess-room.

"It was good fun, Dicky; but I tell you, for a time I was quite as much scared as anyone else. I never thought that it would have gone quite so far. When it came to all the troops turning out, and Sir John and everyone, I felt that there would be an awful row if we were ever found out."

"It was splendid, Terence. I knew that we could not be found out when we had not told a soul. Did you ever see such a funk as the Spaniards were all in, and after all their bragging and the airs that they had given themselves. Our men were so savage at their cowardice, that I believe they would have liked nothing better than an order to pitch into them. And didn't the women yell and howl? It is the best lark we have ever had."

"It is good fun to look back at, Dicky, but I shall be glad when we are out of this. The Spanish authorities are making all sorts of inquiries, and I have no doubt that they will get hold of some of the men in that wine-shop, and it will come out that two British officers started the alarm."

"What if it did?" Ryan said. "There were only two wretched candles burning in the place, and they could not have got a fair sight at us, and indeed they all jumped up and bolted the moment we spoke. I will bet that there is not one among them who would be able to swear to us though we were standing before him; and I have no doubt if they were questioned every man would give a different account of what we were like. I have no fear that they will ever find us out. Still, I shall be glad when we are out of this old place. Not because I am afraid about our share in that business being discovered, but we have been here nearly a fortnight now, and as we know there is a strong French force within ten miles of us, I think that it is about time that the fun began. You don't think that we are going to retreat, do you?"

"I don't know any more about it than you do, Dicky; but I feel absolutely sure that we shall retreat. I don't see anything else for us to do. Every day fresh news comes in about the strength of the French, and as the Spanish resistance is now pretty well over, and Madrid has fallen, they will all be free to march against us; and even when Hope has joined us we shall only be about 20,000 strong, and they have, at the least, ten times that force. I thing we shall be mighty lucky if we get back across the frontier into Portugal before they are all on us."

Sir John Moore, however, was not disposed to retire without doing something for the cause of Spain. The French armies had not yet penetrated into the southern provinces, and he nobly resolved to make a movement that would draw the whole strength of the French towards him, and give time for the Spaniards in the south to gather the remains of their armies together and organize a resistance to the French advance. In view of the number and strength of the enemy, no more heroic resolution was ever taken by a military commander, and it was all the more to be admired, inasmuch as he could hope to win no victory that would cover himself and his army with glory, no success that would satisfy the public at home, and at best he could but hope, after long, fatiguing, and dangerous marches, to effect his retreat from the overwhelming forces that would be hurled against him.

While remaining at Salamanca, Sir John, foreseeing that a retreat into Portugal must be finally carried out, took steps to have magazines established on two of the principal routes to the coast, that a choice might be left open to him by which to retire when he had accomplished his main object of diverting the great French wave of invasion from the south.

On the 11th of December the march began, and for the next ten days the army advanced farther and farther into the country. So far Moore had only Soult's army opposing his advance towards Burgos, and it might be possible to strike a heavy blow at that general before Napoleon, who was convinced that the British must fall back into Portugal if they had not already begun to do so, should come up. He had been solemnly assured that he should be joined by Romana with 14,000 picked men, but that general had with him but 5,000 peasants, who were in such a miserable condition that when the British reached the spot where the junction was to be effected, he was ashamed to show them, and marched away into Leon.

The British, in order to obtain forage, were obliged to move along several lines of route. Sir David Baird's division joined them as they advanced, and when they reached the Carrion their effective force amounted to 23,583 men, with sixty pieces of artillery. On the French side, Soult had—on hearing of the British advance to the north-east, by which, if successful, they would cut the French lines of communication between Madrid and the frontier—called up all his detached troops, and wrote to the governor of Burgos to divert to his assistance all troops coming along the road from France, whatever their destination might be.

On the 21st Lord Paget, with the 10th and 15th Hussars, surprised a French cavalry force at Sahagun, and ordered the 15th to turn their position and endeavour to cut them off. When with the 10th Hussars Lord Paget arrived in the rear of the village, he found six hundred French dragoons drawn up and ready to attack him. He at once charged and broke them and pursued them for some distance. Twenty were killed, thirteen officers and 154 men taken prisoners. On the 23d, Soult had concentrated his forces at the town of Carrion, and that night the British troops were got in motion to attack them, the two forces being about even in numbers; but scarcely had he moved forward when reports, both from Romana and his own spies, reached Sir John Moore to the effect that his march had achieved the object with which it was undertaken. Orders had been sent by Napoleon for the whole of the French armies to move at once against the British, while he himself, with the troops at Madrid, 70,000 strong, had started by forced marches to fall upon him.

The instant Moore received this information he arrested the forward movement of his troops. His object had been attained. The French invasion of the south was arrested, and time given to the Spaniards. There was nothing now but to fall back with all speed. It was well indeed that he did not carry out his intention of attacking Soult. The latter had that day received orders from the emperor not to give battle, but to fall back, and so tempt Moore to pursue, in which case his line of retreat would have been intercepted and his army irretrievably lost.

The order to retreat was an unwelcome one indeed to the troops. For twelve days they had marched through deep snow and suffered fatigues, privations, and hardships. That evening they had expected to be repaid for their exertions by a battle and a victory on the following morning, and the order to retreat, coming at such a moment, was a bitter disappointment indeed.

They were, of course, ignorant of the reasons for this sudden change, and the officers shared the discontent of the troops, a feeling that largely accounted for the disorders and losses that took place during the retreat.

Napoleon led his troops north with his usual impetuosity.

The deep snow choked the passes through the mountains. The generals, after twelve hours of labour, reported the roads impracticable, but Napoleon placed himself at the head of the column, and, amidst a storm of snow and driving hail, led them over the mountain. With tremendous efforts he reached Desillas on the 26th; while Houssaye entered Valladolid on the same day, and Ney, with the 6th corps, arrived at Rio Seco.

Full of hope that he had caught the British, the emperor pushed on towards Barras, only to find that he was twelve hours too late. Moore had, the instant he received the news, sent back the heavy baggage with the main body of infantry, himself following more slowly with the light brigade and cavalry, the latter at times pushing parties up to the enemy's line and skirmishing with his outposts to prevent Soult from suspecting that the army had retreated. On the 26th the whole army, moving by different routes, approached the river Esla, which they crossed in a thick fog, which greatly hindered the operation. A brigade remained on the left bank to protect the passage, for the enemy's cavalry were already close at hand, and Soult was hotly pressing in pursuit.

A strong body of horse belonging to the emperor's army intercepted Lord Paget near Mayorga, but two squadrons of the 10th Hussars charged up the rising ground on which they had posted themselves, and, notwithstanding their disadvantage in numbers and position, killed twenty and took a hundred prisoners. Moore made but a short pause on the Esla, for that position could be turned by the forces advancing from the south. He waited, therefore, only until he could clear out his magazines, collect his stragglers, and send forward his baggage. He ordered the bridge by which the army had crossed to be broken down, and left Crawford to perform this duty.

Short as the retreat had been, it had already sufficed to

damage most seriously the morale of the army. The splendid discipline and order that had been shown during the advance was now gone; many of the regimental officers altogether neglected their duties, and the troops were insubordinate. Great numbers straggled, plundered the villages, and committed excesses of all sorts, and already the general had been forced to issue an order reproaching the army for its conduct, and appealing to the honour of the soldiers to second his efforts. Valiant in battle, capable of the greatest efforts on the march, hardy in enduring fatigue and the inclemency of weather, the British soldier always deteriorates rapidly when his back is turned to the enemy. Confident in his bravery, regarding victory as assured, he is unable to understand the necessity for retreat, and considers himself degraded by being ordered to retire, and regards prudence on the part of his general as equivalent to cowardice.

The armies of Wellington deteriorated with the same rapidity as this force, when upon two occasions it was necessary to retreat when threatened by overwhelming forces; and yet, however disorganized, the British soldier recovers his discipline the instant he is attacked, and fiercely turns upon his pursuers. At the bridge across the Esla two privates of the 3d gave an example of splendid courage and determination. It was night. Some of the baggage was still on the farther bank, and the two men were posted as sentries beyond the bridge, their orders being that if an enemy appeared, one should fire and then run back to the bridge and shout to warn the guard whether the enemy were in force or not. The other was to maintain his post as long as possible.

During the night the light cavalry of the imperial guard rode down. Jackson, one of the sentries, fired and ran back to give the alarm. He was overtaken, and received over a dozen sabre cuts; nevertheless he staggered on until he reached the

"WHAT DO YOU MEAN, TERENCE? WE WOULD HAVE THRASHED
THEM OUT OF THEIR BOOTS IN NO TIME."

bridge, and gave the signal. Walton, the other sentry, with equal resolution stood his ground and wounded several of his assailants, who, as they drew off, left him unhurt, although his cap, knapsack, belt, and musket were cut in over twenty places, and his bayonet bent double.

Terence O'Connor's duties had been light enough during the advance, but during the three days of the retreat to the Esla he had been incessantly occupied. He and Trevor had both been directed to ride backwards and forwards along the line of the brigade to see that there was no straggling in the ranks, and that the baggage carts in the rear kept close up. The task was no easy one, and was unpleasant as well as hard. Many of the officers plodded sulkily along, paying no attention whatever to their men, allowing them to straggle as they chose ; and they were obliged to report several of the worst cases to the brigadier. With the Mayo Fusiliers they had less trouble than with others. Terence had, when he joined them at their first halt after the retreat began, found them as angry and discontented as the rest at the unexpected order, and was at once assailed with questions and complaints.

He listened to them quietly, and then said :

" Of course, if you all prefer a French prison to a few days' hard marching, you have good reason to grumble at being baulked in your wishes ; that is all I have to say about it."

" What do you mean, Terence ? " O'Grady asked, angrily. " Soult's force was not stronger than ours, at least so we heard ; and if it had been it would make no difference, we would have thrashed them out of their boots in no time."

" I dare say we should, O'Grady, and what then ? "

" Well, I don't know what then," O'Grady said, after a moment's silence ; " that would have been the general's business."

" Quite so ; and so is this. There you would have been

with perhaps a couple of thousand wounded and as many French prisoners, and Napoleon with 60,000 men or so, and Ney with as many more, and Houssaye with his cavalry division, all in your rear cutting you off from the sea. What would have been your course then?"

A general silence fell upon the officers.

"Is that so?" the colonel asked at last.

"That is so," Terence said, gravely. "All these and other troops are marching night and day to intercept us. It is no question of fighting now. Victory over Soult, so far from being of any use, would only have burdened us with wounded and prisoners, and even a day's delay would be absolutely fatal. As it is, it is a question whether we shall have time to get back to the coast before they are all posted in our front. Every hour is of the greatest importance. You all know that we have talked over lots of times how dangerous our position is. General Fane told us, when the orders to retreat were issued, that he believed the peril to be even more imminent than we thought. We all know when we marched north from Salamanca, that, without a single Spaniard to back us, all that could be hoped for was to aid Saragossa and Seville and Cadiz to gather the levies in the south and prepare for defence, and that erelong we should have any number of enemies upon us. That is what has precisely happened, and now there is grumbling because the object has been attained, and that you are not allowed to fight a battle that, whether won or lost, would equally ruin us."

"Sure ye are right," O'Grady said, warmly, "and we are a set of omadhouns. You have sense in your head, Terence, and there is no gainsaying you. I was grumbling more than the rest of them, but I won't grumble any more. Still, I suppose that there is no harm in hoping we shall have just a bit of fighting before we get back to Portugal."

"We shall be lucky if we don't have a good deal of fighting, O'Grady, and against odds that will satisfy even you. As to Portugal, there is no chance of our getting there. Ney will certainly cut that road, and the emperor will, most likely, also do so, as you can see for yourself on the map."

"Divil a map have I ever looked at since I was at school," O'Grady said. "Then if we can't get back to Portugal, where shall we get to?"

"To one of the northern seaports; of course, I don't know which has been decided upon; I don't suppose the general himself has settled that yet. It must depend upon the roads and the movements of the enemy, and whether there is a defensible position near the port that we can hold in case the fleet and transports cannot be got there by the time we arrive."

"Faith, Terence, ye're a walking encyclopeydia. You have got the matter at your finger ends."

"I don't pretend to know any more than anyone else," Terence said, with a laugh. "But of course I hear matters talked over at the brigade mess. I don't think that Fane knows more of the general's absolute plans than you do. I dare say the divisional generals know, but it would not go further. Still, as Fane and Errington and Dowdeswell know something about war besides the absolute fighting, they can form some idea as to the plans that will be adopted."

"Well, Terence," the colonel said, "I didn't think the time was coming so soon when I was going to be instructed by your father's son, but I will own that you have made me feel that I have begun campaigning too late in life, and that you have given me a lesson."

"I did not mean to do that, Colonel," Terence said, a good deal abashed. "It was O'Grady I was chiefly speaking to."

"Your supeyrior officer!" O'Grady murmured.

"My superior officer, certainly," Terence went on, with a smile; "but who, having, as he says, never looked at a map since he left school—while I have naturally studied one every evening since we started from Torres Vedras—can therefore know no more about the situation than does Tim Hoolan. But I certainly never intended my remarks to apply to you, Colonel."

"They hit the mark all the same, lad, and the shame is mine and not yours. I think you have done us all good. One doesn't care when one is retreating for a good reason, but when one marches for twelve days to meet an enemy, and then, when just close to him, one turns one's back and runs away, it is enough to disgust an Englishman, let alone an Irishman. Well, boys, now we see it is all right, we will do our duty as well on the retreat as we did on the advance, and divil a grumble shall there be in my hearing."

From that moment, therefore, the Mayo Fusiliers were an example to the brigade. Any grumble in the ranks was met with a cheerful "Whist, boys! do you think that you know the general's business better than he does himself? It is plenty of fighting you are likely to get before you have done, never fear. Now is the time, boys, to get the regiment a good name. The general knows that we can fight. Now let him see that we can wait patiently till we get another chance. Remember, the better temper you are in, the less you will feel the cold."

So, laughing and joking, and occasionally breaking into a song, the Mayo Fusiliers pushed steadily forward, and the colonel that evening congratulated the men that not one had fallen out.

"Keep that up, boys," he said. "It will be a proud day for me when we get to our journey's end, wherever that may be, to be able to say to the brigadier: 'Except those who have been killed by the enemy, here is my regiment just as it was when it started from the Carrion—not a man has fallen out, not a man has straggled away, not a man has made a baste of himself and was unfit to fall in the next morning.' I know them," he said to O'Driscol, as the regiment was dismissed from parade. " They will not fall out, they will not straggle, but if they come to a place where wine's in plenty, they will make bastes of themselves; and after all," he added, " after the work they have gone through, who is to blame them ?"

At the halt the next evening at Bembibre the colonel's forebodings that the men could not be trusted where liquor was plentiful were happily not verified. There were immense wine-vaults in the town. These were broken open, and were speedily crowded by disbanded Spaniards, soldiers, camp-followers, muleteers, women and children—the latter taking refuge there from the terrible cold. The rear-guard, to which the Mayo regiment had been attached the evening before, found that Baird's division had gone on, but that vast numbers of drunken soldiers had been left behind. General Moore was himself with the rear-guard, and the utmost efforts were made to induce the drunkards to rejoin their regiments. He himself appealed to the troops, instructing the commanders of the different regiments to say that he relied implicitly upon the soldiers to do their duty. The French might at any moment be up, and every man must be in his ranks. No men were to fall out or to enter any wine-house or cellar, but each should have at once a pint of wine served out to him, and as much more before they marched in the morning.

After the colonel read out this order, he supplemented it by saying, " Now, boys, the credit of the regiment is at stake. It is a big honour that has been paid you in choosing you to join the rear-guard, and you have got to show that you deserve it. As soon as it can be drawn, you will have your pint of wine each, which will be enough to warm your fingers and toes. Wait here in the ranks till you have drunk your wine and eaten some of the bread in your haversacks, and by that time I will see what I can do for you. You will have another pint before starting; but mind, though I hope there isn't a mother's son who would bring discredit on the regiment, I warn you that I shall give the officers instructions to shoot down any man who wanders from the ranks in search of liquor. The French may be here in half an hour after we have started, and it is better to be shot than to be sabred by a French dragoon, which will happen surely enough to every baste who has drunk too much to go on with the troops."

Only a few murmurs were heard at the conclusion of the speech.

"Now, gentlemen," the colonel said, "will half a dozen of you see to the wine. Get hold of some of those fellows loafing about there and make them roll out as many barrels as will supply a pint to every man in the regiment, ourselves as well as the men. O'Grady, take Lieutenant Horton and Mr. Haldane and two sergeants with you. Here is my purse. Go through the town and get some bread and anything else in the way of food that you can lay your hands upon. And, if you can, above all things get some tobacco."

O'Grady's search was for a time unsuccessful, as the soldiers and camp-followers had already broken into the shops and stores. In an unfrequented street, however, they came across a large building. He knocked at the door with the hilt of his sword. It was opened after a time by an old man.

"What house is this?"

"It is a tobacco factory," he replied.

"Be jabers, we have come to the right place. I want

about half a ton of it. We are not robbers, and I will pay for what we take." Then another idea struck him. "Wait a moment, I will be back again in no time. Horton, do you stay here and take charge of the men. I am going back to the colonel."

He found on reaching the regiment that the men were already drinking their wine and eating their bread.

"I am afraid I shall never keep them, O'Grady," the colonel said, mournfully. "It is scarcely in human nature to see men straggling about as full as they can hold, and know that there is liquor to be had for taking it and not to go for it."

"It is all right, Colonel. I know that we can never keep the men if we turn them into the houses to sleep; but I have found a big building that will hold the whole regiment, and the best of it is that it is a tobacco factory. I expect it is run by the authorities of the place, and as we are doing what we can for them, they need not grudge us what we take; and faith, the boys will be quiet and contented enough, so that they do but get enough to keep their pipes going, and know that they will march in the morning with a bit in their knapsacks."

"The very thing, O'Grady! Pass the word for the regiment to fall in the instant they have finished their meal."

It was not long before they were ready, and in a few minutes, guided by O'Grady, the head of the regiment reached the building.

"Who is the owner of this place?" the colonel asked the old man, who, with a lantern in his hand, was still standing at the door.

"The Central Junta of the Province has of late taken it, your Excellency."

"Good! Then we will be the guests of the Central Junta of

the Province for the night." Then he raised his voice, "Boys, here is a warm lodging for you for the night, and tobacco galore for your pipes; and, for those who haven't got them, cigars. Just wait until I have got some lights, and then file inside in good order."

There was no difficulty about this, for the factory was in winter worked long after dark set in. In a very few minutes the place was lighted up from end to end. The troops were then marched in and divided amongst the various rooms.

"Now, boys, tell the men to smoke a couple of pipes, and then to lie down to sleep. In the morning each man can put as much tobacco into his knapsack and pockets as they will hold, and when we halt they can give some of it away to regiments that have not been as lucky as themselves."

The men sat down in the highest state of satisfaction. Boxes of cigars were broken open, and in a couple of minutes almost every man and officer in the regiment had one alight in his mouth. There were few, however, who got beyond one cigar; the warmth of the place after their long march in the snow speedily had its effect, and in half an hour silence reigned in the factory, save for a murmur of voices in one of the lower rooms where the officers were located.

"O'Grady, you are a broth of a boy," the colonel said. "The men have scarce had a smoke for the last week, and it will do them a world of good. We have got them all under one roof, and there is no fear that anyone will want to get out, and they will fall in in the morning as fresh as paint. Half an hour before bugle-call three or four of you had best turn out with a dozen men, and roll up enough barrels from the vaults to give them the drink promised to them, before starting. Who will volunteer?"

Half a dozen officers at once offered to go, and a captain and three lieutenants were told off for the work.

"They know how to make cigars, if they don't know anything else," Captain O'Driscol said; "this is a first-rate weed."

"So it ought to be by the brand," another officer said. "I took the two boxes from a cupboard that was locked up. There are a dozen more like them, and I thought it was as well to take them out; they are at present under the table. I have no doubt that they are real Havannas, and have probably been got for some grandee or other."

"He will have to do without them," O'Grady said, calmly, as he lighted his second cigar; "they are too good for any Spaniard under the sun. And, moreover, if we did not take them you may be sure that the French would have them to-morrow, and I should say that the Central Junta of the Province will be mighty pleased to know that the tobacco was smoked by their allies instead of by the French."

"I don't suppose that they will care much about it one way or another," O'Driscol remarked; "their pockets are so full of English gold that the loss of a few tons of tobacco won't affect them much. I enjoy my cigar immensely, and have the satisfaction of knowing that for once I have got something out of a Spaniard—it is the first thing since I landed."

"Well, boys, we had better be off to sleep," the colonel said. "I am so sleepy that I can hardly keep my eyes open, and you ought to be worse, for you have tramped well-nigh forty miles to-day. See that the sentry at the door keeps awake, Captain Humphrey; you are officer of the day; upon my word I am sorry for you. Tell him he can light up if he likes, but if he sees an officer coming round he must get rid of it. Mind the sentries are changed regularly, for I expect that we shall sleep so soundly that if all the bugles in the place were sounding an alarm we should not hear them."

"All right, Colonel! I have got Sergeant Jackson in

charge of the reliefs in the passage outside, and I think that I can depend upon him, but I will tell him to wake me up whenever he changes the sentries. I don't say I shall turn out myself, but as long as he calls me I shall know that he is awake, and that it is all right. I had better tell him to call you half an hour before bugle-call, Sullivan, so that you can wake the others and get the wine here; he mustn't be a minute after the half-hour. Thank goodness, we don't have to furnish the outposts to-night."

In ten minutes all were asleep on the floor, wrapped in their greatcoats, the officer of the day taking his place next the door so that he could be roused easily. Every hour one or other of the two non-commissioned officers in charge of the guard in the passage opened the door a few inches and said softly, " I am relieving the sentries, sir ; " and each time the officer murmured assent.

Sullivan was called at the appointed time, got up, and stretched himself, grumbling :

" I don't believe that I have been asleep ten minutes."

On going out into the passage, however, where a light was burning, his watch told him that it was indeed time to be moving. He woke the others, and with the men went down to the cellars. Here the scene of confusion was great; drunken men lay thickly about the floor, others sat, cup in hand, talking, or singing snatches of song, Spanish or English. Hastily picking out enough unbroken casks for the purpose, he set the men to carry them up to the street, and they were then rolled along to the factory. Just as they reached the door the bugle-call sounded ; the men were soon on their feet, refreshed by a good night's sleep. The casks were broached, and the wine served out.

" It is awful, Colonel," Sullivan said. " There will be hundreds of men left behind. There must have been over that number in the cellar I went into, and there are a dozen others in the town. I never saw such a disgusting scene."

Scarcely had they finished when the assemble sounded, and the regiment at once fell-in outside the factory, every man with knapsack and haversack bulging out with tobacco. They then joined the rest of the troops in the main street. General Moore had made a vain attempt to rouse the besotted men. A few of those least overcome joined the rear-guard, but the greater number were too drunk to listen to orders, or even to the warning that the French would be into the town as soon as the troops marched out.

CHAPTER X

CORUNNA

AS the confusion in the streets increased from the pouring out from the houses and cellars of the camp-followers—women and children, together with men less drunk than their comrades, but still unable to walk steadily—who filled the air with shouts and drunken execrations, Colonel Corcoran rode along the line.

"Just look at that, boys," he said. "Isn't it better for you to be standing here like dacent men, ready to do your duty, than to be rolling about in a state like those drunken blackguards, for the sake of half an hour's pleasure? Sure it is enough to make every mother's son of you swear off liquor till ye get home again. When the French get inside the town there is not one of the drunken bastes that won't be either killed or marched away a thousand miles to a French prison, and all for half an hour's drink."

The lesson was indeed a striking one, and careless as many

of the men were, it brought home to them with greater force than ever before in their lives, not only the folly but the degradation of drunkenness. A few minutes later, General Moore, who was riding up and down the line, inspecting the condition of the men in each regiment, came along.

"Your men look very well, Colonel," he said, as he reached the Fusiliers. "How many are you short of your number?"

"Not a man, General; I am happy to say that there was not a single one that did not answer when his name was called."

"That is good, indeed," the general said, warmly. "I am happy to say that all the regiments of the rear-guard have turned out well, and shown themselves worthy of the trust reposed in them; none, however, can give so good a report as you have done. I selected your regiment to strengthen this division from the excellent order that I observed you kept along the line of march, and I am glad indeed that it has shown itself so worthy of the honour. March your regiment across to the side of the street, let the others pass you, and fall in at the rear of the column. I shall give the Mayo Fusiliers the post of honour, as a mark of my warm approbation for the manner in which they have turned out."

Scarcely had the troops left the town when the French cavalry poured in. Now that it was too late, the sense of danger penetrated the brains of the revellers, and the mob of disbanded Spanish and British soldiers and camp-followers poured out from the cellars. Few of the soldiers had the sense even to bring up their muskets. Most of those who did so were too drunk to use them, and the French troopers rode through the mob, sabring them right and left, and trampling them under foot, and then, riding forward without a pause, set out in pursuit of the retiring columns. As they came clattering along the road the colonel ordered the last two companies to halt, and when the head of the squadron was within fifty yards of them, and the troopers were beginning to check their horses, a heavy volley was poured in, which sent them to the right-about as fast as they had come, and emptied a score of saddles. Then the two companies formed fours again, and went on at the double until they reached the rear of the column.

All day the French cavalry menaced the retreat, until Lord Paget came back with a regiment of hussars and drove them back in confusion, pursuing them a couple of miles, with the view of discovering whether they were followed by infantry. Such, however, was not the case, and the column was not further molested until they reached Cacabolos, where they were halted. The rest of the army had moved on, the troops committing excesses similar to those that had taken place at Bembibre, and plundering the shops and houses.

The division marched over a deep stream crossed by a stone bridge, and took up their ground on a lofty ridge, the ascent being broken by vineyards and stone walls. Four hundred men of the rifles and as many cavalry were posted on a hill two miles beyond the river to watch the roads. They had scarcely taken their post when the enemy were seen approaching, preceded by six or eight squadrons of cavalry. The rifles were at once withdrawn, and the cavalry, believing that the whole French army was advancing, presently followed them, and, riding fast, came up to the infantry just as they were crossing the bridge.

Before all the infantry were over the French cavalry came down at a furious gallop, and for a time all was confusion. Then the rifles, throwing themselves among the vineyards and behind the walls, opened a heavy fire. The French general in command of the cavalry was killed, with a number of his troops, and the rest of the cavalry fell back. A regiment of light infantry had followed them across the bridge, and two companies of the 52d and as many of the Mayo regiment went down the hill and reinforced the rifles. A sharp fight ensued until the main body of the French infantry approached the bridge. A battery of artillery opened upon them, and seeing the strength of the British division, and believing that the whole army was before him, Soult called back his troops. The voltigeurs retired across the bridge again, and the fight came to an end. Between two and three hundred men had been killed or wounded.

As soon as night came on the British force resumed its march, leaving two companies of the rifles as piquets at the bridge. The French crossed again in the night, but after some fighting, fell back again without having been able to ascertain whether the main body of the defenders of the position were still there. Later on the rifles fell back, and at daybreak rejoined the main body of the rear-guard, which had reached Becerréa, eighteen miles away. Here General Moore received the report from the engineers he had sent to examine the harbours, and they reported in favour of Corunna, which possessed facilities for defence which were lacking at Vigo. Accordingly he sent off orders to the fleet, which was lying at the latter port, to sail at once for Corunna, and directed the various divisions of the army to move on that town.

The rear-guard passed the day without moving, enjoying a welcome rest after the thirty-six miles they had covered the day before. By this march they had gained a long start of the enemy and had in the evening reached the town the division before them had quitted that morning. The scene as they marched along was a painful one. Every day added to the numbers of the stragglers. The excesses in drink exhausted the strength of the troops far more than did the fatigue of the marches. Their shoes were worn out; many of them limped along with rags tied round their feet. Even more painful than the sight of these dejected and worn-out men was that of the camp-followers. These, in addition to their terrible hardships and fatigue, were worn out with hunger, and almost famished. Numbers of them died by the roadside, others still crawled on in silent misery.

Nothing could be done to aid these poor creatures. The troops themselves were insufficiently fed, for the evil conduct of the soldiers who first marched through the towns defeated all the efforts of the commissariat; for they had broken into the bakers' shops and so maltreated the inhabitants that the people fled in terror, and no bread could be obtained for the use of the divisions in the rear. Towards evening the next day the reserve approached Constantina. The French were now close upon their rear. A bridge over a river had to be crossed to reach the town, and as there was a hill within a pistol-shot of the river, from which the French artillery could sweep the bridge, Sir John Moore placed the riflemen and artillery on it. The enemy, believing that he intended to give battle, halted, and before their preparations could be made the troops were across the bridge, and were joined by the artillery, which had retired at full speed.

The French advanced and endeavoured to take the bridge. General Paget, however, held the post with two regiments of cavalry, and then fell back to Lugo, where the whole army was now assembled. The next day Sir John Moore issued an order strongly condemning the conduct of the troops, and stating that he intended to give battle to the enemy. The news effected an instant transformation. The stragglers who had left their regiments and entered the town by twos and threes at once rejoined their corps. Fifteen hundred men had been lost during the retreat, of whom the number killed formed but a small proportion. But the army still amounted to its former strength, as it was here joined by two fresh battalions, who had been left at Lugo by General Baird on his march from the coast. The force therefore numbered 19,000 men; for it had been weakened by some 4,000 of the light troops having, early in the retreat, been directed towards other ports, in order to lessen as far as possible the strain on the commissariat.

The position was a strong one, and when Soult at mid-day came up at the head of 12,000 men he saw at once that until his whole force arrived he could not venture to attack it. Like the British, his troops had suffered severely from the long marches, and many had dropped behind altogether. Uncertain whether he had the whole of the British before him, he sent a battery of artillery and some cavalry forward; when the former opened fire, they were immediately silenced by a reply from fifteen pieces. Then he made an attack upon the right, but was sharply repulsed with a loss of from three to four hundred men; and, convinced now that Moore was ready to give battle with his whole force, he drew off.

The next day both armies remained in their positions. Soult had been joined by Laborde's division, and had 17,000 infantry, 4,000 cavalry, and 50 guns; the English had 16,000 infantry, 1,800 cavalry, and 40 guns. The French made no movement to attack, and the British troops were furious at the delay. Soult, however, was waiting until Ney, who was advancing by another road, should threaten the British flank or cut the line of retreat. Moore, finding that Soult would not fight alone, and knowing that Ney was approaching, gave the order for the army to leave its position after nightfall and march for Corunna. He exhorted them to keep good order, and to make the effort which would be the last demanded from them. It was indeed impossible for him to remain at Lugo, even if Ney had not been close at hand, for there was not another day's supply of bread in the town.

He took every precaution for securing that no errors should take place as to the route to be followed in the dark, for the ground behind the position was intersected by stone walls and a number of intricate lanes. To mark the right tracks, bundles of straw were placed at intervals along the line, and officers appointed to guide the columns. All these precautions, however, were brought to naught by the ill-fortune that had dogged the general along the whole line of retreat. A tremendous storm of wind and rain set in, the night was pitch dark, the bundles of straw were whirled away by the wind, and when the army silently left their post at ten o'clock at night, the task before them was a difficult one indeed. All the columns lost their way, and one division alone recovered the main road; the other two wandered about all night, buffeted by the wind, drenched by the rain, disheartened and weary.

Some regiments entered what shelters they could find, the men soon scattered to plunder, stragglers fell out in hundreds, and at daybreak the remnants of the two divisions were still in Lugo. The moment the light afforded means of recovering their position, the columns resumed their march, the road behind them being thickly dotted by stragglers. The rearguard, commanded by the general himself, covered the rear, but fortunately the enemy did not come up until evening; but so numerous were the stragglers that when the French cavalry charged, they mustered in sufficient force to repel their attack, a proof that it was not so much fatigue as insubordination that caused them to lag behind. The rear-guard halted a few miles short of Friol and passed the night there, which enabled the disorganized army to rest and re-form. The loss during this unfortunate march was greater than that of all the former part of the retreat, added to all the losses in action and during the advance.

The next day the army halted, as the French had not come up in sufficient numbers to give battle, and on the following day marched in good order into Corunna, where, to the bitter disappointment of the general, the fleet had not yet arrived. At the time, Sir John Moore was blamed by the ignorant for having worn out his troops by the length of the marches; but the accusation was altogether unfounded, as is proved by the fact that the rear-guard—upon whom the full brunt of the fighting had fallen, who had frequently been under arms all night in the snow, had always to throw out very strong outposts to prevent surprises, and had marched eighty miles in two days, had suffered far more than the other troops, owing to the fact that the food supply intended for all had been several times wasted and destroyed by the excesses of those who had preceded them—yet who, when they reached Corunna, had a much smaller number missing from their ranks than was the case with the three other divisions.

After all the exertions that had been made, and the extraordinary success with which the general had carried his force through a host of enemies, all his calculations were baffled by the contrary winds that delayed the arrival of the fleet, and it remained but to surrender or fight a battle, which, if won, might yet enable the army to embark. Sir John did not even for a moment contemplate the former alternative. The troops on arriving were at once quartered in the town. The inhabitants here, who had so sullenly held aloof from Baird's force on its arrival, and had refused to give him the slightest aid, now evinced a spirit of patriotism seldom exhibited by the Spaniards, save in their defence of Saragossa, and on a few other occasions.

Although aware that the army intended, if possible, to embark, and that the French on entering might punish them for any aid given to it, they cheerfully aided the troops in removing the cannon from the sea-face and in strengthening the defences on the land side. Provisions in ample quantity were forthcoming, and in twenty-four hours the army, knowing that at last they were to engage the foe who had for the last fortnight hunted them so perseveringly, recovered its confidence and discipline. This was aided by the fact that Corunna had large magazines of arms and ammunition, which had been sent out fifteen months before, from England, and were still lying there, although Spain was clamouring for arms for its newly raised levies.

To the soldiers this supply was invaluable. Their muskets were so rusted with the almost constant downfall of rain and snow of the past month as to be almost unserviceable, and these were at once exchanged for new arms. The cartridge-boxes were re-filled with fresh ammunition, an abundant store served out for the guns, and, after all this, two magazines containing four thousand barrels of powder remained. These had been erected on a hill, three miles from the town, and were blown up so that they should not fall into the hands of the enemy. The explosion was a terrible one, and was felt for many miles round. The water in the harbour was so agitated that the shipping rolled as if in a storm, and many persons who had gone out to witness the explosion were killed by falling fragments.

The ground on which the battle was to take place was unfit for the operations of cavalry. The greater portion of the horses were hopelessly foundered, partly from the effects of fatigue, partly from want of shoes; for although a supply of these had been issued on starting, no hammers or nails had been sent, and the shoes were therefore useless. It would in any case have been impossible to ship all these animals, and accordingly, as a measure of mercy, the greater portion of them were shot. Three days were permitted Moore to make his arrangements, for it took that time for Soult to bring up his weary troops and place them in a position to give battle. Their position was a lofty ridge which commanded that upon which Sir John Moore now placed his troops, covering the town. On the right of the French ridge there was another eminence upon which Soult had placed eleven heavy guns.

On the evening of the 14th there was an exchange of artillery fire, but it led to nothing. That afternoon the sails of the long-expected fleet were made out, and just at nightfall it entered the harbour. The dismounted cavalry, the sick, the remaining horses, and fifty guns were embarked, nine guns only being kept on shore for action. On the 15th Soult occupied himself in completing his preparations. Getting his great guns on to the rocks on his left, he attacked and drove from an advanced position some companies of the 5th Regiment, and posted his mass of cavalry so as to threaten the British right, and even menace its retreat to the town from the position it held. Had the battle been delayed another day, Sir John Moore had made every preparation for embarking the rest of his troops rather than await a battle in which even victory would be worthless, for Ney's corps would soon be up. The French, however, did not afford him an opportunity of thus retiring.

Terence O'Connor speedily paid a visit to his regiment at Corunna, for he had, of course, accompanied Fane's brigade during the retreat. He was delighted to find that there had been only a few trifling casualties among the officers, and that the regiment itself, although it had lost some men in the fighting that had taken place, had not left a single straggler behind, a circumstance that was mentioned with the warmest commendation by General Paget in his report of the doings of the rear-guard.

"I was awfully afraid that it would have been quite the other way," Terence said. "I know how all the three other divisions suffered, though they were never pressed by the enemy, and had not a shadow of excuse for their conduct."

"You did not know us, me boy," O'Grady said. "I tell ye, the men were splendid. I expect if we had been with the others we should have behaved just as badly; but being chosen for the rear-guard put our boys all on their mettle, and every man felt that the honour of the regiment depended on his good conduct. Then, too, we were lucky in lighting on a big store of tobacco, and tobacco is as good as food and drink. The men gave a lot away to the other regiments, and yet had enough to last them until we got here."

"Then they were not above doing a little plundering," Terence laughed.

"Plunder is it!" O'Grady repeated, indignantly. "It was a righteous action, for the factory belonged to the Central Junta of the Province, and it was just stripping the French of their booty to carry it away. Faith, it was the most meritorious action of the campaign."

"Have you got a good cigar left, O'Grady?"

"Oh, you have taken to smoking, have you?"

"I was obliged to, to keep my nose warm. On the march, Fane and the major and Errington all smoked, and they looked so comfortable and contented that I felt it was my duty to keep them company."

"I have just two left, Terence, so we will smoke them together, and I have got a bottle of dacent spirits. Think of that, me boy; thirty-two days without spirits! They will never believe me when I go home and tell 'em I went without it for thirty-two mortal days."

"Well, you have had wine, O'Grady."

"It's poor stuff by the side of the cratur, still I am not saying that it wasn't a help. But it was cold comfort, Terence, a mighty cold comfort."

"You are looking well on it, anyhow. And how is the wound?"

"Och, I have nigh forgot I ever had one, save when it comes to ateing. Tim has to cut my food up for me, and I never sit down to a male without wishing bad cess to the French. When we get back I will have a patent machine for holding a fork fixed on somehow. It goes against me grain to have me food cut up as if I was a baby; if it wasn't for that I should not miss my hand one way or the other. In fact, on the march it has been a comfort that I have only had five fingers to freeze, instead of ten. There is a compensation in all things. So we are going to fight them at last? There is no chance of the fleet coming to take us off before that, I hope?" he asked, anxiously, "for we should all break our hearts if we were obliged to go without a fight."

"I don't think there is any chance of that, O'Grady, though I should be very glad if there were. I am not afraid of the fighting, but we certainly sha'n't win without heavy loss, and every life will be thrown away, seeing that we shall, after all, have to embark when the battle is over. Ney, with 50,000 men, is only two or three marches away.

"Well, Dicky, how do you do?" he asked, as Ryan came up.

"I am well enough, Mr. Staff Officer. I needn't ask after yourself, for you have been riding comfortably about, while we have been marched right off our legs. Forty miles a day, Terence, and over such roads as they have in this country; it is just cruelty to animals."

"I would rather have been with you, Dicky, than see to the horrible confusion that has been going on. Why, as soon as the day's march was over we had to set to work to go about trying to keep order. A dozen times I have been nearly shot by drunken rascals whom I was trying to get to return to their corps. Worse still, it was heartrending to see the misery of the starving women and camp-followers. I would rather have been on outpost duty, with Soult's cavalry hovering round, ready to charge at any moment."

"It is all very well to say that, Terence!" O'Grady exclaimed. "But wait until you try it a bit, my boy. I had five nights of it, and that widout a drop of whisky to cheer me. It was enough to have made Samson weep, let alone a man with only one hand, and a sword to hold in it, and a bad could in his head. It was enough to take the heart out of any man entoirely, and if it hadn't been for the credit of the regiment, I could often have sat down on a stone and blubbered. It is mighty hard for a man to keep up his spirits when he feels the mortal heat in him oozing out all over, and his fingers so cold that it is only by looking that one knows one has got a sword in them, and you don't know whether you are standing on your feet or on your knee-bones, and feel as if your legs don't belong to you, but are the property of some poor chap who has been kilt twenty-four hours before. Och, it was a terrible time! and a captain's pay is too small for it, if it was not for the divarsion of a scrimmage now and then!"

"How about an ensign's pay?" Ryan laughed. "I think that on such work as we have had, O'Grady, the pay of all the officers, from the colonel down, ought to be put together and equally divided."

"I cannot say whether I should approve the plan, Ryan, until I have made an intricate calculation, which, now I am comfortable at last, would be a sin and a shame to ask me brain to go through; but as my present idea is that I should be a loser, I may say that your scheme is a bad one, and not to say grossly disrespectful to the colonel, to put his value down as only equal to that of a slip of a lad like yourself. Boys nowadays have no respect for their supeyrior officers. There is Terence, who is not sixteen yet——"

"Sixteen three months back, O'Grady," Terence put in.

"Yes, I remember now, but a week or two one way or the other makes no difference. Here is Terence, just sixteen, who ought to be at school trying to get a little learning into his head, laying down the law to his supeyrior officers, just because he has had the luck to get onto the brigadier's staff. I think sometimes that the world is coming to an end."

"At any rate, O'Grady," Terence laughed, "I am half a head taller than you are, and could walk you off your legs any day."

"There! And he says this to a man who has gone through all the fatigues of the rear-guard, while he has been riding about the country like a gentleman at aise."

"Well, I cannot stop any longer," Terence said. "I am on my way up to see how they are getting on with the earth-works, and the general may want me at any moment."

"I would not trouble about that," O'Grady said, sarcastically; "perhaps he might make a shift to do widout you, widout detriment to the service."

Terence made no reply, but, mounting, rode off up the hill behind the town. At two o'clock on the 16th a general movement of the French line was observed, and the British infantry, 14,500 strong, drew up in order of battle along the position marked for them. The British were fighting under a serious disadvantage, for not only had Soult over 20,000 infantry, with very powerful artillery and great strength in cavalry, but owing to their position on the crest running somewhat obliquely to the higher one occupied by the French, the heavy battery on the rocks to their right raked the whole line of battle. Hope's division was on the British left, Baird's on the right. Fraser's division was on another ridge some distance from the others, and immediately covering the town of Corunna; and Paget, with his division to which the Mayo regiment was still attached, was posted at the village of Airis, on the height between Hope's division and the harbour, and looking down the valley between the main position and the ridge held by Fraser.

From here he could either reinforce Hope and Baird, or advance down the valley to repel any attack of the French cavalry, and cover the retreat of the main body if forced to fall back. The battle commenced by the French opening fire with their field-guns, which were distributed along the front of their position, and by the heavy battery on their left, while their infantry descended the mountain in three heavy columns, covered by clouds of skirmishers. The British piquets were at once driven in, and the village of Elvina, held by a portion of the 50th, carried. The French column on this side then divided into two portions; one endeavoured to turn Baird's right and enter the valley behind the British position, while the other climbed the hill to attack him in front. The second column moved against the British centre, and the third attacked Hope's left, which rested on the village of Palavia Abaxo.

The nine English guns were altogether overmatched by those of Soult's heavy battery. Moore, seeing that the half-column advancing by Baird's flank made no movement to penetrate beyond his right, directed him to throw back one regiment and take the French in flank. Paget was ordered to advance up the valley, to drive back the French column, and menace the French battery, uniting himself with a battalion previously posted on a hill to keep the threatening masses of French cavalry in check. He also sent word to

Fraser to advance at once and support Paget. Baird launched the 50th and 42d Regiments to meet the enemy issuing from Elvina. The ground round the village was broken by stone walls and hollow roads, but the French were forced back, and

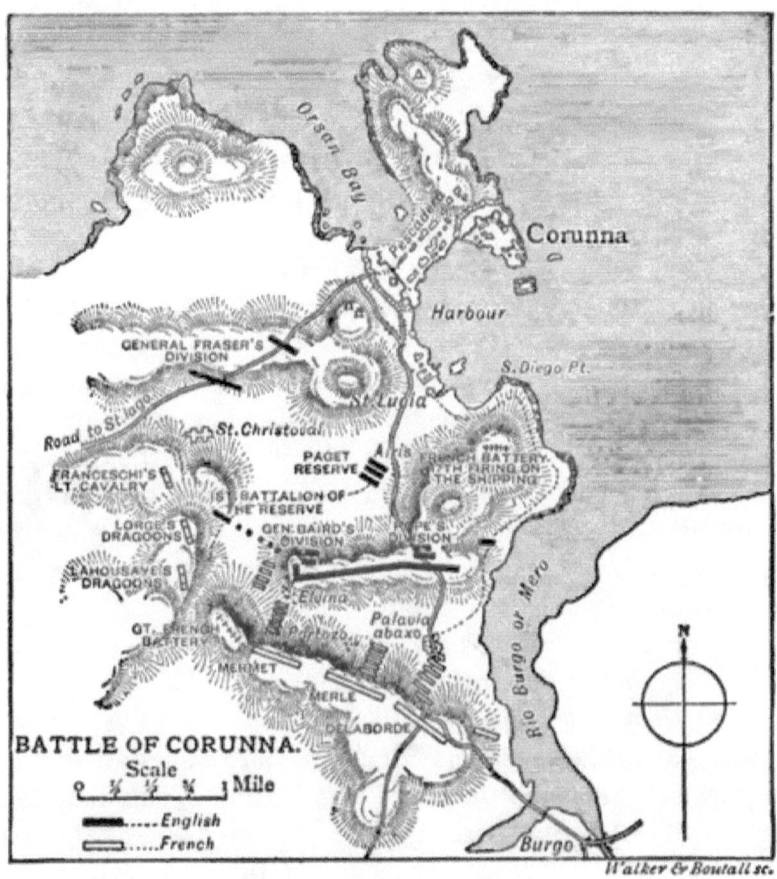

the 50th, entering the village with the fleeing enemy, drove them, after a struggle, beyond the houses.

The 42d, misunderstanding orders, retired towards the hill, and the French, being reinforced, again attacked Elvina, which the 50th held stubbornly until again joined by the 42d, which had been sent forward by Moore himself. Paget was now engaged in the valley, the advance of the enemy was arrested, and they suffered very heavily from the fire of the regiments on the height above their flank, while Paget steadily gained ground. The centre and left were now hotly engaged, but held their ground against all the attacks of the enemy, and on the extreme left advanced and drove the French out of the village of Palavia Abaxo, which they had occupied. Elvina was now firmly held, while Paget carried all before him on the right, and, with Fraser's division behind him, menaced the great French battery.

Had this been carried, the two divisions could have swept along the French position, crumpling up the forces as they went, and driving them down towards the river Moro, in which case they would have been lost. Owing, however, to the battle having been begun at so late an hour, darkness now fell. The general himself, while watching the contest at Elvina, had been struck by a cannon-ball and mortally wounded. General Baird had also been struck down. This loss of commanders combined with the darkness to arrest the progress of the victorious troops, and permitted the French, who were already falling back in great confusion, to recover themselves and maintain their position.

The object for which the battle had been fought was gained. Night, which had saved the French from total defeat, afforded the British the opportunity of extricating themselves from their position, and General Hope, who now assumed the command, ordered the troops to abandon their positions and to march down to the port, leaving strong piquets with fires burning to deceive the enemy. All the arrangements for embarkation had been carefully arranged by Sir John Moore, and without the least hitch or confusion the troops marched down to the port, and before morning were all on board with the exception of a rear-guard, under General Beresford, which occupied the citadel.

At daybreak the piquets were withdrawn and also embarked, and a force under General Hill, that had been stationed on the ramparts to cover the movement, then marched down to the citadel, and there took boats for the ships. By this time, however, the French, having discovered that the British position was abandoned, had planted a battery on the heights of San Lucia and opened fire on the shipping. This caused much confusion among the transports. Several of the masters cut their cables, and four vessels ran ashore. The troops, however, were taken on board of other transports by the boats of the men-of-war. The stranded ships were fired, and the fleet got safely out of harbour.

The noble commander, by whose energy, resolution, and talent this wonderful march had been achieved, lived only long enough to know that his soldiers were victorious, and was buried the same night on the ramparts. His memory was for a time assailed with floods of abuse by that portion of the press and public that had all along vilified the action of the British general, had swallowed eagerly every lie promulgated by the Junta of Oporto, and by the whole of the Spanish authorities; but in time his extraordinary merits came to be recognized to their full value, and his name will long live as one of the noblest men and best generals Great Britain has ever produced.

Beresford held the citadel until the 18th, and then embarked with his troops and all the wounded; the people of Corunna, remaining true to their promises, manned the ramparts of the town until the last British soldier was on board.

The British loss in the battle was estimated at 800 men; that of the French was put down at 3,000. Their greater loss was due to the fact that they assumed the offensive, and were much more exposed than the defenders; that the nine little guns of the latter were enabled to sweep them with grape, while the British were so far away from the French batteries that the latter were obliged to fire round shot; and lastly that the new muskets and fresh ammunition gave a great advantage to the British over the rusty muskets and often damaged powder of the French. Paget's division had suffered but slightly, the main loss of the English having occurred in and around Elvina, and from the shot of the heavy battery that swept the crest held by them. Two officers killed and four wounded were the only casualties in that division, while but thirty of the rank and file were put out of action.

CHAPTER XI

AN ESCAPE

WHILE the battle was at its height Terence was despatched by the brigadier to carry an order to one of the regiments that had pushed too far forward in its ardour. Scrambling over rough ground, and occasionally leaping a wall, he reached the colonel. "The general requests you to fall back a little, sir; you are farther forward than the regiment on your flank. The enemy are pushing a force down the hill in your direction, and as there is no support that can be sent to you at present, he wishes your extreme right to be in touch with the left of the regiment holding Elvina."

"Very good. Tell General Fane that I will carry out his instructions. Where is he now?"

"He is in the village, sir." Terence turned his horse to ride back. The din of battle was almost bewildering. A desperate conflict was going on in front of the village, where every wall was obstinately contested, the regiment being hotly engaged with a French force that was rapidly increasing in strength. The great French battery was sending its missiles far overhead against the British position on the hill, the British guns were playing on the French troops beyond the village, and the French light field-pieces were pouring their fire into Elvina. Terence made his way across the broken ground near the village. Galloping at a low stone wall, the horse was in the act of rising to clear it when it was struck in the head by a round shot. Terence was thrown far ahead over the wall, and fell heavily head-foremost on a pile of stones covered by some low shrubs.

The shock was a terrible one, and for many hours he lay insensible. When he recovered consciousness, he remained for some time wondering vaguely where he was. Above him was a canopy of foliage, through which the rays of the sun were streaming. A dead silence had succeeded the roar of battle. He put his hand to his head, which was aching intolerably, and found that his hair was thick with clotted blood.

"Yes, of course," he said to himself at last; "I was carrying a message to Fane. I was just going to jump a wall and there was a sudden crash. I remember—I flew out of the saddle—that is all I do remember. I have been stunned, I suppose. How is it so quiet? I suppose the battle is over."

Then he sat suddenly upright.

"The sun is shining," he said. "It was getting dusk when I was riding back to the village. I must have lain here all night."

Suddenly he heard a gun fired; it was quickly followed by others. He rose on his knees and looked cautiously over the bushes.

"It is away there," he said, "on those heights above the harbour. The army must have embarked, and the French are firing at the ships."

"POOR OLD JACK! HE HAS CARRIED ME WELL EVER SINCE I GOT HIM AT TORRES VEDRAS."

His conjecture was speedily verified, for, looking along the crest which the British had held during the fight, he saw a large body of French troops just reaching the top of the rise. He stood up now and looked round. No one could be seen moving in the orchards and vineyards round. He peered over the wall; his horse lay there in a huddled-up heap.

"A round shot in the head!" he exclaimed; "that accounts for it. Poor old Jack! he has carried me well ever since I got him at Torres Vedras."

He climbed down and got what he was in search of—a large flask full of brandy-and-water, which he carried in one of the holsters. He took a long drink, and felt better at once.

"I may as well take the pistols," he said, and, putting them into his belt, climbed over the wall again, and lay down among the bushes.

He was now able to think clearly. Should he get up and surrender himself as a prisoner to the first body of French troops that he came across? or should he lie where he was until nightfall, and then try to get away? If he surrendered, there was before him a march of seven or eight hundred miles to a French prison; if he tried to get away, no doubt there were many hardships and dangers, but at least a possibility of rejoining sooner or later. At any rate, he would be no worse off than the many hundreds who had straggled during the march, for it was probable that the great majority of these were spread over the country, as the French, pressing forward in pursuit, would not have troubled themselves to hunt down fugitives, who, if caught, would only be an encumbrance to them.

He was better off than they were, for at any rate he could make himself understood, which was more than the majority of the soldiers could do; and at least he would not provoke the animosity of the peasants by the rough measures they would be likely to take to satisfy their wants. The worst of it was that he had no money. Then suddenly he sat up again and looked at his feet.

"This is luck!" he exclaimed; "I had never given the thing a thought before."

On his arrival at Corunna he had thrown away the riding-boots he had bought at Salamanca. The constant rains had so shrunk them that he could no longer wear them without pain, and he had taken again to the boots that he carried in his valise.

From the time when, at his father's suggestion, he had had extra soles placed on them, above which were hidden fifteen guineas, the fact of the money being there had never once occurred to him. He had had sufficient cash about him to pay for purchases at Salamanca and on the road, and, indeed, had five guineas still in his pocket, though he had drawn no pay from the time of leaving Torres Vedras.

This discovery decided him. With twenty guineas he could pay his way for months, and he determined to make the attempt to escape.

The firing continued for some time and then ceased.

"The fleet must have got out," he said to himself. "It is certain that the French have not taken Corunna. We were getting the best of it up to the time I was hurt, and it would be dark in another half-hour, and there could be no fighting on such ground as this, after that. Besides, Corunna is a strong fortress, and we could have held out there for weeks, for Soult can have no battering train with him; besides, everything was ready for embarkation, and I know that it was intended, whether we won or lost, that the troops should go on board in the night."

As he lay there he could occasionally hear the sound of drums and trumpets as the troops marched from their positions of the night before, to take up others nearer to the town. At times he heard voices, and knew that they were searching for wounded over the ground that had been so desperately contested; but the spot where he was lying lay between the village and the ground where the regiment he had gone to order back had been engaged with the enemy, and as no fighting had taken place there, it was unlikely that the search-parties would go over it. This, indeed, proved to be the case, and after a time he fell off to sleep, and did not wake until night was closing in. He was hungry now, and again crossing the wall he took half a chicken and a piece of bread that his servant had thrust into his wallet just before starting, and made a hearty meal. He unbuckled his sword and left it behind him; he had his pistols, and a sword would be only an encumbrance.

As soon as it became quite dark he made his way cautiously down the valley, passed the spot where the French column had suffered so heavily, and then, turning to the left, traversed the narrow plain that divided the position on which the French heavy battery had been placed and the plateau on which their cavalry had been massed. Numerous fires blazed in the wide valley behind, where the reserve had been stationed on the previous morning, and he doubted not that the French cavalry were there, especially as he found no signs of life on the plateau above. Coming presently on a small stream he bathed his head for a considerable time, and then proceeded on his way, feeling much brighter and fresher than he had done before.

The ground began to ascend more steeply, and after an hour's walking he stood on the crest of the hill and looked down on the position that the French had held, and beyond it on Corunna and the sea. The cold was extreme. He had brought with him his greatcoat and blanket, and, wrapping himself in these, lay down in a sheltered position and slept again till morning broke. His head was now better, and he was able to think more clearly than he could the day before. The first thing was to decide as to his course. It would be dangerous to make direct for the frontier of Portugal. Now that the British army had embarked, Soult would be free to undertake operations in that country, and would doubtless shortly put his troops in motion in that direction, and his cavalry would be scattering all over the province collecting provisions. Moreover, there would be the terrible range of the Tras-os-montes to pass, and no certainty whatever of being well received by the Portuguese peasants north of Oporto.

His constant study of the staff maps was now of great assistance to him. He determined to turn west until he reached the river Minho some distance below Lugo, which he could do by skirting the top of the hills. He would therefore strike it somewhere about the point where the river Sil joined it, and, following this, would find himself at the foot of the Cantabrian Hills, dividing the Asturias from Leon. Then he could be guided by circumstances, and could either cross these mountains and make for a seaport, or could journey down through Leon to Ciudad-Rodrigo, which was still held by a Spanish garrison, and from there make his way through Portugal to Lisbon.

He questioned whether it would be wise for him to attempt to get the dress of a Spanish peasant instead of his uniform, but he finally decided that until he was beyond any risk of being captured by parties from either Soult or Ney's armies, it would be better to continue in uniform. If taken in that dress it would be seen that he was a straggler from Moore's army, and he would be simply treated as a prisoner of war; while, if taken in the dress of a peasant, he would be liable to be treated as a spy and shot. Having made up his mind, he started at once, and in three hours was at the foot of the hills on the other side of which ran the road from Lugo to Corunna, which proved so disastrous to the army. He presently arrived at a small hamlet, and the children in the streets ran shrieking away as they saw him. Women appeared at the doors and looked out anxiously; they had not before seen a British uniform, and at once supposed that he was French. Seeing that he was alone, several men armed with clubs and picks came out.

"I am an English officer," he said, "and I desire food and shelter for a few hours. I have money to pay for it."

The peasants at once came round him. Confused accounts had reached them of the doings on the other side of the hills. They knew that an English army had marched from Lugo to Corunna, hotly pursued by the French, but they had heard nothing of what had happened afterwards. They eagerly asked for news. Terence told them that there had been a great battle outside Corunna, that the French had been repulsed with much loss, and that the English had embarked on board ships to take them round to Lisbon, there to march east to meet the French again.

Nothing could be kinder than the treatment he received. They told him that Ney's army was between the Sil and Lugo, but that no French troops had crossed the Minho as yet.

They were eager to know why the English, if they had beaten the French, sailed away. But when he said that Soult would have been joined by Ney in a couple of days, and would then be well-nigh double the strength of the British, who would be so hotly pressed that they would be unable to embark, the peasants saw that what they considered their desertion could not have been avoided. The news of the terrible defeats that had, a month before, been inflicted upon their armies had not reached them, and Terence did not think it necessary to enlighten them. He told them that the march north of the English had been intended to bring all the French forces in that direction, and so to enable the Spanish armies to operate successfully, and that not only Soult and Ney, but Napoleon himself, had been drawn off from the south in pursuit of them.

They were filled with satisfaction, and he was at once taken into one of the cottages. A good meal was shortly placed before him, his head was carefully bandaged, and he was then asked how it was that he had not embarked with the rest of the army. He related how he had been left behind, and then asked them their opinion as to his best course, telling them the plan he himself had formed. They agreed at once that this was the wisest one, but that it would be dangerous to try it until Ney's force had moved from its present position. They knew that he had a division at Orense on the Minho, and that parties of his cavalry had scoured the plain as far as the river Ulla, and urged upon him to remain with them until some news was obtained of the movements of the French army.

He gladly accepted the invitation, and for a couple of days remained at the little hamlet. One of the peasants came in at the end of that time, saying that the French in Corunna had crossed the mountains and had arrived at Santiago, twenty miles distant, and that their cavalry were scouring the country. They also brought news that Romana was at Toabado, and that he had but two or three thousand men with him, the rest having been routed and cut up by the French cavalry. Terence at once determined to join him.

The fact that he still had some troops with him had no influence in causing him to form this resolution. Romana had been so often defeated that he knew that his men would, after their recent misfortunes, scatter at once before even the weakest French detachment. But Romana himself knew the country well, was a man of great resource and activity, and was likely to evade all efforts to capture him. He thought then that by joining him and sharing his fortunes he was more likely to have some opportunity of making his way to Lisbon than he would have if left to his own resources, especially as he had no doubt that Soult would at once prepare to invade Portugal by occupying all the passes, and thus render it next to impossible to journey thither alone and on foot. One of the peasants offered to guide him across the hills to Toabado. They started at once, and at daybreak next morning reached the village.

As Romana had been several times in personal communication with Sir John Moore, Terence was acquainted with his appearance, and seeing him standing at the door of the principal house of the village, went up to him and saluted him. The latter looked upon him with great surprise.

"How have you managed to pass through the French?" he asked.

"I have seen none of them, Marquis. I was wounded in the battle of Corunna, and after lying insensible all that night, found, when I recovered in the morning, that the French had advanced and that I was in their rear. I heard their guns from the heights above the town, and knew that our army had gained their transports. I lay concealed all day and then crossed the mountains, and have been resting for two days at a village on the other side of the hills. The news came that you were here, and I decided to join you at once. I was on the staff of General Fane, and, knowing the duties of an aide-de-camp, thought I might make myself useful to you until there was an opportunity of my rejoining a British force."

"You are welcome, sir," Romana said, courteously. "It was only this morning that we learned from a prisoner that my men took that you had driven back Soult before Corunna and had embarked safely. I was in great fear that your army would have been captured. I see that you have been wounded on the head."

"It can scarcely be called a wound, Marquis. I was carrying a message on the battle-field; when I was taking a wall my horse was struck with a round shot. I was thrown over his head onto a heap of rough stones, and it was a marvel to me that I was not killed."

"I am just going to breakfast, señor, and shall be glad if you will join me. I have no doubt that you will do justice to it."

Romana, who had commanded the Spanish troops which had escaped from Holland, was the most energetic of the Spanish generals. Defeated often, he was speedily at the head of fresh gatherings, and ready to take the field again. As a partisan chief he was excellent, but possessed no military talent, and was, like the Spaniards generally, full of grand but utterly impracticable schemes, and in spite of his experience to the contrary, confident that the Spaniards would overthrow the French.

"I have been unfortunate," he said, in reply to the inquiry as to how many troops he had with him. "At your English general's request I took a different course with my army to that which he was pursuing, in order that his magazines should be untouched. I crossed his line of retreat, but unfortunately Franceschi's cavalry come down upon us, cut up my artillery and infantry, and scattered my force entirely. However, some three thousand have rejoined, and I expect in a short time to be at the head of 20,000. I ought to have more, but these Galician peasants are stubborn fellows. They know nothing of the affairs of Spain, and although they will fight in defence of their own villages, they have no interest in anything beyond, and hang back from joining an army that might operate outside their province. You see, until now it has been untouched by war. They have suffered in no way from French extortions and outrages. As soon as they feel the smart themselves, I doubt not they will be as full of hatred of the invaders as people are elsewhere, and as ready to take up arms against them."

Romana's troops were but a motley gathering. The force that he had brought with him from Holland had been landed at Santander, marched to Bilbao, and joined Blake's army, and had shared in the crushing defeat suffered by that general at Espinosa, where most of them were taken prisoners. They were again incorporated in the French army, and afterwards took part in the Russian campaign, and in the retreat no less than four thousand of them were taken prisoners by the Russians and handed over by them to British transports sent to Cronstadt to fetch them. Romana himself had escaped from the battle-field, and afterward raised a fresh force. This had dwindled away from 15,000 to 5,000 when he joined Moore on his advance, and now amounted to barely 2,000, of whom the greater portion had thrown away their arms in their flight.

On the following day Romana, with a small body of cavalry, left Toabado, crossed the Minho, descended into the valley of the Tamega, and took refuge close to the Portuguese frontier line. Here he was, for a time, safe from the pursuit of the French, the insignificance of his force being his best protection. Soult lost no time. As soon as the English army had left, Corunna opened its gates to him, as did Ferrol, although neither of these towns could have been taken without a siege, and Soult must have been delayed until a battering-train was brought from Madrid.

The magazines of British powder and stores that had been lying for months in Ferrol were invaluable to him.

The soldiers were set to work to make fresh cartridges, and then, after six days' halt to give rest to his weary and footsore men, he began to prepare to carry out Napoleon's orders to invade Portugal. Ney, with 20,000 men, was to maintain Galicia, and, reinforced by a fresh division, Soult was to march direct upon Oporto with 25,000 men, leaving 12,000 in hospital, and 8,000 to keep up the line of communication with Ney. It took some time to complete all the arrangements and to gather the force at St. Jago Compostella, and it was not until the first of February that he was able to move.

On the day of his arrival on the frontier, Romana despatched Terence to Sir John Cradock, who now commanded the British troops in Portugal, which had been augmented by fresh arrivals from England until their numbers almost equalled that of the force with which Sir John Moore marched into Spain.

Romana asked that arms and money should be sent to him, promising to harass the French advance, and cut their communications from the rear. Terence gladly consented to carry his despatch; he was furnished with one of the best horses in the troop, and at once started on his journey. It was a long and harassing one; many ranges of mountains and hills had to be crossed, by roads difficult in the extreme at the best of times, but almost impassable in winter. Three times he was seized by parties of Portuguese militia and raw levies, but was released on convincing their leaders that he was the bearer of a communication to the English general.

The distance to be travelled was, in a direct line, over two hundred and thirty miles. This was greatly increased by the circuitous nature of the route through the mountainous country, so that it took nine days, and would have much exceeded this time, had Terence not found a British force at Coimbra, and there exchanged his worn-out animal for a fresh one, placed at his disposal by the officer in command.

Cradock was experiencing exactly the same difficulties that

Moore had done. The Spanish and Portuguese authorities united in pressing him to advance, the former urging upon him that his presence would be the signal for the Spanish armies in the south to unite and entirely overthrow the French, while the latter were desirous that he should march to Ciudad-Rodrigo, defeat the French at Salamanca, and so protect Portugal from invasion from that side.

That Portugal might be attacked from the north and south simultaneously by Soult and Victor did not enter into their calculations, but while urging an advance, the Junta would take no steps whatever to enable the army to move; they would neither afford him facilities for collecting transport, nor order the roads that he would have to traverse to be put in order, and thwarted all his efforts to raise a strong force among the Portuguese.

There was, indeed, some improvement in the latter respect. At their own request, Lord Beresford had been sent out from England to take the command of the Portuguese armies, and as he had brought many British officers with him, some 20,000 men had been armed and drilled, and could be reckoned upon to do some service, if employed with British troops to give them backbone. The Portuguese peasantry were strong and robust, and by nature courageous, and needed only the discipline—that they could not receive from their own officers—to turn them into valuable troops. According to the law of the country every man was liable for service, and had the corrupt Junta been dismissed, and full power been given to the British, an army of 250,000 men might have been placed in the field for the defence of the country, with a proper supply of arms and money.

But so far from assisting, the Junta threw every possible impediment in the way. They feared that any real national effort, if successful, would get altogether beyond their control, and that they would lose the power that enabled them to enrich themselves at the expense of the people. Not only that, but they were engaged in a struggle for supremacy with the Junta of Oporto, which was striving by every means to render itself the supreme authority of the whole of Portugal.

Terence had hoped that when he arrived at Lisbon he should meet the army he had left at Corunna, for Sir John Moore's instructions had been precise that the fleet was to go thither. These instructions, however, had been disobeyed, and the fleet had sailed direct for England. It had on the way encountered a great storm, which had scattered it in all directions. Several of the ships were wrecked on the coast of England, and the army which would have been of inestimable service at Lisbon, now served only, by the tattered garments and emaciated frames of the soldiers, to excite a burst of misplaced indignation against the memory of the general whose genius had saved it from destruction.

On arriving at head-quarters and stating his errand, Terence was at once admitted to the room where Sir John Cradock was at work.

"I am told, sir, that you are the bearer of a despatch from the Spanish general, Romana. Before I open it, will you explain how it was that you came to be with him?"

Terence gave a brief account of the manner in which, after being left behind on the field of Corunna, he had succeeded in joining Romana.

The general's face, which had at first been severe, softened as he proceeded.

"That is altogether satisfactory, Mr. O'Connor," he said. "I feared that you might have been one of the stragglers, among whom I hear were many officers, as well as thousands of men belonging to Sir John Moore's army. We received news of his glorious fight at Corunna and the embarkation of his army, by a ship that arrived here but three days since from that port. Have you heard of the death of that noble soldier himself?"

"No, sir," Terence replied, much shocked at the news. "That is a terrible loss, indeed. He was greatly loved by the army. He saw into every matter himself, was with the rear-guard all through the retreat, and laboured night and day to maintain order and discipline, and it was assuredly no fault of his if he failed."

"Was your own regiment in the rear-guard?"

"Yes, sir. It had the honour of being specially chosen by Sir John Moore for its steadiness and good conduct. I was not with it, but was one of Brigadier-general Fane's aides-de-camp. It was while carrying a message to him that my horse was killed and I myself stunned by being thrown onto a heap of stones."

Sir John Cradock nodded, and then opened Romana's despatch. He raised his eyebrows slightly. He had been accustomed to such appeals for arms and money, and knew how valueless were the promises that accompanied them.

"What force has General Romana with him?"

"Some two hundred cavalry and three or four thousand peasants, about a quarter of whom only are armed."

"He says that he expects to be joined by twenty thousand men in a few days. Have you any means of judging whether this statement is well founded?"

"That I cannot say. General Romana seems to me to be a man of greater energy than any Spaniard I have hitherto met, and I know that he has already sent messages to the priests throughout that part of Galicia urging upon them the necessity of using their influence among the peasantry. He got a force together in a very short time, after the complete defeat and capture of his own command by the French, at the time of Blake's defeat, and I think that he might do so again, though whether they would be of any use whatever in the field I cannot say; but should Soult advance into Portugal, I should think that bands of this sort might very much harass him."

"No doubt they might do so. I will see, at any rate, if I can obtain some money from the political agents. I have next to nothing in my military chest, and our forces are at a standstill for the want of it. But that does not seem to matter. While our troops are ill-fed, ragged, almost shoeless, and unpaid, every Spanish or Portuguese rascal who holds out his hand can get it filled with gold. As to arms, they are in the first place wanted for the purpose of the Portuguese militia, who are likely to be a good deal more useful than these irregular bands; and in the second place, there are no means whatever of conveying even a hundred muskets, let alone the ten thousand that Romana is good enough to ask for. By the way, are you aware whether Sir John Moore intended the army to sail to England?"

"Certainly not, sir. I know that up to the moment the battle began the preparation for the embarkation went on unceasingly, and General Fane told me the night before that we were to be taken here. Whether Sir John may, at the last moment, have countermanded that order I am unable to say."

"Yes, I know that it was his intention, for I received a letter from him, written after his arrival at Corunna, saying that the embarkation could not be effected without a battle, and that if he beat Soult he should at once embark and bring the troops round here, as Ney's approaching force would render Corunna untenable. Just at present the arrival of 20,000 tried troops would be invaluable. General Baird will, of course, have succeeded Sir John Moore?"

"General Baird was severely wounded, sir. He had just

ridden up to General Fane when he was struck. General Hope would therefore be in command after Sir John Moore was killed."

"I have heard no particulars of the battle," Sir John said, "beyond that it has been fought and Soult has been driven back, that Sir John Moore is killed, and that the army has embarked safely. And do I understand you that it was towards the end of the battle that you were hurt?"

"It was getting dusk at the time, General, but I cannot say how long fighting went on afterwards."

"Will you please to sit down at that table and give me, as nearly as you can, a sketch of the position of our troops and those of the French, and then explain to me, as far as you may have seen or know, the movements of the corps and the course of events."

As Terence had, the evening before the battle, seen a sketch-map on which General Fane had written the names and positions of the British force and those of the French, he was able to draw one closely approximating to it. In ten minutes he got up and handed the sketch to Sir John Cradock.

"I am afraid it is very rough, sir," he said, "but I think that it may give you an idea of the position of the town and the neighbouring heights, and the position occupied by our troops."

"Excellent, Mr. O'Connor!"

"I had the advantage of seeing a sketch-map that the brigadier drew out, sir."

"Well, benefited from it. Now point out to me the various movements. It seems to me that this large French battery must have galled the whole line terribly; but, on the other hand, it is itself very exposed."

"General Fane said, sir, that he thought Soult was likely to be over-confident. Our army was in frightful confusion on the retreat from Lugo, and the number of stragglers was enormous. Although many came in next day, the field-state showed that over 2,000 were still absent from the colours. The brigadier was observing that there was one advantage in this, namely, that Soult would suppose that the whole army was disorganized, and might, therefore, take more liberties than he would otherwise have done; and that, at any rate, he was likely to rely upon his great force of cavalry on this plateau to cover the battery hill from any attack on its left flank. It was for that purpose that General Paget posted one of the regiments on this eminence on the right of the valley, which had the effect of completely checking the French cavalry."

He then related the incidents of the battle as far as they had come under his notice.

"A very ably fought battle," Sir John Cradock said, as he followed on the map Terence's account of the movements. "Soult evidently miscalculated Sir John's strength and the fighting powers of his troops. He hurled his whole force directly against the position, specially endeavouring to turn our right, but the force he employed there was altogether insufficient for the purpose. From his position I gather that he could not have known of the existence of Paget's reserve up the valley, but he must have seen Fraser's division on the hill above Coranto. I suppose he reckoned that this turning movement would shake the British position, throw them into confusion, and enable his direct attack to be successful before Fraser could come to their support. I am much obliged to you for your description, Mr. O'Connor; it is very clear and lucid. I will write a note, which you shall take to Mr. Villiers, and it is possible that you may get help from him for Romana. I shall be glad if you will dine with me here at six o'clock."

"I am much obliged to you, General, but I have nothing

but the uniform in which I stand, which is, as you see, almost in rags, and stained with mire and blood."

"I think it is probable that you will have no difficulty in buying a fresh uniform in the city; so many officers have come out here with exaggerated ideas of the amount of transport, that they have had to cut down their wardrobes to a very large extent."

He touched the bell. "Will you ask Captain Nelson to step in," he said to the clerk who answered. "Captain Nelson," he said, as one of his staff entered, "I want you to take Mr. O'Connor under your charge. He has just arrived from the north, and was present at the battle of Corunna. He was on Brigadier Fane's staff. As at present he is unattached, I shall put him down in orders to-morrow as an extra aide-de-camp on my staff. He will be leaving to-morrow for the northern frontier. I wish you to see if you cannot get him an undress uniform. He belongs to the infantry. I will give you an order on the paymaster, Mr. O'Connor, to honour your draft for any amount that you may need. I dare say you are in arrears of pay."

"Yes, Sir John. I have drawn nothing since we marched from Torres Vedras in October."

CHAPTER XII

A DANGEROUS MISSION

CAPTAIN NELSON at once took Terence under his charge. "You certainly look as if you wanted a new uniform," he said. "You must have had an awfully rough time of it. If only for the sake of policy, we ought to get you into a new one as soon as possible, for the very sight of yours would be likely to demoralize the whole division by affording a painful example of what they might expect on a campaign."

Terence laughed. "I know I look a perfect scarecrow. Do you think that you can find me something? I really don't know what I should have done if I had not had my greatcoat, for I could never have ventured to walk through the street from the little inn where I put up my horse, if I could not have hidden myself in it."

"I can, fortunately, put you in the right way without difficulty. There is a man here who has made a business of buying up uniforms. I believe he sends most of them to England, where they would certainly fetch a good deal more than he gave for them; but I know that he keeps a stock by him, for there is a constant demand. The work out in the country here does for a uniform in no time, and many men who, before marching for the frontier, parted with all their extra kit for a song, are glad enough to write to him for a fresh outfit at three times the price he gave them two or three months before."

"I wonder they don't send their surplus outfit back to England direct," Terence said.

"Well, you see, there is the risk of the things being lost or stolen on the way home, or being ruined by damp before they are wanted again. Besides, a man thinks there is no saying whether he shall ever want them again, or how long the war will last, and is glad to take anything he can get to save himself any further bother about them."

Terence was fortunate in being able to buy an undress uniform, with facings similar to those of his own regiment, and to lay in a stock of underclothes at a very much lower price than he could have purchased them for even at home. Before leaving the shop he put on his new uniform and left the old one to be thrown away.

"Now,' Captain Nelson said, when they left the shop, "it is just our lunch time. You must come with me and tell us all about your wonderful march and the fight at the end of it."

"I was going down to see about my horse."

"Oh, that is all right! I sent down an orderly to bring him up to our stables. There, this is where we mess," he said, stopping before a hotel. "We find it much more comfortable than having it in a room at head-quarters. Besides, one gets away from duty here. Of course, the chief knows where we are, and can send for us if we are wanted; but one gets off being set to do a lot of office work in the evening, and we find ourselves much more free and comfortable when we haven't got two or three of the big-wigs of the staff. So they have a little mess of their own there, and we have a room kept for ourselves here."

There were more than a dozen officers assembled when the two entered the room, where a meal was laid; for Captain Nelson had looked into the hotel for a moment on their way to the tailor's, to tell his companions who Terence was, and to say that he should bring him in to lunch. They had told some of their acquaintances. Terence was introduced all round, and as soon as the first course was taken off the table he was asked many questions as to the march and battle; and by the time when, an hour later, the party broke up, they had learned the leading incidents of the campaign.

"You may guess how anxious we were here," one of them said, "when Moore's last despatch from Salamanca arrived, saying that he intended to advance, and stating his reasons. Then there was a long silence; all sorts of rumours reached us. Some said that, aided by a great Spanish army, he had overthrown Napoleon, and had entered Madrid; others, again, stated that his army had been crushed, and he, with the survivors, were prisoners, and were on their way to the frontier—in fact, we had no certain news until three days ago, when we heard of the battle, his death, and the embarkation of the army, and its sailing for England. The last was a terrible blunder."

"Only a temporary one, I should think," Captain Nelson said. "From Mr. O'Connor's account of the state of the army, I should think that it is just as well that they should have gone home to obtain an entirely new rig-out; there would be no means of fitting them out here. A fortnight ought to be enough to set them up in all respects, and as we certainly shall not be able to march for another month——"

"For another three months, you mean, Nelson."

"Well, perhaps for another three months, the delay will not matter materially."

"It won't matter at all, if the French oblige us by keeping perfectly quiet, but if Soult menaces Portugal with invasion from the north, Lapisse from the centre, and Victor from the south, we may have to defend ourselves here in Lisbon before six weeks are out."

"Personally, I should not be sorry," another said, "if Soult does invade the north and captures Oporto, hangs the bishop, and all the Junta. It would be worth ten thousand men to us, for they are continually at mischief. They do nothing themselves, and thwart all our efforts. They are worse than the Junta here—if that is possible—and they have excited the peasants so much against us that they desert in thousands as fast as they are collected, while the population here hate us, I believe, quite as much as they hate the French. But why they should do so Heaven knows, when we have spent more money in Portugal than the whole country contained before we came here."

After the party had broken up, Captain Nelson took Terence to Mr. Villiers, who, on reading the general's letter and hearing from Terence how Romana was situated, at once said that he would hand over to him 20,000 dollars to take to the Spanish general.

"How am I to carry it, sir? It will be of considerable weight, if it is in silver."

"I will obtain for you four good mules," Mr. Villiers said, "and an escort of twelve Portuguese cavalry under an officer."

"May I ask, sir, that the money shall be packed in ammunition-boxes, and that no one except the officer shall know that these contain anything but ammunition?"

"You have no great faith in Portuguese honesty, Mr. O'Connor."

"As to their honesty as a general thing, sir, I express no opinion," Terence said, bluntly; "as to the honesty of their political partisans, I have not a shadow of belief. Moreover, there is no love lost between them and the Spaniards, and though possibly money for any of the Portuguese leaders might be allowed to pass untouched by others—and even of this I have great doubt—I feel convinced that none of them would allow it to go out of the country for the use of the Spaniards if they could lay hold of it by the way."

"Those being your sentiments, sir, I think that it is a pity the duty is not intrusted to some officer of broader views."

"I doubt whether you would find one, sir; especially if he has, like myself, been three or four months in the country. I have simply accepted the duty, and not sought it, and should gladly be relieved of it. General Romana sent me here with a despatch, and it is my duty, unless General Cradock chooses another messenger, to carry back the reply, and anything else with which I may be intrusted. I have for the past three months been incessantly engaged on arduous and fatiguing duty. I have ridden for the last nine days by some of the worst roads to be found in any part of the world, I should say, and have before me the same journey. Besides, if I receive the general's orders to that effect, I may have to stay with the Spanish general, and in that case shall, I am sure, be constantly upon the move, and that among wild mountains. If this treasure is handed over to me I shall certainly do my best to take it safely and to defend it, if necessary, with my life; but it is assuredly a duty of which I would gladly be relieved. But that, sir, it seems to me, is a question solely for the commander-in-chief."

Mr. Villiers gazed in angry surprise at the young ensign; then thinking, perhaps, that he would put himself in the wrong, and as his interferences in military matters with Sir John Cradock had not met with the success he desired for them, he checked the words that rose to his lips, and said, shortly: "The convoy will be ready to start from the treasury at daybreak to-morrow."

"I shall be there—if so commanded by General Cradock."

As soon as they had left the house Captain Nelson burst into a shout of laughter.

"What is it?" Terence asked, in surprise.

"I would not have missed that for twenty pounds, O'Connor; it is the first bit of real amusement I have had since I landed. To see Villiers—who regards himself as the greatest man in the country, who not only thinks that he regulates every political intrigue in Spain and Portugal, but assumes to have the direction of every military movement also, and tries to dictate to the general on purely military matters—quietly cheeked by an ensign, is the best thing I ever saw."

"But he has nothing to do with military matters, has he?"

"No more than that mule-driver there, but he thinks he

has; and yet, even in his own political line, he is the most ill-informed and gullible of fools, even among the mass of incompetent agents who have done their utmost to ruin every plan that has been formed. I doubt whether he has ever been correct in a single statement that he has made, and am quite sure that every prophecy he has ventured upon has been falsified, every negotiation he has entered into has failed, and every report sent home to government is useful only if it is assumed to be wrong in every particular; and yet the man is so puffed up with pride and arrogance that he is well-nigh insupportable. The Spaniards have fooled him to the top of his bent; it has paid them to do so. Through his representations the ministry at home have distributed millions among them. Arms enough have been sent to furnish nearly every able-bodied man in Spain, and harm rather than good has come of it. Still, he is a very great man, and our generals are obliged to treat him with the greatest civility, and to pretend to give grave consideration to the plans that, if they emanated from any other man, would be considered as proofs that he was only fit for a mad-house. And to see you looking calmly in his face and announcing your views of the Spanish and Portuguese was delightful." And Captain Nelson again burst into laughter at the recollection.

Terence joined in the laugh. "I had no intention of offending him," he said. "Of course I have often heard how he was pressing General Moore to march into Spain, and promising that he should be met by immense armies that were eager and ready to drive the French out of that country, and were only waiting for his coming to set about doing so. I know that the brigadier and his staff used to talk about what they called Villiers' phantom armies, but as I only said what everyone says who has been in Spain, it never struck me that I was likely to give him serious offence."

"And if you had thought so, I don't suppose it would have made any difference, O'Connor."

"I don't suppose it would," Terence admitted; "and perhaps it will do him good to hear a straightforward opinion for once."

"It will certainly do him no harm. Now, you had better tell the chief that you are to have the money. I should think that he will probably send a trooper with you as your orderly. Certainly, he has no reason to have a higher opinion of the Portuguese than you have."

"I will go back with you, Captain Nelson; but as you were present, will you kindly tell the general? I don't like bothering him."

"Certainly, if you wish it."

On arriving at head-quarters Terence sat down in the ante-room and took up an English paper, as he had heard no home news for the last three months. Presently Captain Nelson came out from the general's room and beckoned to him. He followed him in. Four or five officers of rank were with the general, and all were looking greatly amused when he entered.

"So you have succeeded in obtaining money for Romana," the general said.

"Yes, sir, there was no difficulty about it. Mr. Villiers asked me a few questions as to the situation on the frontier, and at once said that I should have £5,000 to take him."

"Captain Nelson tells us that you were unwise enough to express an opinion as to the honesty of the Portuguese escort that he proposed to send with you."

"I said what I thought, General, and had no idea that Mr. Villiers would take it as an offence, as he seemed to."

"Well, he has his own notions on these things, you see," the general said, dryly, "and they do not exactly coincide with our experience; but then Mr. Villiers claims to understand these people more thoroughly than we can do."

Terence was silent for a moment. "I only went by what I have seen, you know," he said, after a pause, "and certainly had no intention of angering Mr. Villiers. But it seemed to me that, as I was responsible for taking this money to Romana, it was my duty to suggest a precaution that appeared to me necessary."

"Quite right, quite right; and it is just as well, perhaps, that Mr. Villiers should occasionally hear the opinions of officers of the army frankly expressed. Certainly, I think that the precaution you suggested was a wise one, and if Mr. Villiers does not do so, I will see that it is carried out.

"I have asked Captain Nelson to go with you, taking the treasure, to the barracks and see that the money is taken out of the cases and repacked in ammunition-boxes. It would be unwise in the extreme to tempt the cupidity of any wandering parties that you might fall in with by the sight of treasure-cases. Your suggestion quite justifies the opinion that I had formed of you from the brief narrative that you gave me of the battle of Corunna. For the present, gentlemen, I have appointed Mr. O'Connor as an extra aide-de-camp on my staff. He served in that capacity with Brigadier-general Fane from the time that the troops marched from here, which is in itself a guarantee that he must, in the opinion of that general, be thoroughly fit for the work.

"I think, Mr. O'Connor, that, going as you will as an officer on my staff, it is best that you should be accompanied by a couple of troopers, and I have just spoken to Colonel Gibbons, who will detach two of his best men for that service. In addition to your being in charge of the treasure, you will also carry a despatch from myself to General Romana, with suggestions as to his co-operation in harassing the advance of the French. I will not detain you further now. Don't forget the dinner hour."

A large party sat down to table. There were the officers Terence had seen there in the afternoon, and several colonels and heads of departments of the army, and Terence, although not shy by nature, felt a good deal embarrassed when, as soon as the meal was concluded, several maps were, by the general's orders, placed upon the table, and he was asked to give as full an account as he was able of the events that had happened from the time General Moore marched with his army from Salamanca, and so cut himself off from all communication.

It was well that Terence had paid great attention to the conversations between General Fane and the officers of the brigade staff, had studied the maps, and had made himself, as far as he could, master of the details of the movements of the various divisions, and had gathered from Fane's remarks a fair knowledge of General Moore's objects and intentions. Therefore, when he had overcome his first embarrassment, he was able to give a clear and lucid account of the campaign, and of the difficulties that Moore had encountered and overcome in the course of his retreat. The officers followed his account upon the maps, asked occasional questions, and showed great interest in his description of the battle.

When he had done, Sir John Cradock said: "I am sure, gentlemen, that you all agree with me that Mr. O'Connor has given us a singularly clear and lucid account of the operations of the army, and that it is most creditable that so young an officer should have posted himself up so thoroughly, not only in the details of the work of his own brigade, but in the general plans of the campaign and the movements of the various divisions of the army."

There were also hearty compliments from all the officers as they rose from the table.

"I doubt, indeed, Sir John," one of them said, "whether we should ever have got so clear an account as that he has given from the official despatches. I own that I, for one, have never fully understood what seemed a hopeless incursion into the enemy's country, and I cannot too much admire the daring of its conception. As to the success which has attended it, there can be no doubt, for it completely paralysed the march of the French armies, and has given ample time to the southern provinces of Spain to place themselves in a position of defence. If they have not taken advantage of the breathing time so given them, it is their fault, and in no way detracts from the chivalrous enterprise of Moore."

"No, indeed," Sir John agreed; "the conception was truly an heroic one, and one that required no less self-sacrifice than daring. There are few generals who would venture on an advance when certain that it must be followed by a retreat, and that at best he could but hope to escape from a terrible disaster. It is true that he gained a victory which, under the circumstances, was a most glorious one, but this was the effect of accident rather than design. Had the fleet been in Corunna when he arrived, he would have embarked at once, and in that case he would have been attacked with ferocity by politicians at home, and would have been accused of sacrificing a portion of his army on an enterprise that everyone could have seen was ordained to be a failure before it commenced."

"Did you know General Fane personally before you were appointed to his staff?"

"No, General; he commanded the brigade of which my regiment formed part, and of course I knew him by sight, but I had never had the honour of exchanging a word with him."

"Then, may I ask why you were appointed to his staff, Mr. O'Connor?"

Terence hesitated. There was nothing he disliked more than talking of what he himself had done. "It was a sort of accident, General."

"How an accident, Mr. O'Connor? Your conduct must have attracted his attention in some way."

"It was an accident, sir," Terence said, reluctantly, "that General Fane happened to be on board Sir Arthur Wellesley's ship at Vigo when my colonel went there to make a report of some circumstances that occurred on the voyage."

"Well, what were these circumstances?" the general asked. "You have shown us that you have the details of a campaign at your finger ends, surely you must be able to tell what those circumstances were that so interested General Fane that he selected you to fill a vacancy on his staff."

Terence felt that there was no escape, and related as briefly as he could the account of the engagement with the two privateers, and of their narrow escape from being captured by a French frigate.

"That is a capital account, Mr. O'Connor," Sir John Cradock said, smiling, as he brought it to a conclusion. "But, so far, I fail to see your particular share in the matter."

"My share was very small, sir."

"I think I can fill up the facts that Mr. O'Connor's modesty has prevented him from stating," one of the officers said.

"It happened that before we sailed from Ireland six weeks ago, an officer of the Mayo Fusiliers, who had been invalided home in consequence of a wound, dined at our mess, and he told the story very much as Mr. O'Connor has told it, but he added the details that Mr. O'Connor has omitted. He stated that really the escape of the wing of the regiment was entirely due to an ensign who had recently joined—a son of one of the captains of the regiment. He said that, in the first place, when the cannon were found to be so honeycombed with rust that it would have been madness to attempt to fire them, this young officer suggested that they should be bound round with rope just like the handle of a cricket bat. This suggestion was adopted, and they were therefore able to pour in the broadside that crippled the lugger and brought her sails down, leaving her helpless under the musketry fire of the troops. In the second place, when the ship was being pounded by the other privateer without being able to make any reply, and must shortly have either sunk or surrendered, this young officer suggested to one of the captains that the lugger, lying helpless alongside, should be boarded, and her guns turned on the brig, a suggestion that led not only to the saving of the ship, but the capture of the brig itself.

"Lastly, when the French frigate hove in sight, the troops were transferred to the two prizes, and were about to make off, in which case one of them would almost certainly have been captured. He suggested that they should hoist French colours, and that both should be set to work to transfer some of the stores from the ship to the privateers. This suggestion was adopted, with the result that on the frigate approaching, and seeing, as was supposed, two French privateers engaged in rifling a prize, she continued on her way without troubling herself further about them. Sir Arthur Wellesley issued a most laudatory notice of Mr. O'Connor's conduct in general orders."

Most of those present remembered seeing the order, now that it was mentioned, and the general, turning to Terence, who was colouring scarlet with embarrassment and confusion, said, kindly:

"You see, we have got at it after all, Mr. O'Connor. I am glad that it came from another source, for I do not suppose that we should have got all the facts from you, even by cross-questioning. You may think, and I have no doubt that you do think, that you received more credit than you deserved for what you consider were merely ideas that struck you at the moment; but such is not my opinion, nor that, I am sure, of the other officers present. The story which we have just heard of you, and the account that you have given of the campaign, afford great promise, I may almost say a certainty, of your attaining, if you are spared, high eminence in your profession.

"Your narrative showed that you are painstaking, accurate, and intelligent. The facts that we have just heard prove you to be exceptionally quick in conceiving ideas, cool in action, and able to think of the right thing at the right time—all qualities that are requisite for a great commander. I warmly congratulate you, that at the very commencement of your career you should have had the opportunity afforded you for showing that you possess these qualities, and of gaining the warm approbation of men very much older than yourself, and all of wide experience in their profession. I am sorry now that you are starting to-morrow on what I cannot but consider a useless, as well as a somewhat dangerous, undertaking. I should have been glad to have utilized your services at once, and only hope that you will erelong rejoin us."

So saying, he rose. The hour was late, for Terence's description of the campaign and battle had necessarily been a very long one, and the party at once broke up, all the officers present shaking the lad warmly by the hand.

"You are a lucky fellow, O'Connor," Captain Nelson said, as he accompanied him to his room, in which a second bed had been set up for the young ensign's accommodation. "You will certainly get on after this. There were a dozen colonels and two generals of brigade among the party, and I fancy that there is not one of them that will not bear you in mind and say a good word for you, if opportunity occurs, and

Sir John himself is sure to push you on. I should say that not an officer of your rank in the army has such good chances, and you look such a lad, too. You did not show it so much when you first arrived; of course you were fagged and travel-stained then, but now I should not take you for more than seventeen. Indeed, I suppose you are not, as you only joined the service six months ago."

"No; I am not more than seventeen," Terence said, quietly, not thinking it necessary to state that he wanted a good many months yet to that age, for to do so would provoke questions as to how he obtained his commission before he was sixteen. "But, you see, I have had a good many advantages. I was brought up in barracks, and I suppose that sharpens one's wits a bit. When I was quite a young boy I used to be a good deal with the junior officers; of course, that made me older in my ideas than I should have been if I had always associated with boys of my own age. Still, it has been all luck, and though Sir John was kind enough to speak very warmly about it, I really can't see that I have done anything out of the way."

"Luck comes to a good many fellows, O'Connor, but it is not every one who has the quickness to make the most of the opportunity. You may say that they are only ideas; but you see you had three valuable ideas, and none of your brother officers had them, and you cannot deny that your brains worked more quickly than those of the others.

"Well, we may as well turn in at once, as we have all got to be up before daylight. I am very glad that Sir John has given you a couple of troopers. It will make you feel a good deal more comfortable anyhow, even if you don't get into any adventure where their aid may be of vital importance."

"It will indeed; alone I should have very little influence with the Portuguese guard. These might be perfectly honest themselves, but they might not be at all disposed to risk their lives by offering any opposition to any band that might demand the ammunition they would believe were in the cases. I was twice stopped by bands of scantily armed peasants on my way down, and although they released me on seeing the letter that I carried to the general, it was evident that they felt but little good-will towards us, and had I had anything about me worth taking, my chance of reaching Lisbon would have been small."

"The Junta of Oporto has spared no pains in spreading all sorts of atrocious lies against us ever since the escort of the French prisoners interfered to save them from the fury of the populace, though perhaps the peasants in this part of the country still feel grateful to us for having delivered them from the exactions of the French.

"In the north, where no French soldier has set foot, they have been taught to regard us as enemies to be dreaded as much as the French. Up to the present time all the orders for the raising of levies have been disregarded north of the Douro, and though great quantities of arms have been sent up to Oporto, I doubt whether a single musket has been distributed by the Junta. That fellow Friere, the general of what they call their army, is as bad as any of them. I hope that if Soult comes down through the passes he will teach the fellow and his patrons a wholesome lesson."

"And do you think that the troops here will march north to defend Oporto?"

"I should hardly think that there is a chance of it. Were our force to do so, Lisbon would be at the mercy of Victor and of the army corps at Salamanca. Cuesta is, what he calls, watching Victor. He is one of the most obstinate and pig-headed of all the generals. Victor will crush him without difficulty, and could be at Lisbon long before we could get back from Oporto. No, Lisbon is the key of the situation; there are very strong positions on the range of hills between the river and the sea at Torres Vedras, which could be held against greatly superior forces. The town itself is protected by strong forts, which have been greatly strengthened since we came. The men-of-war can come up to the town, aid in its defence, and bring reinforcements; and provisions can be landed at all times.

"The loss of Lisbon would be a death-blow to Portuguese independence, and you may be sure that the ministry at home would eagerly seize the opportunity of abandoning the struggle here altogether. Do you know that at the present moment, while urging Sir John Cradock to take the offensive with only 15,000 men against the whole army of France in the Peninsula, they have had the folly to send a splendid expedition of from thirty to forty thousand good troops to Holland, where they will be powerless to do any good, while their presence here would be simply invaluable. Well, we will not enter upon that subject to-night; the folly and the incapacity of Mr. Canning and his crew is a subject that, once begun, would keep one talking until morning."

CHAPTER XIII

AN AWKWARD POSITION

WHEN Captain Nelson and Terence went out, just as the morning was breaking, they found the two troopers waiting in the street. Each held a spare horse; the one was that upon which Terence had ridden from Coimbra, the other was a fine English horse.

"What horse is this?" Terence asked.

"It is a present to you from Sir John Cradock," Captain Nelson said. "He tōld me last night that the troopers had been ordered to ask for it when they took your horse this morning, and that his men were ordered to hand it over to them. He wished me to tell you that he had pleasure in presenting the horse to you as a mark of his great satisfaction at the manner in which you had mastered the military details of Sir John Moore's expedition, and the clearness with which you had explained them."

"I am indeed greatly obliged to the general; it is most kind of him," Terence said. "Will you please express my thanks to him in a proper way, Captain Nelson."

They rode to the Treasury, where they found the Portuguese escort, with the mules, waiting them. The officer in charge of the Treasury was already there, and admitted the two officers.

"I have packed the money in ammunition-boxes," he said. "I received instructions from Mr. Villiers to do so."

"It is evident that your words had some effect, Mr. O'Connor," Captain Nelson said aside to Terence. "I suppose that when he thought it over he came to the conclusion that, after all, your suggestions, were prudent ones, and that it would add to the chance of the money reaching Romana were he to adopt it."

"I am glad that he did so, for had the money been placed in the ordinary chests and then brought to the barracks to be packed in ammunition-cases, the Portuguese troopers would all have been sure of the nature of the contents; whereas now, whatever they may suspect, they cannot be sure about it, because there is a large amount of ammunition stored in the same building."

Some of the guard stationed in the Treasury carried the chests out, and assisted the muleteers to lash them in their places.

TERENCE RECEIVES A PRESENT OF A HORSE FROM SIR JOHN CRADOCK.

"I cannot thank you too warmly, Captain Nelson, for the kindness that you have shown me," Terence said.

"Not at all," that officer replied; "I simply carried out the general's orders, and the duty has been a very pleasant one. No, I don't think I would mount that horse if I were you," he went on, as Terence walked towards his acquisition. "I would have him led as far as Coimbra, while you ride the horse you borrowed there, then he will be fresh for the further journey."

"That would be the best way, no doubt, though our stages must all be comparatively short ones, owing to our having mules with us."

"I should not press them if I were you. I don't suppose that it will make much difference whether Romana gets the money a few days sooner or later."

"None whatever, I should say," Terence laughed, as he mounted his horse. "Still, I do think that he will be able to gather a mob of peasants. Of course, being almost without arms, they will be of no use whatever for fighting, but still they may harass Soult's communications, cut off stragglers, and compel him to move slowly and cautiously."

Terence now saluted the Portuguese officer, who said, as he returned the salute:

"My name, señor, is Juan Herrara."

"And mine is Terence O'Connor, señor. Our journey will be a somewhat long one together, and I hope that we shall meet with no adventures or accidents by the way."

"I hope not, señor. My instructions are simple; I am to place myself under your orders, and to convey eight cases of ammunition to the northern frontier, and to follow the routes that you may point out. I was ordered also to pick the men who are to form the escort. I have done so, and I think I can answer that they can be relied upon to do their duty under all circumstances."

Terence now turned, and with a hearty farewell to Captain Nelson, rode on by the side of Lieutenant Herrara. The two British troopers followed them, the four mules with their two muleteers kept close behind, and the twelve Portuguese troopers brought up the rear.

"It is a strong escort for four mules carrying ammunition," the Portuguese officer said, with a smile.

"It may seem so," Terence laughed, "but you see the country, especially north of the Douro, is greatly disturbed."

"Very much so, and I think that the precaution that has been taken is a very wise one. I have been informed what is really in the cases. Were I going by myself with a sergeant and twelve men, I should say that to put the money in ammunition-cases was not only absolutely useless but dangerous, the disproportion between the force and the value of the ammunition would be so great that it would attract attention at once, but as you are with us it is more likely to pass without observation. You are an officer on the staff of the English general. You have your own two orderlies, and, as you are carrying despatches, it is considered necessary that you should have an escort of our people. The cases in that event would seem to be of little importance, but to be simply travelling with us to have the advantage of the protection of our escort."

"You are quite right, Señor Herrara, and it would have been vastly better had the money been stowed in sacks filled up with grain; then they could follow a short distance behind us, and it would seem that they were simply carrying forage for our use on the road."

"That would have been very much better, señor. You might have it done at Torres Vedras."

"The money is in bags, each containing two hundred dollars. There will be no trouble in transferring them to sacks filled with plenty of forage. Two of your soldiers have behind them a bundle or two of faggots, a basket of fowls, and other matters; these can be piled on the top of the sacks, so that the fact that the principal load was forage would hardly be noticed. You might mention to the muleteers that I thought that it would be a considerable saving of weight if we used sacks instead of those heavy cases, and that the ammunition would travel just as well in the one as the other. We must arrange so that the muleteers do not suspect anything."

"As a rule," Herrara said, "they are very trustworthy. There is scarcely a case known in which they have stolen goods intrusted to them, however valuable; but it would be easy to place a few packets of ammunition in the mouth of each sack, and call them in to cord them up firmly. The sight of the ammunition would go far to lessen any suspicions they might have."

They reached Torres Vedras that night. Terence spoke to the officer in command there, and was furnished with the sacks he required, and enough forage to fill them. The boxes were put into a room in the barracks, and here Terence, with his two orderlies, opened the cases and transferred the bags of money to the centre of the sacks. Two or three dozen packets of ammunition were obtained, and a few put into the mouths of the sacks. These were left open, and the room locked up, two of the Portuguese soldiers being placed on guard before it. Terence and Lieutenant Herrara were invited to dine at mess and had quarters assigned to them, and Terence, after dinner, again, but much more briefly than before, gave the officers at the station a sketch of the retreat and battle.

The next morning the muleteers were called in to fasten up the sacks. At the suggestion of the officer in command, a tent was also taken.

"You may want it badly before you are done," he said. "If I were you I should always have it pitched, except when you are at a village, for you can have the sacks in as beds, and so keep them under your eye; and if, as you tell me, you are giving out that they contain ammunition, it would seem but a natural step, as you are so able to keep it dry."

The mules looked more heavily laden than upon the preceding day, but they were carrying no heavier burden, for the weight of the tent, its poles, the basket of fowls, Terence's valise, and other articles, were considerably less than those of the eight heavy cases that had been left behind. The two officers now rode at the head of the detachment, and two only of the Portuguese soldiers kept in rear of the mules, which now followed at a distance of thirty or forty yards behind them. They stopped that night at Rolica and the next at Leirya. This was a long march, and a short one the next day brought them to Pombal, and the following afternoon they arrived at Coimbra. Here they spent another pleasant evening with the regiment stationed in the town.

"By the way, O'Connor," one of the officers said, after the dinner was over and cigars lighted, " I suppose you don't happen to have any relations at Oporto?"

"Well, I do happen to have some," Terence answered, in some surprise. "Why do you ask?"

"Well, that is singular," the officer said; "I will tell you how it happened. I was with the party that escorted the French prisoners down to Oporto. Just as we had got into the town—it was before the row began, and being early in the morning, there were very few people about—a head appeared at a window on the second floor of a big convent standing on the left side of the road. I remember the name was carved over the door—it was the Convent of Santa Maria. I happened to catch sight of the nun, and she at once dropped a little letter, which fell close to me. I picked it up and stuck it into my glove, and thought no more about it for a time, for the mob soon began to gather, to yell and threaten the prisoners, and my hands were too full, till we had got them safely on board a ship, to think any more of the matter. When I took off my glove the letter fell out. It was simply addressed 'to an English officer.'

"'I, an English girl, am detained here, a prisoner, principally because my Spanish relations wish to seize my property. I have been made a nun by force, though my father was a Protestant, and taught me his religion. I pray you to endeavour to obtain my freedom. I am made most miserable here, and am kept in solitary confinement. I have nothing to eat but bread and water, because I will not sign a renunciation of my property. The Bishop of Oporto has himself threatened me, and it is useless to appeal to him. Nothing but an English army being stationed here can save me. Have pity upon me, and aid me.'

"It was signed '*Mary O'Connor.*' Of course no British troops have been there since, but if we are sent there I had made up my mind to bring the matter before the general, and ask him to interfere on the poor girl's behalf; though I know that it would be an awkward matter. For if there is one thing that the Portuguese are more touchy about than another, it is any interference in religious matters, and the bishop, who is a most intolerant rascal, would be the last man who would give way on such a subject."

"I have not the least doubt in the world but that it is a cousin of mine," Terence said. "Her father went out to join a firm of wine merchants in Oporto. I know that he married a very rich Portuguese heiress, and that they had one daughter. My father told me that he gathered from his cousin's letters that he and his wife did not get on very well together. He died two years ago, and it is quite possible that the mother, who may perhaps want to marry again, has shut the girl up in a convent to get rid of her altogether, and to make her sign a document renouncing her right to the property in favour of herself, or possibly, as the bishop seems to have meddled in the affair, partly of the Church.

"I quite see that nothing can be done now, but if we do occupy Oporto, some day, which is likely enough, I will speak to the general, and if he says that it is a matter that he cannot entertain, I will see what I can do to get her out."

"It is awkward work, O'Connor, fooling with a nunnery either here or in Spain. The Portuguese are not so bigoted as the Spaniards across the frontier, but there is not much difference, and if anyone is caught meddling with a nunnery they would tear him to pieces, especially in Oporto, where men who are even suspected of hostility to the bishop are murdered every day."

"I don't want to run the risk of being torn to pieces, certainly, but after what you have told me of her letter, I will not let my little cousin be imprisoned all her life in a nunnery, and robbed of her property, without making some strong effort to save her."

"I will give you the letter presently, O'Connor; I have it in a pocket-book at my quarters. By the by, how old is your cousin?"

"About my own age, or a little younger."

The subject of the conversation was then changed, and half an hour later the officer left the room and returned with the letter.

"At any rate," he said, "if we do go to Oporto you will have more opportunity for getting the general to move than I should."

Terence had handed over the horse he had borrowed, with many thanks for its use, and received his own again, which was in good condition after its rest of seven or eight days. It was by no means a valuable animal, but he thought it as well to take it on with him in case any of the other horses should meet with an accident or break down during the journey through the mountains.

Coimbra was the last British station through which they would pass, and the real difficulties of the journey would now begin. Terence had, before starting, received a sum of money for the maintenance of himself and his escort upon the way, and he had done all in his power to see that the troopers were comfortable at their various halting-places.

The journey as far as the Douro passed without any adventure. They encountered on the road several bands of peasants armed with pikes, clubs, hoes, and a few guns. These were for the most part ordenanças or levies, called out when a larger force than the regular troops and militia was required. They were on their way to join the forces assembling under the edicts, and beyond pausing to stare at the British officer with the two dragoons behind him and an escort of their own troops, they paid no attention to the party.

They crossed the Douro at St. Joa de Pesquiera, and on stopping at a large village some ten miles beyond, found it occupied by a rabble of some two thousand men, absolutely useless for service in the field, but capable of offering an obstinate defence to the passage of a river, or of impeding an enemy's advance through a mountain defile. As they stopped before the principal inn a man, dressed in some attempt at a uniform, came out from a door.

"You are a British officer, sir?" he asked Terence, raising his broad hat courteously.

"I am an officer on the English general's staff, and am proceeding on a mission from him to the northern frontier to ascertain the best means of defence, and the route that the enemy are most likely to move by if they attempt to invade Portugal from that direction."

"The French general would hardly venture to do that," the officer said, disdainfully, "when there will be 50,000 Portuguese to bar his way."

"He may be in ignorance of the force that will gather to meet him," Terence said, gravely, and with difficulty restraining a smile at the confident tone of this leader of an armed mob. "However, I have my orders to carry out. Do you not think," he said, turning to Herrara, "that it will be better for us to go on to the next hamlet, if there is one within two or three miles. I fear there is little chance of obtaining any accommodation for our men here."

"There is no need for that," the Portuguese colonel broke in. "There is a large house at the end of the village that is at present vacant; the proprietor, who was a disturber of the peace, and who belonged to the French faction, was killed last week in the course of a disturbance created by him. I, as Commissioner of the Junta here, had the house closed up, but it is quite at your service."

As the march had already been a long one, Terence thought it best to accept the offer. The colonel called a man, who presently brought a key, and accompanied them to the house in question. It showed signs at once of mob violence. The snow in the garden was trampled down, the windows broken, and one of the lower ones smashed in as if an entry had been effected here. The door was riddled with bullet holes. Upon this being opened the destruction within was seen to be complete, rooms being strewn with broken furniture and litter of all sorts.

"At any rate there is plenty of firewood," the lieutenant said, as he ordered his men to clear out one of the rooms. "There has been dastardly work here," he went on, as the man who had brought the key left the place.

"Yes, I have no doubt the proprietor, whoever he was, has been foully murdered, and as likely as not by the orders of that fellow we met, who says he is Commissioner of the Junta. I should not be surprised if we have trouble with him before we have done. I should think, Herrara, you had better send off a couple of men to get what they can in the way of provisions and a skin of wine. This is a cheerless-looking place, and these broken windows are not of much use for keeping out the cold. Bull, you had better see if you can find something among all this rubbish to hang up in front of the window, for in its present state it merely creates a draught."

The orderly went out, and returned with two torn curtains.

"There has been some bad work going on here, sir," he said. "There are pools of blood in three of the rooms upstairs, and it is evident that there has been a desperate struggle. One of the doors is broken in, and there are several shot-holes through it."

"I am afraid there has been bad work. I suppose the man here was obnoxious to somebody, so they murdered him. However, it is not our business."

Some of the horses were stabled in a large shed, the others in the lower rooms of the house, the soldiers and muleteers taking possession of the large kitchen, where they soon had a huge fire burning. The windows on this side of the house were unbroken. The two orderlies soon fastened up the curtains across the windows of the officers' room, and when the fire was lighted it had a more cheerful aspect. The burdens of the mules were brought into the room opposite, where there was a key in the door and bars across the windows. Presently the soldiers returned with some meat, a couple of fowls, bread, and some wine, together with a bunch of candles. The fowls were soon plucked, cut in two, and grilled over the fire, and in a quarter of an hour after the men's return the two officers sat down to supper. The meal was just finished when there was a knock at the outer door, and the soldier acting as sentry came in and said that Colonel Cortingos desired to speak to them.

"I suppose that is the fellow we saw in the town," Terence said; "show him in."

The supposition was a correct one, for the man entered, accompanied by two others. Terence had no doubt that this fellow was the author of the attack upon the house, and the murderer of the proprietor and others. He did not feel disposed to be exceptionally civil to him, but as he had a couple of thousand men under his command and had certainly put the only available place in the village at their disposal, he rose as he entered.

"These two gentlemen," the colonel began, "form, with myself, the committee appointed by the Junta of Oporto to organize the national resistance here and in the surrounding neighbourhood, to keep our eye upon persons suspected of being favourable to the enemy, and to arrest and send them to Oporto for trial. We are also enjoined to make close inquiries into the business of all persons who may pass through here."

"I have already told you," Terence said, quietly, "that I am an officer on the staff of the English general, and that I have a mission from him to see what are the best means of defending the northern passes, and, I may add, to enter into such arrangements as I may think proper with the leaders of any bands who may be gathered for the purpose of defending them. As I am acting under the direct orders of the general, I in no way recognize the right of any local authority to interfere with me in any way."

"And I, Lieutenant Herrara, have been ordered by the colonel of my regiment to command the escort of Portuguese cavalry told off to accompany this British officer, and also feel myself free from any interference or examination by civilians."

"I am a colonel!" Cortingos said, angrily.

"By whom appointed, if I may ask?"

"By the Junta of Oporto."

"I was not aware that they possessed the right of granting high commissions," Herrara said, "although, of course, they can grant temporary rank to those who command irregular forces. This British officer has assured you as to the object of his journey, and unless that object has had the approval of the military authorities at Lisbon he would not have been furnished with an escort by them."

"I have only his word and yours as to that," Cortingos said, insolently. "I am acting under the orders of the supreme authority of this province."

"You are doing your duty, no doubt," the lieutenant said, "in making these inquiries. This officer has answered them, and I will answer any further questions if I consider them to be reasonable."

"We wish, in the first place," Cortingos said, "to examine any official passes you may have received."

"Our official passes are our uniforms," Herrara replied, haughtily.

"Uniforms have been useful for purposes of disguise before now," Cortingos replied. "I again ask you to show me your authority."

"Here is an authority," Terence broke in. "Here is a despatch from General Sir John Cradock to General Romana."

"Ah, ah, a Spaniard."

"A Spanish general, a marquis and grandee of Spain, who has been fighting the French, and who is now with a portion of his army preparing to defend the passes into Portugal."

Cortingos held out his hand for the paper, but Terence put it back again into the breast-pocket of his uniform.

"No, sir," he said; "this communication is for the Marquis of Romana, and for him only. No one else touches it so long as I am alive to defend it."

The colonel whispered to his two associates.

"We will let that pass for the present," he replied, and turning to Terence again, said, "In the next place we wish to know the nature of the contents of the sacks that are being carried by the mules that accompany you."

"They contain ammunition, and forage for our horses," Lieutenant Herrara said. "You can, if you choose, question the muleteers, who fastened up the sacks and had an opportunity of seeing the ammunition."

"In the name of the Junta I demand that ammunition!" Cortingos said, with an air of authority. "It is monstrous that ammunition should be taken to Spaniards, who have already shown that they are incapable of using it with any effect, while here we have loyal men ready to die in their country's defence, but altogether unprovided with ammunition."

"For that, sir, you must apply to your Junta. Since they give you orders, let them give you ammunition; there is enough in Oporto to supply the whole population, had they arms; and you may be assured that I and my men will see that the convoy intrusted to our charge reaches its destination."

"I believe that there is not only ammunition, but money in those sacks," said Cortingos. "It would be an act of treachery to allow it to pass, when, even if not taken to them directly, it might fall into the hands of the French. It is needed here; my men lack shoes and clothes, and as you say the object of your mission is to see to the defence of our frontier, any money you may have cannot be better applied than to satisfy the necessities of my soldiers. However, we do

"IN THE NAME OF THE JUNTA, I DEMAND THAT AMMUNITION,"
SAID CORTINGOS.

not wish to take steps that might appear unfriendly. And, therefore, if you will allow us to inspect the contents of those sacks, we will let you pass on if we find that they contain no money—confiscating only the ammunition for the use of the troops of the province."

"I refuse absolutely," Herrara said, "to allow anything confided to my charge to be touched."

"That is your final decision," the man said, with a sneer.

"Final and absolute."

"I also shall do my duty;" and then, without another word, the colonel with his two associates left the house.

"We shall have trouble with that fellow," Herrara said.

"So much the better," Terence replied. "We have evidence here that the scoundrel is a murderer. No doubt he had some private enmity against the owner of this establishment, and so denounced him to the Junta, and then attacked the place, murdered him, and perhaps some of his servants, and sacked the house. They won't find it so easy a job as it was last time; all the windows are barred, and there are only three on this floor to defend. The shutters of two of them are uninjured, so it is only the one where they broke in before that they can attack, while our men at the windows upstairs will make it hot for them as they approach. But I should hardly think that the men he calls soldiers will venture to attack a party of regular troops."

The lieutenant shrugged his shoulders.

"He will tell them some lies, probably assert that we are French agents in disguise taking money to the French army. Indeed, there is neither order nor discipline among these bands, and, roused to a pitch of fury, they would murder their own leaders as readily as anyone else. The Junta acts as if the province were altogether independent, and numbers of men of position have been butchered on the pretence of their being adherents of the French, when their sole crime was that they disapproved of the doings of the bishop and his tools. You will see that the night will not pass off without something happening. Of course, I shall be sorry to have to order the men to fire. In the first place it would render it very difficult for us to resume our journey; and in the second, if we succeed in getting out alive, they will send a lying account of the affair to Lisbon, and there will be all sorts of trouble. Still, of course, if they attack the house we shall defend ourselves."

The two officers then made a tour of the house and carefully examined the means of defence. The broken shutters were replaced in their position in the window, and were backed with a pile of the fragments of furniture. The horses were all brought in from the shed outside, the soldiers were warned that the mob in the place were likely to attack them, and four of them were placed as sentries at the upper windows; and, by the looks of the men when the lieutenant made the communication to them, Terence saw that they could be relied upon.

"I have no doubt that we shall be able to defend the place successfully," Terence said to the two British troopers; "but if the worst comes to the worst we will all mount inside the house, throw open the door behind, and then go right at them. But I hope that we shall avoid a fight, for if we have one, it will be very difficult for us to make our way to the north, or to get back across the Douro."

In an hour one of the sentries at the upper window brought news that a large number of men were approaching. Terence at once gave some orders that he and the lieutenant had agreed upon to the two soldiers, and four of the Portuguese troopers, and then went up with the lieutenant to the window over the door. He threw it open just as a crowd of men poured into the garden in front.

"What is it?" he asked. "What do you want?"

"I demand entrance to this house in the name of the Junta of Oporto," a voice which he recognized as that of Cortingos replied. "If that is refused I shall denounce you as traitors to Portugal, and your blood will be on your own heads."

"We respect the orders of the Junta," Herrara replied, "and are ready to open the door as you demand; but I must first be assured that it is really the committee appointed by the Junta that demand it."

Several of the men had torches, and these were brought forward, and they saw the man and his two associates standing in front.

"Good, I will open the door," the lieutenant said, and he and Terence went down. The bars were removed and the door thrown open, the two officers walked a few paces outside, and then halted.

Followed closely by their armed followers, the three men approached, confident in the strength of their following.

"Enter, gentlemen," Terence said. "I protest against this invasion, by force, but I cannot oppose it."

The three men entered the door, the two officers standing aside and allowing them to pass. The instant the three Portuguese had entered Terence and the lieutenant threw themselves suddenly upon those following them. Two or three rolled over with the suddenness of the assault, and the rest recoiled a step or two. Before they could recover themselves Herrara and Terence dashed through the door, which was slammed to and barred by the two English troopers. Meanwhile, the three men had been seized by the Portuguese troopers, their coats torn off them, and their hands tied behind their backs, and then they were hurried upstairs.

Yells of fury filled the air outside, shots were fired at the windows, and men began to beat the door and shutters with bludgeons and hatchets. Suddenly a light appeared from a window above, and Cortingos and his two friends were seen standing there. By the side of each stood a trooper, holding a rope with a noose round the prisoners' necks. For a moment there was a silence of stupefaction outside, followed by a yell of fury from the mob. Herrara went to the window and shouted: "My friends." Again there was a moment of silence, as each wanted to hear what he said. "My friends, at the first shot that is fired, or the first blow that is struck at the doors of this house, these three men will be hung out of the window. They have deceived you grossly. I am an officer of the National Army, these troopers are men of the 2d Portuguese Dragoons. We have been appointed by the military authorities of Lisbon to escort this British officer, who is on the staff of the British general, and whose commission is to make arrangements with the Spanish general, Romana to harass the rear of the French, and attack their convoys should they attempt to enter the northern passes.

"These three scoundrels have deceived you, in order, as they hoped, to obtain some money that they believed us to be escorting. As loyal Portuguese, I warn you against attempting to aid the fellows in a deed which would bring disgrace upon the national name, and would result in the British general refusing to assist in the defence of your country. You are brave men, but you see these three cowards are trembling like children. We advise you to appoint fresh officers among yourselves, and to remain faithful to your duty, which is to march when ordered to the defence of the defiles. These three fellows we shall take with us, and will see that they do not further deceive you. Already they have done harm enough by goading you to theft, and to murder a man whose only fault was that he was more patriotic than they are. Be assured that in no case would you be able to carry this house. It is defended by sixteen well-armed men, and hundreds of you would throw away your lives in the attempt. Therefore, I advise you to go back to your quarters, and in the morning assemble and choose your officers."

The crowd stood irresolute.

"Tell them to go, you cur," Herrara said to Cortingos, standing back from the window and giving him a kick that almost sent him on his face. "Tell them to disperse at once, if you don't want to be dangling from the end of this rope."

Cortingos stepped forward, and in a quavering voice told the men to disperse to their quarters.

"We have made a mistake," he said. "I am now convinced that these officers are what they appear to be. I beseech you do not cause trouble, and disperse at once quietly."

Hoots of derision and scorn rose from the peasants.

"I have a good mind to fire a shot before I go," one of the peasants shouted, "just for the pleasure of seeing three such cowards hung."

Another yell of disgust and anger arose, and then the crowd melted away.

"Keep these three fellows at the window. Remove the ropes from their necks, and take your place behind them; you will be relieved every hour. If they move, bayonet them at once."

"We shall die of cold," one of the men whimpered.

"That would be a more honourable death than you are likely to meet," Terence said, scornfully. "I fancy if I don't hang you, those men in the village will do so if they can lay hands on you."

"How about the sentries, sir?" the corporal of the escort asked Herrara as they went downstairs.

"They can all be removed except the one keeping guard over these men—he is to be relieved every hour—and one inside the door, he can be relieved every two hours."

The night passed quietly. Just as they were preparing to start next morning, the soldier on guard over the prisoners shouted, "There is a crowd of men coming!"

"Get your arms ready," Herrara said to the escort; "but I don't think there will be any occasion to use them."

Terence went to the door. "Bull, do you and Macwitty keep close behind; but whatever happens don't use your weapons, unless I order you to do so."

The crowd stopped at the gate, two of them only coming forward.

"We are ready to fight, sir," one said, addressing Terence, "but we have no officers; none of us know anything about drill. We will follow you, if you will command us, and you will find that we won't turn our backs to the enemy. We know that English officers will fight."

"Wait a minute or two," Terence said, after a moment's hesitation, "I will then give you my answer."

Herrara had followed him out and heard the offer.

"I don't know what to do, Herrara," Terence said, as he re-entered the house. "My instructions are to join Romana, and to remain with him for a time, sending word to Lisbon as to the state of things, and aiding him in any way in my power. Here are between two and three thousand stout, healthy fellows, evidently disposed to fight. If they were armed I would not hesitate a moment, but I don't suppose that there are a hundred muskets among them, and certainly Romana has none to give them. Still, in the defiles we might give a good deal of trouble to the French by rolling stones down, breaking up bridges, and that sort of thing."

"It would be good fun," Herrara laughed. "As for myself," he said, "I have orders to return as soon as I have seen the treasure safely in Romana's camp. If it hadn't been for that I should have liked nothing better, though there would not have been much chance for cavalry work in these defiles."

"I will talk to them again," Terence said. "It is not often that one gets the chance of an independent command. It is just the sort of work I should like."

He went out again. "I should like to command a number of brave fellows," he said, "but the question is about arms. There have been any quantity sent out by England for your use; but instead of being served out, the Juntas keep them all hidden up in magazines. Even now, when the French are going to invade your country, they still keep them locked up, and send you out with only pikes and staves to fight against a well-armed army. It is nothing short of murder."

"Down with the Juntas!" cried half a dozen of the men standing near enough to hear what was said.

"I don't say 'Down with the Juntas!'" Terence replied; "but I do say take arms if you can get them. Are there any magazines near here?"

"There is one at Castro, ten miles away," the man said. "I know that there are waggon-loads of arms there."

"Well, my friends, the matter stands thus: I, as a British officer, cannot lead you to break open magazines; but I say this, if you choose to go in a body to Castro and do it yourselves, and arm yourselves with all the muskets that you can find there, and bring with you a good store of ammunition in carts that you could take with you from here, and then come to me at a spot where I will halt to-night five or six miles beyond Castro, I will take command of you. But mind, if I command, I command. I must have absolute obedience. It is only by obeying my orders without question that you can hope to do any good. The first man who disobeys me I shall shoot on the spot, and if others are disposed to support him I shall leave you at once."

"I will consult the others," the man said. "Many of us, I know, will be glad to fight under an English officer, and agree to obey him implicitly."

"Very well, I will give you a quarter of an hour to decide."

Before that time had elapsed a dozen men came to the door with the principal spokesman.

"We have made up our minds, señor. We will follow you, and we will arm ourselves at Castro. It is a sin that the arms should be lying there idle with so many hands ready to use them."

"That is good," Terence said. "Now, my first order is that you wait until I have been gone an hour; then, that you form up in military order, four abreast; the men with guns in front, the others after them. You must go as soldiers, and not as a mob. You must march into Castro peacefully and quietly, not a man must straggle from the ranks. You must go to the authorities and demand the arms and ammunition; if they refuse to give them to you, march—always in regular order—to the magazine and burst it open; then distribute the muskets and a hundred rounds of ammunition to each man having one, take the rest of the stores in carts, and then march away along the road north until you come to the place where we are halted.

"Observe the most perfect order in Castro. If any man plunders or meddles in any way with the inhabitants and is reported to me, I shall know how to punish him. From the moment that you leave this place remember that you are soldiers of Portugal, and you must behave so as to be an honour to it as well as a defence. Now let us all shout 'Viva Portugal!'"

A great shout followed the words, and then Terence went indoors, and five minutes later started with his convoy, telling the three prisoners they could go where they liked.

CHAPTER XIV

AN INDEPENDENT COMMAND

AS they left the village the Portuguese lieutenant burst into a sudden fit of laughter.

"What is it, Lieutenant?" Terence asked.

"I am laughing at the way in which you—who, as you tell me, have only been six months in the army—without hesitation organize what is really a rising against the authorities, you having already taken representatives of the Junta prisoners——"

"Yes; but you must remember that they took upon themselves to endeavour to forcibly possess themselves of the treasure in my charge."

"That is true enough; still, you did capture them. You treated them with considerable personal indignity, imprisoned them, and threatened their lives. Then you incite, say 2,500 ordenanças to break open magazines."

"No, no, Lieutenant, I did not incite them. You will remember they expressed a desire to march under my command to fight against the French. I simply pointed out to them that they had no arms, and asked if they could get any; and hearing that there were plenty lying useless a few miles away, suggested that those arms would do more good in their hands than stowed away in magazines. Upon their agreeing with me on this head, I advised them to proceed in a quiet and orderly way, and to have no rioting or disturbance of any sort. I said that if they, after arming themselves, came to me and still wished to follow me, I would undertake to command them. You see, everything depends upon the manner in which the thing is put."

"But you must remember, señor, that the Junta will naturally view the matter in the light in which their representatives will place it before them."

"I think it unlikely," Terence replied, "that they will have any opportunity of doing so. I took care that they were removed from the window before I met the deputies of the men. They will consequently be unaware of the arrangements made, and will, perhaps, go out as soon as we have left and try to persuade the men to follow and attack us. As it was possible that they might take this course, I took the precaution of sending out one of the muleteers, with instructions to mention casually to the men that I was leaving the three fellows behind me, and that it might be as well for them to confine them under a guard so as to prevent their going to Oporto at present and making mischief."

"I agree with you, señor, that they are certainly not likely to make any report as to the proceedings here."

"I fancy not; in fact I should not be at all surprised if at the present moment they are hanging from the windows of the house of the man they caused to be murdered. They will most richly deserve their fate, and it may save us some trouble. No doubt the Junta will hear some day that the ordenanças here rose, killed the three members of their committee, obtained arms at Castro, and marched into the mountains. The Junta will care nothing whatever for the killing of its three agents; plenty of men of the same kind can be found to do their work. That the mutineers afterwards fell in with a British officer, and placed themselves under his command, will not concern the Junta one way or the other, and they will certainly be a great deal more useful in that way than they would be in remaining unarmed here.

"They may even, when the French once get in motion, come to regard the affair altogether as satisfactory. If all the new levies were to act in exactly the same way, Portugal would be very materially benefited."

"But how are you going to feed them?"

"That is rather a serious question. I suppose they will have to be fed in the same way as other irregular bands. However, I shall consider myself fully justified in devoting a fifth of the money I am carrying to that purpose. I obtained from Villiers £5,000 to enable Romana to support the levies he is raising. Those levies will be for the most part unarmed, and therefore practically useless; and as these Portuguese will be at any rate fairly armed, and are likely to be of very much greater service than a horde of Galician peasants, a portion at least of the money can be very much more usefully employed in feeding them than were it all given to Romana. I have no doubt whatever that when I explain the circumstances to General Cradock, he will entirely approve of my appropriating a small portion of the money that Villiers has chosen to throw away on Romana. When you return I shall get you to carry a report from me to the general, stating what I have done. I have no doubt he will warmly approve of it."

On approaching Castro they made a detour to avoid the town.

"There may be more representatives of the Junta there," Terence said, "and we may have even more trouble with them than we had with the last. I don't want any more bother, especially as I have much greater interest in the money now than I had before. I have not a shadow of belief in those bands of Portuguese peasants, but I do think that, with the aid of my two troopers, I shall be able to lick these fellows into some sort of shape, and to annoy Soult, if I cannot stop him. I hope they will find a good supply of powder, besides the muskets and ammunition at Castro; we shall want it for blowing up bridges and work of that sort."

"I wish I could go with you," Herrara said.

"I really don't see why you should not. I would take the blame on my own shoulders. One of your troopers could carry my report to the general, and I will say that under the circumstances I have taken upon myself to retain you with me in order to assist me in drilling and organizing this band, conceiving that your services with me would be very much more useful than with your regiment. You see, you were placed under my orders, so that no blame can fall upon you for obeying them, and at any rate you certainly will be doing vastly better service to the country than if you were stationed at Lisbon, with no prospect of an advance for a long time to come. Still, of course, I will not retain you against your will."

"I should like it of all things," Herrara said; "but do you really think that the general would approve?"

"I have not the least doubt that he would, and at any rate if he did not he would only blame me, and not you. Your help would certainly be invaluable to me, and so would that of your men. They are all picked soldiers, and if we divided the force up into twelve companies, they would very soon teach them as much drill as is necessary for work like this. Each trooper would command one of the companies, my two orderlies would act as field officers; you would be colonel, and I should be political officer in command."

Herrara burst into a fit of laughter.

"You are the strangest fellow I ever met, señor. Here is a very serious business, and you take it as easily as if it were a game of play. However, it does seem to me that we might do some good service. At any rate I am quite willing to obey your orders. It would be an adventure to talk of all one's life."

"That is right," Terence said; "and there will be some credit to be gained, too. Indeed, we can safely say that our band will be very much better organized than nineteen out of twenty of the irregular bands."

The track they followed was a very bad one, and the point at which they regained the main road was eight miles north of Castro. There was a small village here, and they at once halted. Although they had travelled slowly they knew that the men could not come along for some time, as they were not to start until an hour after them, and would be detained for some considerable time at Castro. It was indeed nearly three hours before a column marching in good order was seen coming along the road.

"That is a good sign," Terence said; "they have obeyed orders strictly; whether they have got the arms I cannot tell yet. The men at the head of the column have certainly muskets, but as the armed men were to go in front that is no proof."

However, as the column approached, it could be seen that at any rate a very considerable number were armed.

"We had better form them up as they come, Herrara. If the head of the column stops it will stop them all, and then there will be confusion."

The road through the village was wide. When a hundred ranks had passed they were halted, faced round, and marched forward, and so they continued until the village was filled with a dense mass of men, twenty deep. Terence observed with satisfaction that they had with them six bullock carts filled with ammunition-cases, spare muskets, and powder-barrels. The men who had first spoken to Terence had headed the column, and these had stopped by his side as the others marched in.

"You have succeeded, I see," he said. "I hope that you were enabled to accomplish it without violence."

"They were too much surprised to offer much resistance. Five fellows, who said they were the committee appointed by the Junta, came to us and told us that unless we dispersed at once we should be severely punished. We told them that we had come out of our homes at the orders of the Junta, but that as the Junta had not supplied us with arms we had come for them, as we were not going to fight the French with nothing but sticks. They then threatened us again, and we told them that if they hindered us from defending the country we should hang them at once; and as they saw we meant it, they went quietly off to their houses. Then we broke down the door of the magazine. We found four thousand muskets there. Each man took one, and we left the remainder and enough ammunition for them, and have brought the rest here, together with a hundred spare muskets.

"We have observed excellent order, and no one was hurt or alarmed. The only men who left the ranks were a score who went round to the bakers' shops by my orders, and bought up all the bread in the place. We found a bag with a thousand dollars at the quarters of Cortingos."

"What became of him and his two associates?"

"They had the impudence to come out and harangue us when you had gone; but we tied them up to the branch of a tree, so there is an end of them."

"And a very fitting end, too," Terence said. "What have you done with the money?"

"The bag is in that cart, señor."

"You had better appoint four of your number as treasurers. I would rather not touch it. You must be as careful as you can, and spend it only on the barest necessaries of life. We shall have few opportunities of buying things in the mountains, but when we do come upon them they must be paid for. Of course, we shall go no farther to-night. How many men have you?"

"About two thousand five hundred, señor."

"They must be told off into twelve companies. That will be two hundred and ten to each company. I shall appoint one of these soldiers to each company to drill and command it. I propose that each company shall elect its other officers. Lieutenant Herrara will, under my orders, command the regiment. The two English soldiers with me will each take command of six companies. The first thing to be done is to tell off the men into companies."

"This we will at once do. After that they can be marched just outside the village, and each company will then fall out and elect its officers. When that is done the men will be quartered in the village. I have set apart one room in each house for the inhabitants, and the men must pack as tightly as they can into the others; and of course the sheds and stables must also be utilized."

With the assistance of the troopers the work of dividing the force up into companies was accomplished in an hour. Herrara then called his men to him.

"You will each take the command of a company," he said, "and drill them and teach them the use of their arms. This force is now under the command of this British officer. Acting under his orders, I take the command of the force under him. So long as we are out you will each act as captains of your companies, and your British comrades will act as field officers, each taking the command of six companies. We are going to hinder the advance of the French, and to cut their communications with Spain. It will be a glorious and most honourable duty, and I rely most implicitly on your doing your best to make the men under your command fit to meet the enemy. Captain Juan Sanches, you will take the first company;" and so he allotted to each his command.

The soldiers saluted gravely, but with an air of delight.

"You will, in the first place, march your men to various spots around the village; they will then fall out and select six officers each. You will see that each man knows the number of his company, so that they can fall in without hesitation as soon as the order is given. While you are away we shall examine the houses and allot so many to each company."

In the meantime Terence had been similarly instructing the two orderlies. Although standing at attention, a broad grin of amusement stole over their faces as he went on:

"I did not expect this any more than you did," he said; "but my orders were open ones, and were to assist General Romana in hindering the advance of the French, and I think that I cannot do so better than by augmenting his forces by 2,500 well-armed men. I rely greatly upon you to assist me in the work. You will, as you see, each occupy the position of field officers, while the Portuguese troopers will each have the command of a company. In order to support your authority I shall address you each as major, and you can consider that you hold that rank as long as we are out with this force. I have seen enough of you both to know that you will do your duty well. You will understand that this is going to be no child's play; it will be a dangerous service. I shall spare neither myself nor any under my command. There will be lots of fighting and opportunities for you to distinguish yourselves, and I hope that I shall be able to speak in high terms of you when I send in my report to General Cradock."

"We will do our best, sir," Andrew Macwitty said. "How are we to address you?"

"I shall keep to Mr. O'Connor, and shall consider myself a political officer with supreme military authority. Your titles are simply for local purposes, and to give you authority among the Portuguese."

"We don't know enough of the lingo to give the words of command, sir," William Bull said.

"That will not matter. The Portuguese dragoons will teach them as much drill as it is necessary for them to know. If you have to post them in a position you can do that well enough by signs; but at the same time it is most desirable that you should both set to work in earnest and try to pick up a little of the language. You both know enough to make a start with, and if you ride every day with one or other of the captains of companies, and when they are drilling the men stand by and listen to them, you will soon learn enough to give the men the necessary orders. As a rule, the two wings will act as separate regiments; each of them is rather stronger than that of a line regiment at its full war strength, and it will be more convenient to treat them as separate regiments, and, until we get to the frontier, march them a few miles apart.

"In this way they can occupy different villages, and obtain better accommodation than if they were all together. They have money enough to buy bread and wine for some time. You and the captains under you had better each form a sort of mess. You will, of course, draw rations of bread and wine, and I will provide you with money to buy a sheep occasionally or some fowls, to keep you in meat."

The two troopers walked gravely away, but as soon as they were at a little distance they turned round the corner of a house and burst into a shout of laughter.

"How are you finding yourself to-day, Major Macwitty?"

"Just first-rate; and how is yoursel', Major Bull?" and they again went off into another shout of laughter.

"This is a rum start, and no mistake, Macwitty."

"Ay, but it is no' an unpleasant one, I reckon. Mr. O'Connor knows what he is about, though he is little more than a laddie. The orderly who brought our orders to go with him, said he had heard from one of the general's mess waiters that the general and the other officers were saying the young officer had done something quite out of the way, and were paying him compliments on it, and the general had put him on his own staff in consequence, and was saying something about his having saved a wing of his regiment from being captured by the French. The man had not heard it all; but just scraps as he went in and out of the room with wine, but he said it seemed something out of the way, and mighty creditable. And now what do you think of this affair, Bull?"

"There is one thing, and that is that there is like to be, as he said, plenty of fighting, for I should say that he is just the sort of fellow to give us the chance of it, and I do think that these Portuguese fellows really mean to fight."

"I think that mysel', but there is no answering for these brown-skin chaps. Still, maybe it is the fault of the officers as well as the men."

"It will be a rare game anyhow, Macwitty. At any rate I will do my best to get the fellows into order. He is a fine young officer, and a thorough gentleman, and no mistake. He goes about it all as if he had been accustomed to command two regiments all his life, and these Portuguese fellows seem to have taken to him wonderfully. At any rate it will be a thing for us to talk about all our lives—how we were majors for a bit, and fought the French on our own account."

"Yes, if we get home to tell about it," Macwitty said, cautiously. "I dinna think we can reckon much on that yet. It is a desperate sort of a business, and he is ower young to command."

"I would rather have a young officer than an old one," Bull said, carelessly; "and though he is Irish, I feel sure that he has got his head screwed on the right way. Look how well he managed last night. Why, an old general could not have done better. If he hadn't caught those three fellows in a trap, I doubt whether we should have got out of the scrape. Sixteen or seventeen men against over two thousand is pretty long odds. We should have accounted for a lot of them, but they would have done for us in the end."

"You are right there, Bull. I thought mysel' that it was an awkward fix, and certainly he managed those Portuguese fellows well, and turned the lot round his little finger. Ay, ay; he knows what he is doing perfectly well, young as he is."

"Well, we had best be off to look after our commands," Bull laughed. "I suppose they will call mine the first regiment, as I have the right wing."

While the men were away, Terence and Herrara, with the head man of the village, went round to all the houses, and marked on pieces of paper the number of men who could manage to lie down on the floors and passages, with the number of the company, and fixed them on the doors; they also made an arrangement with the proprietor of a neighbouring vineyard to supply as much wine as was required, at the rate of a pint to each man. When the men returned four men were told off from each company to fetch the rations of bread, and another four to carry the wine. They were accompanied by one of the newly elected sergeants to check the quantity, and see that all was done in order. To prevent confusion the companies were kept drawn up until the rations had been distributed; then they were taken into their quarters, filling every room, attic and cellar, barn, granary, and stable in the village. Then Terence and Herrara in one room, and the troopers in another of the little inn, sat down to a meal Terence had ordered as soon as they arrived.

The next morning at daybreak they marched off. Terence rode at their head, Herrara at the rear of the regiment, and each captain at the head of his company. From time to time Terence rode up and down the line, and ordered the men to keep step.

"It is just as easy," he said to the captains, "for the men to do so as to walk along anyhow, and they will find that the sound of all the footfalls together helps them to march steadily and lessens fatigue. Never mind about the slope of their muskets; you must not harass them about little things, else they will get sulky; it will all come gradually."

Four marches of twenty miles each took them over the mountains in four days. The Portuguese marched well, and not a single man fell out from the ranks, while at the end of the day they were still fresh enough to allow of an hour's drill. Even in that short time there was a very appreciable difference in their appearance. They had already learned to keep their distances on the march, to slope their muskets more evenly on their shoulders, and to carry themselves with a more erect bearing. The first two drills had been devoted to teaching them how to load and aim, the other two to changes of formation, from column into line and back again.

"They would make fine soldiers, sir," Bull said, on the fourth evening, "after they have had six months' drill."

"No doubt they would move more regularly," Terence agreed, "but in mountain warfare that makes little difference; as soon as they have learned to shoot straight, and to have confidence in themselves, they will do just as well holding a defile or the head of a bridge as if they had been drilled for months. We must get hold of some horns of some sort, and they must learn a few simple calls, such as the advance, retire, form square, and things of that sort. With such large companies the voice would never be heard in the din of a battle. I hope that we shall get at least a week to practise skirmishing over rough ground and to fall back in good order, taking advantage of every rock and shelter, before we get under fire. Do you know anything about blowing up bridges?"

"Not me, sir. That is engineers' business."

"It is a thing that troopers ought to know something about too, Bull; for if you were far in advance without an engineer near you, you might do good service by blowing up a bridge and checking the advance of an enemy. However, I dare say we shall soon find out how it is best done. Now, to-morrow morning we will have three hours of skirmishing work on these hillsides. By that time the other regiment will have come up, and then we will march together to join Romana."

The Spanish general was much surprised at the arrival of Terence at the head of two well-armed regiments. His force had swelled considerably in point of numbers, for he had sent messengers all over the country to the priests, and these, having a horror of the French, had stirred up the peasants by threats of eternal perdition if they came back; while Romana issued proclamations threatening death to all who did not take up arms. Thus he had some 8,000 men collected, of whom fully half were his own dispersed soldiers. He received Terence with effusion.

"Have you brought me arms?" was his first question.

"No, sir; no transport could be obtained in Lisbon, and it was found impossible to despatch any muskets to you. I have, however, four thousand pounds, in dollars, to hand over. At starting I had five thousand, but of these I have, in the exercise of my discretion, retained a thousand for the purchase of provisions and necessaries for these two Portuguese regiments which are under my command, and with which I hope to do good service by co-operating with your force. Have you not found great difficulty in victualling your men?"

"No, I have had no trouble on that score," the marquis said. "I found that a magazine of provisions had been collected for the use of General Moore's army at Montrui, three miles from here, and have been supporting my troops on the contents. The money will be most useful, however, directly we move. Fully half of my men have guns, for the Galician peasants are accustomed to the use of arms. I wish that it had been more, but four thousand pounds will be very welcome. Do you propose to join my force with your regiments?"

"Not exactly to join them, General; my orders are to give you such assistance as I can, and I think that I can do more by co-operating with you independently. In the first place, I do not think that my Portuguese would like to be commanded by a Spanish general; in the second place, it would be extremely difficult to feed so large a body of troops in these mountains, and the smaller the number the more easily can they move about. Besides, in these defiles a large force of undisciplined men could not act efficiently, and in case of a reverse would fall rapidly into confusion. I propose to use my force as a sort of flying column, co-operating with yours. Thus, if you attack the head of a column, I will fall on their flank or rear, will harass their line of communication, blow up bridges and destroy roads, and so render their movements slow and difficult. By such means I should certainly render you more efficient service than if my regiments were to form a part of your force."

"Perhaps that would be best," Romana said. "Could you supply me with any ammunition? For although the peasants have guns, very few have more than a few rounds of ammunition, and even this is not made up into cartridges."

"That I can do, sir. I can give you 20,000 rounds of ammunition and ten barrels of powder. I have no lead, but you may perhaps be able to obtain that."

"Yes. The priests, in fact, have sent in a considerable amount. They have stripped the roofs off their churches. That will be a most welcome supply indeed, and I am heartily obliged to you."

The gift of the ammunition had the effect of doing away with any discontent the Spaniard may have felt on finding that Terence was going to act independently of him. It had indeed already flashed across his mind that it might be unpleasant always to have a British officer with him, from whose opinion he might frequently differ, and who might endeavour to control his movements. He had hardly expected that, with so much on their hands, and the claims that would be made from Oporto for assistance, they would have sent any money; and the sixteen thousand dollars were therefore most welcome, while the ammunition would be invaluable to him.

Terence had taken out his share of the money, and the cart with the remainder for Romana was now at the door. The sacks were brought in, Romana called in four or five officers, the dollars were counted out and a receipt given to Terence for them.

"I will send the ammunition up in half an hour, Marquis."

"I thank you greatly, señor. I will at once order a number of men to set to work casting bullets and preparing cartridge-cases. In the meantime, please let me hear what are your general's plans for the defence of Portugal."

Terence told him that he was unaware what were the intentions of the British general, but that, from what he learned during the few hours that he was at Lisbon, he thought it improbable in the extreme that Sir John Cradock would be able to send any force to check the advance of the French upon Oporto.

"In the first place," he said, "he is absolutely without transport; and in the second Victor has a large army, and now that Saragossa has fallen, there is nothing to prevent his marching direct upon Lisbon. Lapisse is at Salamanca and can enter Portugal from the east. The whole country is in confusion; with the exception of a force gathering under Lord Beresford there is no army whatever. Lisbon is almost at the mercy of the mob, who, supported by the government, march about with British muskets and pikes, killing all they suspect of being favourable to the French, and even attacking British soldiers and officers in the streets.

"Were the general to march north, he would not get news of Victor's advance in time to get back to save Lisbon, therefore I fear that it is absolutely impossible for him to attempt to check the French until they cross the Douro, perhaps not until they cross the Mondego. The levies of the northern province are ordered to assemble at Villa Real, and I believe, from what I gathered on the march, that some thousands of men are there, but I doubt very greatly whether they are in a state to offer any determined resistance to Soult."

"That is a bad look-out," the general said, gloomily; "still, we must hope for the best, as Spain will soon raise fresh armies, and so occupy the attention of the enemy that Soult will have to fall back. I am in communication with General Silveira, who will advance to Chaves; he has four thousand men. He has written to me that the bishop had collected 50,000 peasants at Oporto."

"Where they will probably do more harm than good," Terence said, scornfully. "I would rather have half a regiment of British troops than the whole lot of them. It is not men that are wanted, it is discipline, and 50,000 peasants will be even more unmanageable and useless than 5,000 would be. By the way, General, I have now to inform you that General

Cradock has done me the honour of placing me on his personal staff."

"I am glad to hear it," the marquis said, courteously; "it will certainly increase your authority greatly."

Terence, leaving Romana, marched his troops to within a mile of Monterey, choosing a spot where there was a wood which would afford some shelter to the troops, and would give them a supply of firewood. At Monterey he would be able to purchase provisions, and he wished to keep them apart from Romana's men, whose undisciplined habits and general insubordination would counteract his efforts with his own men.

The next ten days were spent in almost incessant drilling, and in practising shooting. Bread and wine were obtained from Monterey, and he purchased a large flock of sheep at a very low price, the peasants, in their fear of the French, being very anxious to turn their flocks and herds into money, which could be hid away securely until the tide of invasion had passed. Laborious and frugal in their habits, these peasants seldom touch meat, and the troops were highly gratified at the rations supplied to them, and worked hard and cheerfully at their drill.

Among so many men there were naturally a few who were inclined to be insubordinate. These were speedily weeded out. The offenders were promptly seized, flogged, and expelled from the force, their places being supplied from among the peasants, many of whom were desirous of enlisting. Terence sent these off, save a few he selected, to Silveira, as his own force was quite as large as could properly be handled. With improved food and incessant drill the men rapidly developed into soldiers. Each carried a rough native blanket rolled up like a scarf over one shoulder. This was indeed the only point of regular equipment. They had no regular uniform, but they were all in their peasant dresses. There was no communication between them and Romana's forces, for the animosity between the two peoples amounted to hatred. The Portuguese would indeed have marched to attack them as willingly as they would have received the order to move against the French.

During this week of waiting Silveira with 4,000 men arrived at Chaves, and a meeting took place between him and Romana. Both had plans equally wild and impracticable, neither would give way, and as they were well aware that their forces would never act together, they decided to act independently against the French. At the end of eight days the news came that Soult, having made all his preparations, had left Orense on his march southward.

Terence had bought a quantity of rough canvas, and the men, as they sat round the fires after their day's work was over, made haversacks in which they could carry rations for four or five days. As soon as the news was received that Soult was advancing, Terence ordered sufficient bread to supply them for that time, from the bakehouses of Monterey. A hundred rounds of ball-cartridge were served round to each. A light cart containing eight barrels of powder, a bag with 1,000 dollars, and the tent, was the only vehicle taken, and the rest of the ammunition and powder was buried deep in the wood, and the bulk of the money privately hidden in another spot by Terence and Herrara. Twelve horns had been obtained; several of the men were able to blow them, and these, attached one to each company, had learned a few calls. Terence and Herrara took their post at the edge of the wood to watch the two regiments march past.

"I think they will do," Terence said; "they have picked up marvellously since they have been here; and though I should not like to trust them in the plain with Franceschi's cavalry sweeping down upon them, I think that in mountain work they can be trusted to make a stand."

"I think so," Herrara agreed. "They have certainly improved wonderfully. Our peasants are very docile and easily led when they have confidence in their commander, and are not stirred up by agitators, but they are given to sudden fury, as is shown by the frightful disorders at Lisbon and Oporto. However, they certainly have confidence in you, and if they are successful in the first skirmish or two they can be trusted to fight stoutly afterwards."

CHAPTER XV

THE FIRST SKIRMISH

SOULT had spent a month in making his preparations for the invasion of Portugal. The time, however, had not been wasted by him. Vigo, Tuy, and Guardia had all been occupied without opposition. Salvatierra on the Minho had been taken possession of, and thus three roads were open to him by which to cross low down on the river, namely, at Guardia, Tuy, and Salvatierra. These roads afforded the shortest and easiest line to Oporto. Romana and Silveira had both been of opinion that he would march south from Orense, through Monterey, and up the valley of the Tamega, and their plans were all made with a view of opposing his advance in that direction. The night before Terence marched he called upon Romana.

"It seems to me probable, Marquis, as it does to you, that the French will advance by this line, but it is possible that they may follow the north bank of the Minho and cross at Salvatierra or Tuy. By that route they would have several rivers to cross but no mountains or defiles. Were they to throw troops across there they would meet with no opposition until they arrived at Oporto. It seems to me that my best plan would be to march west and endeavour to prevent such a passage being made. If I could do so it would prevent your position being turned. There are no bridges marked on my map, and if I could secure the boats we should, at any rate, cause Soult much difficulty and delay. No doubt there are some local levies there, and we should be able to watch a considerable extent of the river; indeed, so far as I can see, they must cross, if they cross at all there, at one of the three towns on the north side, for it is only by the roads running through these that they could carry their artillery and baggage."

"I think that will be an excellent plan," Romana said, "for although I believe that they will come this way, I have been very uneasy at the thought that they might possibly cross lower down, and so turn our position altogether. But you will have to watch not only the three places through which the roads pass, but other parts of the river, for they may throw a few hundred men across in boats at any point, and these falling suddenly upon your parties on the bank, might drive them away and enable the main body to cross without resistance."

"I will keep as sharp a look-out as I can, Marquis."

Marching north from Monterey the troops moved through Villa Real and Gingo, and then, turning west, crossed the river Lima, there a small stream, and then following the valley of that river for some distance, turned off and struck the Minho opposite Salvatierra, having covered fifty miles in two days. Here a considerable number of armed peasants and ordenanças were gathered. They were delighted at the arrival of two well-armed regiments; and hearing from Herrara that Terence was a staff-officer of the British general, and was sent by him to direct the defence of the river, they at once placed themselves under his orders.

Terence found, to his satisfaction, that on the approach of the French most of the boats had been removed to the south side of the river and hauled up the bank. His first order was that anyone acquainted with the position of any boats on the other side of the river should at once inform him of it. It was not long before he heard of some twenty or thirty that had been hidden by their owners on the other side, in order that they might have the means of crossing to escape the French exactions. At nightfall several boats were launched, and parties of men, directed by those who had given information, started to cross the river and bring those boats over. The Minho was at this time in flood and was running with great rapidity, and Terence felt confident that in its present state none of the enemy's cavalry would attempt to cross it by swimming.

He decided on placing the largest part of his force opposite Tuy, as the principal road south passed through this town, and he would here be supported by the guns of the fortress of Valenca. He stationed his first battalion here, with orders to line the river for six miles above and below this spot. Half of the second battalion he left under Macwitty, and with the other half determined to march down towards the mouth of the river. The next morning all the boats returned, bringing those for which they had been searching, and after closely questioning the guides he felt assured that there could be so few remaining that the French would hardly attempt to cross the river in the face of the crowd of peasants—whom they could not but see—lining the southern bank.

'As soon as the boats had returned he marched with the three companies. When half-way between Valenca and Caminha he met a peasant, who had crossed from the northern bank in a boat that had escaped the search of the French. He reported that some days before some 10,000 of the French had arrived in the neighbourhood of the village Campo Sancos, and that a division had been hard at work since their arrival transporting some large fishing-boats and heavy guns from the harbour of Guardia to Campo Sancos. The guns had been placed in a battery on a height, and the boats launched in a little river that ran into the Minho village. Terence learned that the work was now nearly completed, and the peasant had risked his life in coming across to give information.

Terence at once sent off a mounted man to Valenca to request Herrara to march down with the first battalion and to send on to Macwitty to leave one company to assist the ordenanças to guard the river between Salvatierra and Valenca, and to take post with the other two in front of the latter town. At nightfall he was joined by Herrara.

After explaining the situation to him, Terence said:

" It will not be necessary to watch the river above Campo Sancos, for it would be impossible to row heavy fishing-boats against this stream, so they must land somewhere between that place and the mouth of the river. Thus we have only some eight miles to guard, and as we have eighteen hundred men, besides the peasants, we ought to be able to do that thoroughly. I expect they will endeavour to make the passage to-night, and they will certainly cross, as nearly as they can, opposite the village. The battery is about a mile below it, and is no doubt intended to cover their landing. I shall post myself with two companies of the first battalion there, and extend another company from that point up to Campos Sancos. You, with the other three companies and the three companies of the second battalion, will watch the river below.

" It is unlucky that there is no moon at present. I do not expect, however, that the attack will take place till morning, for, in the first place, the peasant said that although the guns had been got up to the height they had not yet been placed in position, and as we have noticed no movement there all day, nor seen a French soldier anywhere near the river, they will only be beginning work now, and can hardly have finished it until well on in the night. Besides, when the first party who crossed have obtained a footing here, the boats will have to go backwards and forwards. No doubt the cavalry will be among the first to cross, and they would hardly get the horses on board in the dark. It is of vital importance to repel this attack, for if the French got across they would be at Vianna to-morrow evening, and at Oporto three days later. I don't suppose that place will resist for a day; and if, as is probable, Victor moves up from the south, he and Soult may be in front of Lisbon in ten days' time.

"You had better tell your captains this, in order that they may understand how vital it is to prevent the passage. From what I hear from the peasants, the boats will not be able to carry more than three or four hundred men, and wherever they land we ought to be able to crush them before the boats can cross again and bring over reinforcements."

"Well, Bull, I think we are likely to have fighting to-night," Terence said, as Herrara marched off with his men.

"I hope so, sir. I don't think they will be able to cross in our face, and it will do the men a lot of good to win the first fight."

"If Romana's troops were worth anything, Soult would find himself in an awkward position. He has got his whole army jammed up in the corner here, and if he cannot cross there is nothing for him to do but to march along the river to Orense, and then come down by the road through Monte-rey. There are several streams to cross as he marches up the bank. Romana is sure to have heard of his concentrating somewhere down near the mouth of the river, and I should think that by this time he will have crossed near Orense, and will arrive in time to dispute the passage of these streams. He told me that the Galician peasants have been so enraged by their cattle being carried off for the use of the French army that they will rise in insurrection the instant the French march, and if that is the case, they and Romana ought to be able to give Soult a lot of trouble before he reaches Orense."

"I don't think those fellows with Romana are likely to do much, sir. The French will just sweep them before them."

"I am afraid so, Bull; still, if we can prevent the French from crossing here and compel them to follow the long road through Monterey, we shall have done good service. It would give Portugal another seven or eight days to prepare, and will send the enemy through a country where undisciplined troops ought to be able to make a stand even against soldiers like the French."

All through the night Terence and his major patrolled the bank from the point facing Campo Sancos to a mile below that on which the French were placing their guns. Everything went on quietly, sentries at intervals kept watch, and the men, wrapped in their blankets, lay down in parties of fifty at short intervals.

"The day is beginning to break," Terence said, as he met Bull coming back from the lower end of the line. "I am not afraid now, for if we can but see them coming we can gather two or three hundred men at any point they may be making for. Besides, our shooting would be very wild in the dark."

"That it would, sir; not one shot in fifty would hit the boats, let alone the men; and when the Portuguese saw the boats come on without pause in spite of their fire, they would be likely to lose heart and to get unsteady."

"We may as well stop here, Bull. It will be light enough

to see across the river in another quarter of an hour, and if there are no boats coming then, I think it is pretty certain that they will not begin until to-morrow night. The peasant said that they have only got 10,000 troops there as yet, and we know that Soult has more than double that, and he may wait another day for them all to come up."

Ten minutes later one of the sentries close to them shouted out that he could see boats. Terence ran up to him.

"Where are they, my man?"

"Nearly opposite, sir."

Terence gazed fixedly for a moment, and then said: "I see them; they are heading straight across." Then he gave the order to the man who always accompanied him with a horn, to blow the alarm.

At the sound, the troops sprang to their feet, and some hundreds of peasants, who were lying down a short distance behind, ran up. The horn was evidently heard on the other side of the river, for immediately the guns of the battery opposite opened fire, and their shot whizzed overhead. The boats plied their oars vigorously, and the French soldiers cheered; they were but some three hundred yards away when first discovered. The Portuguese were coming rapidly up at the double. Terence shouted that not a shot was to be fired until he gave the order. He was obeyed by his own men, but the peasants at once began a wild fire at the boats. By the time these were within fifty yards of the shore Terence saw with satisfaction that fully a company had come up. The men stood firmly, although the balls from the French battery ploughed up the ground around them.

"Wait until the first boat grounds," Terence shouted again. Another minute and the first fishing-boat touched the shore. Then the horn sounded, and the front line of the Portuguese poured a terrible volley into it. A few of the

French soldiers only succeeded in gaining the land, and these were at once shot down. Then the troops opened a rolling fire upon the other boats. The French replied with their musketry, but their fire was feeble. They had expected to have effected a landing with but slight opposition, and the concentrated fire of the troops and the peasantry convinced them that, even should they gain the shore, they would be greatly outnumbered, and would be shot down before they could gather in any regular formation. Many of the rowers, who were Spanish peasants forced into the work, had fallen. Most of their comrades left the oars and threw themselves into the bottom of the boats, and the craft drifted down the stream.

Shouts of triumph rose from the Portuguese, who obeyed the signal to form fours, and marched along parallel with the boats, forming line occasionally and firing heavy volleys. The French soldiers now seized the oars and rowed the craft into the middle of the river, and then slowly and painfully made their way to Campo Sancos, having lost more than half of the three hundred men who had left there. The French battery ceased to fire, and the din of battle was succeeded by a dead silence. Once convinced that the French had abandoned the attempt to land, the Portuguese broke into loud shouts of triumph, which were only checked when Terence ordered them to form up in close order. When they did so he addressed a few words to them, complimenting them upon the steadiness that they had shown, and upon their obeying his order to reserve their fire till the French were close at hand.

"I was convinced that you would behave well," he said, "and in future I shall have no hesitation in meeting a body of French equal in numbers to yourselves."

Messengers were at once despatched to order up all the troops that had been posted below, and in two hours the whole force, with the exception of the three companies, between them and Salvatierra, were assembled.

"The question is, Herrara," Terence said, when he and his colonel had exchanged congratulations on the repulse of the French, "what will Soult do next?"

"That is a question upon which everything depends. I don't think he will try again here. He has been eight days in preparing those boats to cross, and now that he knows there is a very strong force here, and that even if he got three or four times as many boats he would scarcely be able to force a passage, my idea is that he will abandon the attack and march at once for Orense. In that case the question is, shall we wait until we have assured ourselves that he has gone, and then follow and harass his rear? or shall we march up the river and then cross to help Romana to bar his passage?"

"I think the latter will be the best plan. You see, we should not be cutting his communication were we to march now, because when he has crossed the river Avia he will have direct communication with Ney, and will of course draw all his supplies from the north, so I think that we had better lose no time in pushing up along the river."

The troops were ordered to light fires and cook their breakfast. While this was going on Terence assembled the peasant bands, and told them that he thought the French would not make another attempt to cross, but that they must remain in a state of watchfulness until they received certain news from the other side that they had marched for Orense.

As soon as breakfast was over and the cooking-pots packed in the cart, the two regiments started on their march. They were in high spirits, and laughed and sang as they tramped along. They had lost but two killed by the French musketry fire, and there were but five so severely wounded as to be unable to take their places in the ranks. These Terence ordered to be taken in a country cart to Pontelima, and he provided them with money for their support there until cured.

The men having been on foot all night, Terence halted them after doing fifteen miles. On the following morning, soon after they had started, they saw a large body of French cavalry following the road by the river. These were La Houssaye's, who had been quartered at Salvatierra. The river here was narrower than it had been below, and halting the troops and forming them in line, two or three volleys were fired across the river. These did some execution, and caused much confusion in the French ranks. The horsemen, however, galloped rapidly up the river, and were soon out of range.

"That settles the question, Herrara. The French are retracing their steps, and bound for Orense. Soult has not let the grass grow under his feet, and the cavalry are evidently sent on to clear out any bands of peasants that may be gathering at the rivers."

La Houssaye, indeed, twice in the course of the day broke up irregular bands, and burned two villages. The infantry and artillery, after passing through Salvatierra, moved by the main road. This, however, was found to be so bad that the artillery were, with ten of the sixteen light guns, and six howitzers, left behind at Tuy, with a great ammunition and baggage train, together with 900 sick. A garrison of 500 men were left in the fort. Orders were given that all stragglers were to be retained at that place.

The march of the French was not unopposed. When they arrived at the river Morenta they found 800 Spaniards had barricaded the bridges and repulsed the advance parties of cavalry. On the 17th, at daybreak, the leading division attacked them fiercely, carried the bridge, and pursued them

"THE FRENCH CAVALRY RODE UP TOWARDS THE SQUARES, BUT WERE MET WITH HEAVY VOLLEYS."

hotly, until at a short distance from Ribadavia the Spaniards rallied upon some 10,000 irregulars arrayed in order of battle in a strong position covering the town. The rest of the division and a brigade of cavalry came up, and, directed by Soult himself, attacked the Spaniards, drove them through the town and across the Avia with great loss. Twenty priests were found among the slain. The next day three or four thousand other irregulars from the valley of Avia were attacked and scattered, and on the 18th the French cavalry, with three brigades of infantry, entered Orense.

An hour earlier Terence had arrived on the other side of the river, and had at once made preparations for blowing up the bridge. The men had been but a short time at work when numbers of the townsmen streamed across the bridge and reported that a great body of the French were entering the town. Terence had a hasty consultation with Herrara, and both agreed that they could not hope to hold the bridge long against the whole French army, especially as they had learned two hours before from a peasant who had ridden up, that strong bodies of French troops had crossed the river by the ferries at Ribadavia and Barbibante, and that they might shortly be attacked in flank. The powder-barrels were therefore hastily repacked, and the troops marched off towards the hills on their left.

They were but half-way across the plain when a regiment of French cavalry were seen riding in pursuit. The regiments were at once formed into squares within fifty yards of each other, and Terence and Bull in the centre of one square, and Herrara and Macwitty in the other, exhorted the men to stand steady, assuring them there was nothing whatever to be feared from the cavalry if they did so. The French rode up towards the squares, but were met by heavy volleys, and after riding round them drew off, having suffered considerable loss, being greatly surprised at finding that instead of a mob of armed men, such as they had met at Avia, they were encountered by soldiers possessing the steadiness of trained troops.

The regiments resumed their march until far up the hill, where they proceeded to cut down trees and brushwood and to form an encampment, as their leader had decided to stay here and await events until Soult's intentions were clearly shown. There were two courses open to the French general. He might advance to Allaritz and then march along the Lima, be joined by his artillery and train from Tuy, and then move direct upon Oporto, or he might follow the valley of the Tamega to Chaves, whence he would have the choice of routes, and take either that over the Sierra de Cabrera to Braga, or continue his course down the valley until he reached the Douro.

It was not until the 4th of March that the French again moved forward. In the meantime Terence was forced to remain quiet, except that each day he marched his men farther among the hills and drilled them for some hours perseveringly. The affair on the Minho and the repulse of the French cavalry had given them great confidence in themselves and their leader, and had shown them the value of steadiness, and of maintaining order and discipline in the ranks. They therefore devoted themselves even more willingly and zealously than before to their military exercises, and the ten days taken by Soult in preparing for the advance were well spent in accustoming the Portuguese to rapid movements among the mountains, and to attaining a fair knowledge of what would be required of them in mountain warfare. Two companies always remained in the camp, and these had several skirmishes with bodies of French marauders, and small parties of cavalry making across the country to ascertain the position and strength of the Portuguese.

The advance of the French was rapid, and on the 5th the cavalry and a portion of the infantry reached Villa Real, where, on the evening of the same day, two divisions of infantry arrived. That night Terence with his men having on the 4th marched along the hills parallel to the road, made a forced march, crossed the road and took up a position on the spur of the mountains between Montalegre and the river. Even yet it was doubtful which route Soult intended to follow, as the division at Villa Real might be intended only to prevent Romana and Silveira falling upon his flank. As he marched down the valley of the Lima, he had learned from Romana that he and Silveira had decided to fall back to Chaves, and that he agreed with Terence's opinion that he had better remain in the rear of the French, and intercept their communications with Orense.

On the following morning the French advanced in force to Monterey. Romana abandoned the position as they advanced, drew off to Verin, and then retired along the road towards Sanabria. He thus left it open to himself either to follow the road to Chaves, as agreed upon, or to retire into Spain through the mountains. Franceschi's cavalry and a battalion of French infantry overtook between two and three thousand men forming the rear of Romana's column. The latter drew up in a great square. Franceschi attacked the rear face with his infantry, passed with his cavalry round the sides of the square, and placed himself between it and the rest of the retiring column. He had with him four regiments of cavalry, and now hurled a regiment at each side of the square.

The Spaniards were at once seized with dismay, broke their formation, and in a moment the French cavalry were upon them, cutting and trampling them down. Twelve hundred were killed and the rest made prisoners. As soon as Romana heard of the disaster that had befallen his rear-guard, he broke his engagement with Silveira and led his force over the mountains into Spain, where the news of his defeat caused the Spanish insurgent bands to disperse rapidly to their homes, where they delivered up their arms; and even the priests, who had been the main promoters of the rising, seeing the failure of all their plans, advised them to maintain a peaceable attitude in future.

Silveira was not more fortunate, for two thousand of his troops with some guns, issuing from the mountains just as Franceschi returned from the annihilation of Romana's rearguard, the French cavalry charged and captured the Portuguese guns, and drove Silveira down the valley.

Soult paused two days at Monterey, the baggage and hospital train, and a great convoy of provisions being brought up from Orense, under the guard of a whole division. This rendered it evident that he intended to cut himself off altogether from Spain, and to subsist entirely upon the country. It was clear then that it was useless to attempt to fall upon his rear, and by a long march through the mountains Terence took his force down to Chaves.

Here he found that Silveira, deserted by Romana and beaten by Franceschi, had fallen back to a mountain immediately behind Chaves. Terence continued his march until he joined him. He found a great tumult going on among his troops; always insubordinate, they were now in a state of mutiny. Many of the officers openly advocated that they should desist from a struggle in which success was altogether hopeless, and should go over and join the French. The troops, however, not only spurned the advice, but fell upon and killed several of those who offered it, and demanded from Silveira that he should lead them down to defend Chaves. This he refused to do, saying that the fortifications were old and useless, the guns worn out, and that were they to shut themselves up there, they would be surrounded and forced to surrender.

This refusal excited the mutineers to the highest pitch, and when Terence arrived they were clamouring for his death. A small party of soldiers who remained faithful to him surrounded him, but they would speedily have been overpowered had it not been for the arrival of Terence's command. As soon as he understood what was happening, he formed his men into a solid body, marched through the excited crowd, and formed up in hollow square round the general. The firm appearance of the force and the fact that they possessed more arms than the whole of Silveira's army, had its effect. The mutineers, however, to the number of 3,500, determined to carry out their intentions, and at once marched away to Chaves. Silveira remained with but a few hundred men, as the 2,000 routed by Franceschi had not rejoined him.

"I owe you my life, señor," he said to Terence, "for those mad fools would certainly have murdered me."

"It is not surprising," Terence said. "A mob of men who are not soldiers cannot be expected to observe discipline, especially when insubordination and anarchy have been absolutely fomented by the authorities, crimes of all sorts perpetrated by their orders, and no efforts whatever made to punish ill-doers."

"Your men seem to be disciplined and obedient," Silveira said.

"They have been taught to be so, General, and I believe that I can rely upon them absolutely. If you had but officers and discipline, I am certain that your soldiers would be excellent; but as it is, with a few exceptions, your officers are worse than useless. They are appointed as a reward for their support of the Junta; they are ignorant of their duties, and many of them favour the French; they regard their soldiers as raised, not for the defense of Portugal, but for the support of the Junta. I have seen enough to know that the peasants are brave, hardy, and ready to fight. But what can they do when they are but half-armed, and no attempt whatever is made to discipline them? Have you heard, since these troubles began, of a single man being shot for insubordination, or of a single officer being punished even for the grossest neglect of orders? It is nothing short of murder to put a mob of half-armed peasants to stand against French troops."

"All that is quite true," Silveira said, heartily. "However, I shall do my best, and shall, I doubt not, soon have another force collected, for now that the French have fairly entered Portugal, and are marching towards the capital, every man will take up arms. And you, señor, what do you mean to do?"

"I shall harass the French as I see an opportunity, but I shall not subject my men to certain disaster by joining any of the new levies. I know what my men can do, and what I can do with them; but if mixed up with thousands of raw peasants they would be swept away by the latter and share in any misfortune that might befall them. What I have seen of your troops to-day, and what I saw of Romana's, is quite enough to show me that to lead peasants into the field is simply to bring misfortune and death upon them. Far better that each leader should collect two or three hundred men and teach them discipline and a little drill instead of taking a mob thousands strong out to battle. Those men that have marched down into Chaves will, you will see, offer no resistance, and will simply be killed or made prisoners to a man. Now, may I ask if you have any stores here, General? We have had great difficulty in buying food up in the mountains, and as it will be useless to you, and certainly cannot be carried off, I should be glad to fill the men's haversacks before we go farther."

"Certainly. I had enough meat and bread for my whole force for a week, and you are welcome to take as much as you require. Which way do you propose marching?"

"I am waiting to see which way the French go after leaving Chaves. Whether they go down the valley or across the mountains to Braga, I shall endeavour to get ahead of them; and as my men are splendid marchers, I have no doubt that I shall succeed in doing so, even if the French have a few hours' start. If I can do nothing else, I can at least make their cavalry keep together instead of riding in small parties all over the country to sweep in food."

Fires were soon lighted, some bullocks killed and cut up, and a hearty meal eaten. They had already made a very long march, and were ordered to lie down until nightfall. Silveira marched away with his men, and Terence and Herrara sat and watched the road, down which bodies of French troops could already be seen advancing from Monterey towards Chaves. As they approached the town, gun after gun was fired. The advance-guard halted and waited until the whole division had come up.

CHAPTER XVI

IN THE PASSES

ON the following day the French cavalry, with a division of infantry, took up their position beyond the town, so as to cut off the retreat of the garrison, who were then summoned to surrender. No reply was made, but for the next twenty-four hours the defenders, although in no way attacked, kept up a random fire from the guns on the walls, and with musketry, to which no reply whatever was made by the French.

On the following day, the whole army having now come up, the town was again summoned, and at once surrendered, when Soult, who did not wish to be hampered with a mob of prisoners, contemptuously allowed them to depart to their homes.

After bringing up his sick from Chaves, and discovering that the passes through the mountains were unoccupied, and that the Portuguese army was at Braga, Soult, on the 14th, began to move in that direction, both for the purpose of crushing Friere and getting into communication with Tuy, and being joined by his artillery from there. As soon as this movement was seen from the hill where Terence's regiments had been for three days resting, preparations were made for marching, and with haversacks well filled with bread and meat, the troops started in good spirits. Terence procured the services of a peasant well acquainted with the mountains, and was led by paths used by shepherds across the hills, and after a twelve hours' toilsome journey came down into the defiles that the French were following. There he learned from peasants, that, with the exception of a small scouting party two days before, there were no signs of any hostile force.

The men were at once set to work to destroy a bridge across a torrent at the mouth of a defile. It was built of stone, but was old and in bad repair, and the men had little difficulty in prising the stones of the side walls from their places, and throwing them down into the stream. Another party made a hole over the key of an arch. A barrel of powder was placed here, and a train having been laid, was covered up by a pile of rocks. A third party formed a barricade six feet high, across the end of the bridge, and also two breastworks, each fifty yards away on either side, so as to flank the approaches to the other end and the bridge. The troops were extended along the hillsides, one battalion on each side of the defile, under the shelter of the rocks and brush.

While these preparations were being made, the horses were taken up to the top of the hills by some paths known to the peasants of a little village near the mouth of the defile, the women and children following them. Terence and Herrara had a consultation, and then the former called Bull and Macwitty to him.

"Now," he said, "you understand that while we will defend this defile as long as we can, we will run no risk of a defeat that might end in a rout. We shall inflict heavy loss upon them before they can repair the bridge, and can certainly force their cavalry to remain quiet until they bring up their infantry. Colonel Herrara, you, with one company of the second battalion, will hold the village, and we shall sweep the column advancing along the bottom of the defile with a fire from each flank, while they will also be exposed to your fire in front. When they succeed in making their way up to within charging distance you will evacuate the village and join Macwitty on the hill.

"They must attack us there on both sides, for no troops could march through until the hillsides are cleared. It is probable that they may do this before they attempt to attack the village, but in any case you must keep up a steady fire until they get within fifty yards of you, then retire up the hill, but leave a party to keep them in check until the rest have gained the crest and formed up in good order. By the time you do this they will have driven in your rear-guard. The French will be breathless with their exertions when they reach you. Wait till a considerable number have gained the crest, then, before they have time to form, pour a heavy volley into them and charge, and then sweep them with your fire until they reach the bottom. The next time they will no doubt attack in much greater force; in that case we will move quietly off without waiting for them, and will reunite at the village of Romar, five miles in the rear. If we find, as we near it, that the French are in possession, we will halt, and I will send orders to the second regiment as to what is to be done. If the force is not too great we will attack them at night."

"How will you know where we shall be, sir?" Macwitty said.

"I have arranged with Colonel Herrara that when you halt you shall light two fires a short distance from each other. I will reply by lighting one, and the fires are then to be extinguished."

This being arranged, Terence went down and applied a match to the train, and then retired at a run. Three minutes later there was a heavy explosion, rocks flew high in the air, and when the smoke cleared away, a cheer from the hillside told that the explosion had been successful. Terence returned to the bridge; a considerable portion of the arch had been blown away, and putting fifty men to work, the gap was soon carried across the road and widened, so that there was a chasm twelve feet across. The parties who were to man the breastworks were now posted. Terence himself took the command here. The defenders consisted of a company of Bull's battalion.

Half an hour later a deep sound was heard, and as it grew louder the head of a column of cavalry was seen approaching. The whole of the force on the hillsides were hidden behind rocks or brushwood; not a head was shown above the breastworks. The cavalry, however, halted, and an officer with four men rode forward. When within fifty yards of the bridge a volley of twenty muskets flashed out from the work behind it. The officer and three men fell, the other galloped back to the main body. He had seen nothing beyond the fact that there was a breastwork across the road, and Franceschi, thinking that he had but a small force of peasants in front of him, ordered a squadron to charge, and clear the obstacle.

As before, they were allowed to approach to within fifty yards of the bridge, when from the breastwork in front, and the two side redoubts a storm of musketry was poured into them. The effect was terrible; the head of the squadron was swept away, but a few men charged forward until close to the break in the bridge. Most of these fell, but a few galloped back, and the remains of the squadron then trotted off in good order.

No further movement took place for an hour, and then a body of infantry, some two thousand strong, appeared. As they passed the cavalry, the first two companies were thrown out in skirmishing order, and were soon swarming down towards the stream. The banks of this, although very steep, were not impassable by infantry, and the defenders of the two side redoubts spread themselves out along the bank, and, as the skirmishers approached, opened fire.

For a time the rattle of firearms was incessant. When the main body of French infantry had, as their commander thought, ascertained the strength of the defenders, they advanced in solid order until near the bridge, and then wheeled off on either flank and advanced with loud shouts. A horn was sounded, and from the hillsides near a scattering fire of musketry opened at once. The French, however, pushed forward without a pause. Terence's horn sounded again, the men fell back from the bank, and the whole company ran at full speed across the narrow valley, and took their place with their comrades on the hillside.

The French crossed the stream under a heavy fire, and, dividing into two portions, prepared to assault both hills simultaneously. The combat was obstinate, the French suffered heavily, but pushed their way up unflinchingly. The Portuguese, encouraged by the shouts of their officers, held their ground obstinately, retreating only at the sound of their horns, and renewing the combat a short distance higher up. Being sheltered by the rocks behind which they lay, their loss was but trifling in comparison to that of the French, who were forced to expose themselves as they advanced, and whose numbers dwindled so rapidly that when half-way up they were on both sides brought to a stand-still, and then, taking shelter behind the rocks, they maintained the contest on more equal terms.

But by this time a column of 4,000 men was marching down to the stream, and, dividing like the first, climbed the hills. The Portuguese now fell back more rapidly, their fire slackened, and the French, with loud shouts, pressed up the hill. Presently the resistance ceased altogether, and, firing as they advanced at the flying figures, of whom they caught an occasional glimpse, the French pressed forward as rapidly as the nature of the ground would permit, cheering loudly. At last they reached the top of the hill, and the leaders paused in doubt as they saw before them some eleven or twelve hundred men drawn up in line four deep at a distance of fifty yards. Every moment added to the number of the French, and as they arrived their officers tried to form them into order. When their numbers about equalled those of the Portuguese, two heavy volleys were poured into them, and then, with loud shouts, the Portuguese rushed at them with levelled bayonets.

The charge was irresistible. The French were hurled over the crest and went down the hill, carrying confusion and dismay among those climbing up. The Portuguese pressed them hotly, giving them no time to rally, and forcing them down to the bottom of the hill without a check. Then at the signal they fell back to the post that they had held at the beginning of the fight. The success was equal on both hillsides, and the regiments cheered each other's victory with shouts which rose high above the roar of musketry. With their usual discipline, the French speedily rallied, in spite of the heavy fire that from both sides swept their ranks, and they prepared, when joined by another regiment which was approaching at the double to their assistance, to renew the assault.

Terence saw that, this time, the odds would be too great to withstand. His horn sounded the retreat, and the Portuguese turned to make their way up the hill just as a French battery opened fire. Sheltered among the rocks, the infantry below were unconscious of the movement, for on either side a company had been left to continue their fire until the main body gained the top of the hill, when they too were summoned by the horns to fall back. The wounded had been all taken up the hill, and were laid in blankets and carried off by their comrades. As the two regiments marched away from the crest of the defile the soldiers were in the highest spirits. They had repulsed with heavy loss a French force of three times their own strength, and they greeted Terence and Bull, as they rode together along the column, with enthusiastic cheers.

The wounded, which in the first battalion numbered forty-three, were despatched with a party a hundred strong to a village four miles away among the mountains, and the regiment marched on until it reached the point agreed upon.

Two men were sent forward to reconnoitre the village, and returned with the report that it had already been occupied by a very strong force of French cavalry. Half an hour later two wreaths of smoke rose on the opposite hill. Sticks had been gathered in readiness, and the answering signal was at once made. Two minutes later the smoke ceased to rise on either side. Terence now received the reports of the captains of the six companies, and found that fifteen men had been killed, and that his strength was thus reduced by fifty-eight. The men were now told that they could lie down, the companies keeping together so as to be ready for instant action.

Trifling wounds, of which there were some two or three and twenty, were then attended to and bandaged. Some of these were quite serious enough to have warranted the men falling out, but the delight and pride they felt at their success had been so great that they had refused to be taken off with their disabled comrades. Terence made a round of the troops and addressed a few words to each company, praising their conduct, and thanking them for the readiness and quickness with which they had obeyed his orders.

"You see, my lads," he said, "what can be done by discipline. Had it not been for the steady drill you have had ever since we marched, we could not have hoped to oppose the French, and I should not have ventured to have done so. Now, you see, you have proved that you are as brave as the enemy, and not only have you beaten them with heavy loss, but the effect of this fight will be to render them more cautious in future and slower in their movements, and the news of the blow you have struck will inspirit your countrymen everywhere."

Having nothing else to do until after darkness fell, Terence, after finishing his round, sat down and added an account of the fight to the report he had written up at their last halting-place. This was written in duplicate, one copy being intended for General Cradock, and the other for the Portuguese authorities at Oporto. Outposts had been thrown out towards the village as soon as they halted, and after opening their haversacks, eating a meal, and quenching their thirst at a little rivulet that ran down to the village, the men lay down to sleep, tired with their long night's march and the excitement of the battle.

Terence was no exception to the general rule, for although

he had had his horse, yet for the greater part of the distance he had marched on foot, as the ruggedness of the ground traversed had in most places been too great to travel in safety on horseback in the dark. When night fell all were on their feet again, refreshed by a long sleep. Two men were now sent down to reconnoitre the village again. They reported that it was still occupied by the cavalry. The infantry, as they could see by the fires along the road, had bivouacked there, and one regiment at least had passed through the village and had occupied the road ahead.

Terence had already written out his instructions to Herrara in triplicate, and three men were despatched with these. They were warned to be extremely careful, for the men who had first been sent, had reported that the French had posted sentries out on their flanks. One of the messengers was to make a long detour to cross the road half a mile ahead of the French, and then to make his way along on the opposite hillside to the spot where Herrara was posted. The other two were to make their way as best they could through the village. The pieces of paper they carried were rolled up into little balls, and they were ordered that, if noticed and an alarm given, these were at once to be swallowed.

Soon after ten o'clock the regiment formed up. Terence had given detailed orders to the captain of each company. These were instructed to call up their men twenty at a time, and to explain their orders to them, so that every man should know exactly what to do. No sound had been heard in the village, and Terence felt sure that Herrara must have received his orders, and at a quarter past ten he with one company moved slowly down towards the village; Bull, with the main body of the force, marching westward along the hills. Six men had volunteered for the service of silencing the French outposts, and these, leaving their muskets behind, stole forward in advance of the company, which halted at some little distance from the French centre.

In a quarter of an hour they returned. Eight French sentries had been surprised and killed, the Portuguese crawling up to them until near enough to spring upon and stab them without the slightest alarm being given. The company now moved silently forward again until within a hundred yards of the village, when they halted until the church clock struck eleven. Then they rushed down into the village. As they entered it shots were fired, and an outcry rose from the other side, showing that Herrara had managed matters as well as they had. The surprise was complete; the street was full of horses, while the soldiers had taken shelter in the houses. A scene of the wildest confusion ensued. The horses were shot, for it was most important to cripple this most formidable arm of the French service, and the men were attacked as they poured out of the houses.

Bull, with a hundred men, made his way straight to the upper end of the village and repelled the desperate attempts of a squadron of horse that were posted beyond it in readiness for action, to break through to the assistance of their comrades, while Terence and Herrara, each with a hundred men, held the road at the lower end of the village to check an infantry attack there. It was not long before it was delivered. The French infantry, disciplined veterans, accustomed to surprises, had sprung to their feet when the first shot was fired, and forming instantly into column, came on at a run, led by their officers. Terence, with fifty men, four deep, barred the way across the road; the rest of his men were stationed along the high ground flanking it on one side, while Herrara with his hundred flanked the opposite side.

As the French came on the Portuguese on the high ground remained silent and unnoticed, but when a flash of fire ran across the road and a deadly volley was poured in upon the enemy, those on the flanks at once opened fire. For a moment the column paused in surprise, and then opened fire at their unseen assailants, whose fire was causing such gaps in the ranks. The colonel and several other officers who had been at its head had fallen; in the din no orders could be heard, and for some minutes the head of the column wasted away under the rain of bullets. Then a general officer dashed up, and another body of Frenchmen came along at a run. Terence's horn rang out loudly; the signal was repeated in the village, the fire instantly ceased, and when the French column rushed into the place not a foe was to be seen, but the street was choked up by dead horses and men.

These reinforcements did not pause, but making their way over the obstacles pressed on to where a roar of fire in front showed how hotly the advance-guard was engaged. Here the surprise had been rather less complete. Some of the outposts had given the alarm, and the French were on their feet before, after pouring terrible volleys into them, a thousand men fell upon them on either side. Great numbers of the French fell under the fire, and the long line was broken up into sections by the impetuous rush of the Portuguese. Nevertheless, the French soldiers hung together, and the combat raged desperately until the head of the relieving column came up. Then, as suddenly as before, the attack ceased. Not a gun was fired, and, as if by magic, their assailants stole away into the darkness, while the French opened a random fire after them.

An hour later the two Portuguese regiments united on the road two miles in advance of the village. Their loss had been eighty-four killed and a hundred and fifty wounded, of which seventy were serious cases. These were, as before, sent off to be cared for in the mountain villages. The French loss, as Terence afterward heard, had been very heavy;

three hundred of the cavalry had been killed, and upwards of four hundred infantry. Great was the enthusiasm when the two regiments met, and after a short halt marched away together into the hills and encamped in a wood two miles from the road.

"What next, Generalissimo?" Herrara, whose left arm had been broken by a bullet, asked.

"I think that we have done enough for the present," Terence said. "We will leave it to the rest of the army to do a little fighting now. We have lost, in killed and wounded, some two hundred men, and I don't wish to see the whole force dwindle away. I propose that we do not go near Braga. I have no idea of putting myself under the command of Friere; I have seen enough of him already. So we will travel by by-roads till we get near Oporto, then we will find out how matters stand there. My own idea is that when the French army approaches, the Junta's courage will ooze out of its finger ends, and that the 50,000 peasants, which it calls an army, will bolt at the first attack of the French. So, as I don't mean to be trapped there, we will rest on our laurels until we see how matters go."

It was well for the corps that Terence abstained from joining the army at Braga. As the French entered the pass of Benda Nova, the peasants rushed furiously down upon them. Many broke into the French columns, and fighting desperately, were slain. The survivors made their way up the hillside, and then making a detour, fell upon the rear of the column, killed fifty stragglers and plundered the baggage. This spontaneous action of the peasants was the only attempt made to bar the advance of the French, and Friere permitted them to pass through defile after defile without firing a shot. His conduct aroused the fury of his troops, and the feeling was fanned by agents of the bishop, who had now become jealous of him, and his men rushing upon him dragged him from a house in which he had taken refuge, and slew him—a fit end to the career of a man who had proved himself as unpatriotic as he was incapable.

On the 18th Soult arrived near Braga, and the Portuguese, who were now commanded by Eben, a German officer in the British service, drew up to meet him. The French began their advance on the 20th, and half an hour later the Portuguese army was a mob of fugitives. The vanquished army lost 4,000 men and all their guns, 400 only being taken prisoners; the rest dispersed in all directions, carrying tales of the invincibility of the French. Had it not been for the stout resistance offered by 3,000 men, placed on a position in the rear commanding the road, which checked the pursuit of the cavalry and enabled the fugitives to make off, scarce a man of the Portuguese would have escaped to tell the tale.

Terence had approached Oporto, and encamped in a large wood, when the fugitives brought him news of the crushing defeat that they had suffered. The soldiers were so furious when they heard of the disgraceful rout, that Terence and Herrara had difficulty in preventing them from killing the fugitives. The result strengthened his position. The troops on arriving at their present camping-place were eager to be led into Oporto. Terence and Herrara had talked the matter over several times, and agreed that such a step might be fatal. Standing, as this town did, on the north side of the river, the only means of leaving it was the bridge of boats, and if anything happened to this all retreat would be cut off.

The defeat at Braga at once confirmed their opinion that the army of peasants that the bishop had gathered round Oporto would be able to make but little resistance to the French attack.

"It would be terrible," Herrara said; "50,000 fugitives,

and a great portion of the inhabitants of the town, all struggling to cross the bridge, with the French cavalry pressing on their rear, and the French artillery playing upon them. It is not to be thought of."

The troops, however, had been full of confidence in the valour of their countrymen, and from their own success against the French believed that the army at Braga would certainly defeat Soult, and there had been some dissatisfaction that they had not been permitted to take part in the victory. The news brought by the fugitives at once dissipated the hopes that they had entertained. They saw that their commander had acted wisely in refusing to join the army there, and their feeling of contempt for the undisciplined ordenanças and peasants equalled the confidence they had before reposed in them. Terence ordered the two regiments to form into a hollow square and addressed them.

"Soldiers," he said, "I know that it was a disappointment to you that I did not take you to Braga. Had I done so, not one of you would have escaped, for when the rest fled like a flock of sheep you could not alone have withstood the attack of the whole French army. I know that you wish to enter Oporto. I have withstood that wish, and now you must see that I was right in doing so. The peasants gathered in its defence are even less disciplined than those at Braga, and Soult will, after two or three minutes' fighting, capture the place. Were you there you could not prevent such a result. You might hold the spot at which you were stationed, but if the French broke in at any other point you would be surrounded and killed to a man. What use would that be to Portugal? You can do more good by living and fighting another day.

"Even if you should fall back with the other fugitives, what chance of safety would there be? You know that there is but one bridge of boats across the river, and that will soon be blocked by a panic-stricken crowd, and your chance of crossing would be slight indeed. The men who fought at Braga, those men who will fight before Oporto, are no more cowards than you are, and had they gained as much discipline as you have, I would march down with you at once and join in the defence. But a mob cannot withstand disciplined troops. When the Portuguese have learned to be soldiers, they may fight with a hope of success; until then it is taking them to slaughter to set them in line of battle against the French. Soult may be here in twenty-four hours, therefore I propose to march you down to the river above Oporto. We are sure to find boats there, and we will cross at once to the other side and encamp near the suburb at the south end of the bridge, and when the fugitives pour over we will take our station there, cover their retreat, and prevent the French from crossing in pursuit."

A murmur of satisfaction broke from the soldiers and swelled into a shout. Soon after evening fell the corps marched from the wood, and two hours later came down on the bank of the Douro. As Terence anticipated, there were plenty of fishermen's boats hauled up, and the regiments passed over by companies. By three in the morning all were across, and by five they encamped in a wood beyond the steep hill rising behind the Villa Nova suburb, on the left bank of the river. As soon as he had seen the soldiers settled Terence borrowed the clothes of one of the men, and putting these on instead of his uniform, he sent for Bull and Macwitty, and the two soldiers soon arrived. They looked in astonishment at their officer.

"I am going into the town," he said, "partly to judge for myself of the state of things there, and partly on a little private business of my own. It is possible that I may get into trouble. I hope that I shall not do so, but it is as well to be prepared for any emergency that might happen. If, then, I do not return, you are to look to Colonel Herrara for orders. When the French enter Oporto, which I am certain they will do as soon as they attack it, you may gather your men at this end of the bridge, cover the retreat, and repulse all efforts of the French to cross. As soon as those attempts have ceased, you will march with the two regiments for Coimbra, and report yourselves to the officer commanding there. Here are my despatches to the general, in which I have done full justice to your bravery and your conduct. Here is also a note to the officer commanding at Coimbra. I have spoken to him about your conduct, and have asked him to allow you to continue with the Portuguese until an order is received from Sir John Cradock. I have given Colonel Herrara a duplicate of my despatches and official orders, in case you should be killed."

"Cannot we go with you, sir?" Bull asked.

"I don't think so, Bull. Dress as you might, you could hardly be taken for anything but an Englishman. Your walk and your complexion, to say nothing of your hair, would betray you both at once. The first person who happened to address you would discover that you were not natives, and the chances are he would denounce you, and that you would be torn to pieces before you could offer any explanation. Now, I think that I can pass readily enough. The wind and rough weather have brought me to nearly the right colour, and I know how to speak Portuguese well enough to ask any question without exciting suspicion."

"But why not take two of the men with you?" Macwitty said. "They could do any talking that was necessary; and should anyone suggest that you are not a native, they could declare that you were a comrade from their own village."

Bull strongly approved of the suggestion, and Terence, though in some respects he would rather have been alone, at last agreed to it.

"They may as well take their arms; not for use, but to give them the appearance of two men from the camp who had come down to make purchases in the city."

Daylight was just breaking as the three crossed the bridge of boats into the town, and passed through it up the hill to the great camp that had been established there. It covered a large extent of ground, and contained tents sufficient for the whole of the 50,000 men assembled. A short distance away was the line of intrenchments on which the peasants had been for some weeks engaged. They consisted of forts crowning a succession of rounded hills, and connected by earthen ramparts, loopholed houses, ditches, and an abattis of felled trees. No less than two hundred guns were in place on the forts. It was a position that two thousand good troops should have been able to hold against an army.

"It is a strong position," Terence said to the two men with him.

"Yes, the French can never pass that," one of them said, exultingly.

"That we shall see. They ought not to, certainly, but whether they will or not is another matter."

They wandered about for a couple of hours. Once one of the Portuguese joined a group of peasants, and learned from them something of the state of things in the town, representing that they had but just arrived.

"You are lucky. You will see how we shall destroy the French army. Our guns will sweep them away. Every man in the town is full of confidence, and the traitors are all trembling in their houses. When the news of the business at Braga came yesterday, and we learned the treachery of our generals, the people rose, dragged fifteen suspected men of rank from the prison and killed them. There is not a day that some of these traitors are not rooted out."

"That is well," the other said; "it is traitors that have brought us to this pass."

"You will see how we shall fight when the French come. The bishop himself has promised to come out in his robes to give us his blessing, and to call down the wrath of heaven on the French infidels."

After having finished his survey of the line, Terence returned to the city, and following the instructions that he had received as to the situation of the convent at Santa Maria, he was not long in finding it. It was a massive building; the windows of the two lower stories were closely barred. He could not see any way of opening communications with his cousin, or of devising any way of escape. He, however, thought that it might possibly be managed if he could send in a rope to her and a pulley, with means of fixing it; in that way he could lower her to the ground. But all this would be very difficult to manage, even if he had ample time at his disposal, and in the present circumstances it was altogether impossible. He stared at the house for a long time in silence, but no idea came to him, and it was with a feeling of hopelessness that he recrossed the bridge and rejoined the troops.

"I am glad to see you back, sir," Bull said, heartily. "I have been in a funk all this morning that something might happen to you."

"It has all gone off quietly. I will now tell you and Macwitty what my business here is. I may need your help, and it is a matter in which none of the Portuguese would dare to offer me any assistance."

"I think they would do maist anything for you, sir," Macwitty said. "They have that confidence in you, they would go through fire and water if you were to lead them."

"They would do almost anything but what I want done now. I have a cousin, a young lady, who is an heiress to a large fortune. Her father is dead, and her mother, a wealthy land-owner, has had her shut up in a convent, where they are trying to force her, against her will, to become a nun. She is kept a prisoner, on bread and water, until she consents to sign a paper surrendering all her rights. Now, what I want to do is to get her out. It cannot be done by force; that is out of the question. It is a strong building, and even if the men would consent to attack a convent, which they would not do, all the town would be up, and we should have the whole populace on us. So that force is out of the question. Now, the French are sure to take the place. When they do, there will be an awful scene. They will be furious at the resistance they have met with, and at the losses that they have suffered. They will be maddened, and reasonably, by the frightful tortures inflicted upon prisoners who have fallen into the hands of the Portuguese, and you may be sure that for some time no quarter will be given. The soldiers will be let loose upon the city, and there will be no more respect for a convent than a dwelling-house. You may imagine how frightfully anxious I am. If it had not been for the French I would have let the matter stand until our army entered Oporto, but as it is, I must try and do something; and, as far as I can see, the only chance will be in the frightful confusion that will take place when the French enter the town."

"We will stand by you, Mr. O'Connor, you may be sure. You have only got to tell us what to do, and you may trust us to do it."

Macwitty, who was a man of few words, nodded. "Mr. O'Connor knows that," he said.

"Thank you both," Terence said, heartily. "I must think out my plan, and when I have decided upon it I will let you know."

CHAPTER XVII

AN ESCAPE

DURING his visit to the other side of the river Terence had seen, with great satisfaction, that a powerful battery, mounting fifty guns, had been erected on the heights of Villa Nova, and its fire, he thought, should effectually bar any attempt of the French to cross the bridge.

It would indeed be madness for them to attempt such an operation, as the boats supporting the bridge could be instantly sunk by the concentrated fire of the battery. He said nothing of this on his return to camp, as it might have given rise to fresh agitation among the men, were they to be aware that their presence was not really required for the defence of the bridge. After a short stay in camp he again went down into the town, with the idea that he was more likely to hit upon some plan of action there than he would be in the camp.

The two men again went with him. Another prolonged stare at the convent failed to inspire him with any scheme that was in the slightest degree practicable. He fell back upon the conclusion he had mentioned to the two troopers, that the only chance would be to take advantage of the wild confusion that would prevail upon the entry of the French. The difficulty that presented itself to him was, that the nuns would be so appalled by the approach of the French that it would be unlikely that they would think of leaving the protection—such as it was—of the convent, and would shrink from encountering the wild turmoil in the streets. Even if they did so, it would be too late for them to have any chance of getting across the bridge, which would be thronged to a point of suffocation by the mob of fugitives, and might readily be destroyed by one or two of the boats being sunk by the French artillery.

The one thing evident was, that he must arrange to get a boat and to station it at the end of some street going down to the river from the neighbourhood of the convent. That part of the city being some distance from the bridge, the streets would soon be deserted, and there would not be a wild rush of fugitives to the boat, which would be the case were it to be lying alongside anywhere near the bridge. Upon the other hand, it would be less likely that the nuns would leave the convent if all was comparatively quiet in that neighbourhood, and did they do so it would be difficult in the extreme to carry off his cousin from their midst, ignorant, too, as he was of her appearance. After looking for some time at the convent, he returned to the more busy part of the town. Presently he heard a great shouting; every window opened, and he saw a crowd coming along the street. By the candles, banners, crucifixes, and canopies it was evident that it was a religious procession. He was about to turn off into a side street when the thought struck him that possibly it was the bishop himself on his way up to the camp; therefore he remained in his place, doffed his hat, and, like all around him, went down on one knee.

The procession was a long and stately one, and in the midst, walking beneath a canopy, came the bishop himself. Terence gazed at him fixedly in order to impress on his mind the features of the man whose ambition had cost Portugal so dearly, and at whose instigation so much blood of the most honest and capable men of the province had been shed. The face fully justified the idea that he had formed of the man. The bishop was of commanding presence, and walked with the air of one who was accustomed to see all bow before him; but on the other hand, the face bore traces of his violent character. There was a set smile on his lips, but his brow was heavy and frowning, while his receding chin contradicted the strength of the upper part of his face. There was, too, a look of anxiety and restlessness betrayed by a nervous twitching of the lips.

"The scoundrel is a coward," Terence said to himself. "He may profess absolute confidence, but I don't think he feels it, and I will bet odds that he won't be in the front when the time for fighting comes."

Terence walked away after the procession had passed.

"If one could get hold of the bishop," he said to himself, "one might get an order on the superior of the convent to hand over Mary O'Connor to the bearer, but I don't see how that can possibly be managed. Of course, he is surrounded by priests and officials all day, and his palace will be guarded by any number of soldiers, for he must have many enemies. There must be scores of relatives of men who have been killed by his orders, who would assassinate him, bishop though he is, had they the chance. And even if I got an order—and it seems to me impossible to do so—it would not be made out in the name of Mary O'Connor. I know that they change their names when they go into nunneries, and she may be Sister Angela or Cecilia, or anything else, and I should not know in the slightest degree whether the name he put down was the one that she really goes by. No, that idea is out of the question."

Returning to the camp, he held counsel with Herrara. The

latter, he knew, had none of the bigotry so general among his countrymen. He had before told him about his cousin being shut up against her will, and of the letter that she had thrown out, but had hitherto said nothing of his intention to bring about her escape if possible.

"I had an idea that that was what was in your mind when you went off so early this morning, O'Connor. I have a high respect for the Church, but I have no respect for its abuses. And the shutting up of a young lady, and forcing her to take the veil in order to rob her of her property, is as hateful to me as it can be to you, so that I should have no hesitation in aiding you in your endeavour to bring about her escape. Have you formed any plan?"

"No; I have thought it over again and again, but cannot think of any scheme."

"If that is the case, O'Connor, I fear that it is useless for me to try to do so; you are so full of ideas always, that if you cannot see your way out of the difficulty, it is hopeless to expect that I could do so. If you can contrive any plan I will promise to aid you in any way you can point out, but as to inventing one, I should never do so if I racked my brain ever so much."

"There must be some way," Terence said. "I used to get into all sorts of scrapes when I was a boy, but found there was always some way out of them, if one could but hit upon it. The only thing that I can think of, is to carry her off in the confusion when the French enter the town."

"I should say that the nuns would never think of leaving their convent, O'Connor; it is their best hope of safety to remain there."

"No doubt it is, but the French don't always respect the convents—very much the contrary, indeed. No, I don't think that they would go out merely to rush into the street; but they might go out if they thought they could get over the bridge before the French arrived."

"They might do that, certainly; indeed, it would be the best thing they could do."

"Do you think that if one were to dress up as a priest, or as one of the bishop's attendants, and to go as from him with an order to the lady superior to take the nuns at once across the bridge to the convent on the other side, she would obey it?"

"Not without some written order," Herrara said. "The bishop would naturally send someone who would be known to her, or if he did send a stranger he would give him a letter or some token she would recognize; otherwise, she could not know that it was his order."

"That is what I was afraid of, Herrara, but it is what I shall try, if I can see no other way. Indeed, I see only one chance of getting over the difficulty. The bishop is a tyrant of the worst kind. Now, as far as I can remember, tyrants of his sort—that is to say, tyrants who rule by working on the passions of the mob—are always cowards. I watched the bishop closely when I saw him to-day, and I am convinced he is one also. Even in that kneeling crowd he could not conceal it. There was a nervous twitching about his lips which, to my mind, showed that he was in a state of intense anxiety, and that under all his swagger and show of confidence he was, nevertheless, in a horrible state of alarm. That being so, it seems to me extremely likely that when the fighting begins he will make a bolt of it. He won't wait for the French to enter, for he would know well enough that in their fury at their defeat, the fugitives, if they came upon him, would be likely to tear him limb from limb, just as they have murdered dozens of infinitely better men; so I think that he will make off beforehand. I imagine that he will go secretly, and with only two or three attendants."

"But you could never carry him off without an alarm being raised, if that is what you are thinking of, O'Connor."

"No, I am not thinking of that; but if I could, say with Bull and Macwitty, suddenly attack him like three robbers, we might carry off something that would serve as a sort of passport to the lady abbess. For instance, he had a tremendously big ring on. I noticed it as he held up his hands, as if on purpose to show it off."

"That was his episcopal ring," Herrara laughed. "Yes, if you could get hold of that, it would be a key that would open the door of any convent."

"Do you think she would hand my cousin over to me if I showed it to her and gave her a message as from the bishop?"

"Yes, if you knew the name. You see, from the day she was made a nun she lost her former name altogether; and certainly the bishop would send for her under her convent name."

"That is what I was thinking myself. Then I must get them all out."

"You have got to get the ring first," Herrara said with a smile.

"Yes, yes, I mean if I get it."

"But if the French have entered the town you can never get them across the bridge."

"No, I know that. I mean to get a boat and have it lying off the end of some quiet street. I could put a couple of our men into that, for they would only regard it, when I had got her on board, as an effort on my part to save one of the nuns from the French. One thing to do would be to get the robe of a priest, or the dress of one of the bishop's officials."

Herrara thought for some time. "I think that I could do that for you, O'Connor. Of course I have a good many acquaintances in Oporto, among them some ladies. I was intending to go across this evening and see some of them, and implore them to leave the town before it is too late. One of these friends of mine might buy some robes for me; a woman can do that sort of thing when a man cannot. She can pretend that she wants to buy the robe as a present for the parish priest, or her father confessor, or something of that sort. At any rate, it is worth trying."

"It is, indeed, Herrara, and if you could manage it I should be greatly obliged to you."

"I will go across at once. I expect Soult will be close up to-morrow morning, or at any rate the next day. It may be another couple of days before he gets his whole force concentrated, but in four days anyhow his shot will be rattling down into the town. I will go and see what I can do. You had better get one of my troopers to get the boat for you."

Herrara did not return until early on the following morning.

"I have managed it," he said, as Terence, who was getting very anxious about him, ran forward to meet him.

"There is one family in Oporto whose eldest son is a brother officer of mine, and I have visited them here with him, and have met them several times at Lisbon. Indeed, I may tell you frankly that had it not been for the troubles, his sister would, ere this time, have been affianced to me. I had hoped that they had left the town before this, but they told me that any movement of that sort might bring disaster on them. Two of her brothers are in the army, and the bishop could not, therefore, pretend that the father was a traitor to the country; being an elderly man, the latter has in fact held aloof altogether from politics; but he is certainly not of the bishop's party, and the bishop considers that all who are not with him are against him. Had they attempted to leave the town there is no doubt he would have made it a pretext for arresting the father, and would certainly do so on the first opportunity.

However, they quite believed that the great force that there is here would be sufficient to defend the fortifications, and were completely taken aback when I told them that I was absolutely convinced that the place would fall at the first attack of the French.

"They agreed to make all preparations for leaving at once. Their horses have been seized, nominally that they should be used on the fortifications, but really, I have no doubt, to prevent their leaving. Of course I told them all about what we had been doing, in which they were intensely interested. For aught they know, their house may be watched; so they will come out in some of their servants' clothes. I told them that they must leave on the night before Soult made his attack. Of course he will summon the town, and the bishop will, of course, refuse to surrender, and you may be sure the French will attack on the following day. They left me alone with Lorenza for a time, and I took that opportunity of telling her about your plan, and what you wanted, and she promised to procure you the dress of an ecclesiastic to-morrow. I told her that you were about my size and height.

"She knew your cousin personally, and was very fond of her, and therefore entered all the more readily into our plans to get her out. She said that she disappeared suddenly some months ago, and that her mother had given out that she had been suddenly seized with the determination to enter a convent, much against her own wishes. Lorenza felt sure that this was not true, for she knew that your cousin had heard from her father much about the Reformed religion, and was in her heart disposed that way. The mother is engaged to be married to a nobleman who is one of the bishop's warmest supporters, and the general idea was that Mary O'Connor had been forced into a nunnery against her will. I sat talking with them until late last night, and they would not hear of my leaving, especially as they said that the town was full of bands of ruffians, who traversed the streets, attacking and robbing anyone of respectable appearance. As I had rather a fancy to try what a comfortable bed was like again, I did not need much pressing."

"Thank you greatly, Herrara, I am indeed obliged to you; things seem to look really hopeful. I have arranged with Bull and Macwitty that on the evening before the attack is likely to take place we will watch all night at this end of the bridge. The bishop won't leave until the last thing, but I would wager any money he will do so that night. He won't go farther than Villa Nova, so as to be ready to cross again at once if the news comes that the French have been beaten off. No doubt he will make the excuse that as an ecclesiastic he could take no active part in the defence, but had been engaged in prayer, which had done more towards gaining the victory than his presence could possibly have done."

"I should not be surprised if that should be his course," Herrara said, smiling. "At any rate, for your sake I hope that it will be. Have you seen about a boat?"

"Yes, I spoke to Francesco Nortis yesterday evening, and told him that I wanted to hire a boat with two boatmen for the next week. They were to be at his service night and day. He was to tell them that he would not want it for fishing, but that, in case, by any possibility, the French took the town, he should be able to go across and bring some friends over. When I told him that money was no object, he said that there would be no difficulty about it. They will be glad enough to get a good week's pay and next to nothing to do for it."

Two days passed quietly. On the first day the news arrived that Silveira had invested Chaves on the day of the battle of Braga, and had forced the garrison, which consisted of but a hundred fighting men, with twelve hundred sick, to capitulate.

Day after day news came of the advance of the French. They had moved in three columns. Each had met with a stout resistance, but had carried the passes and bridges after severe loss. One of the columns had been held for some time in check at the Ponte D'Ave, but had carried it at last, whereupon the Portuguese had murdered their general and dispersed.

On the 26th, six days after the battle of Braga, Franceschi's cavalry were seen approaching the position in front of Oporto. The alarm bells rung, the troops hurried to their positions, but the day passed off quietly, the confidence of the people being still further raised by the arrival of 2,000 regular troops sent by Beresford to their assistance. As there were already seven or eight thousand regular troops in the camp, it seemed to all that as Soult had but 20,000 men fit for action, the defences ought to be held against him for any length of time. The majority, indeed, believed that he would not even venture to attack the town when upon his arrival he perceived its strength, especially when they knew that he had but a few guns with him, his park of artillery being still at Tuy, which was closely invested by the Spaniards.

On the following day the whole French army settled down in front of the Portuguese works, and a wild and purposeless fire was now opened by the defenders, although the French were far beyond musket-range.

Soult sent in a message to the bishop urging him to surrender. He assured him that resistance was hopeless, and that it was his earnest desire to save so great a city from the horrors of a storm. The message was sent by a prisoner, who was seized by the mob in spite of the flag of truce that he carried, and would have been murdered had he not assured the people that he came with a message from Soult, to the effect that, seeing the hopelessness of attacking the town or of marching back to the frontier in safety, he wished to negotiate for a surrender for himself and his army.

At one point the Portuguese displayed a white flag, and shouted that they wished to surrender. A French general advanced with another officer, but when they reached the lines the Portuguese fell upon him, killed his companion, and carried the general a prisoner into the town. The negotiations were prolonged until evening, but the bishop declined all Soult's overtures, and the fire from the intrenchments continued. In the course of the evening Merle's division, in order to divert attention from the points Soult had fixed upon for the attack, moved towards the Portuguese left, when a tremendous fire of artillery and musketry opened upon it. The division made its way forward, and occupied some hollow ground which shielded it from fire, within a very short distance of the intrenchments. Feeling that the crisis was at hand, Terence had everything prepared. The boatmen were told that they might be required that night, and that they were to have the boat in readiness to start at any moment. Herrara had warned his friends, and went to their house with six of his men, as soon as it became dusk, to escort them over. Terence with his two troopers, clad in the dresses of two of the tallest of the men and wrapped in cloaks, with their broad hats pressed low down upon their foreheads, went down to the end of the bridge as soon as it became quite dark. The river was three hundred yards broad, but the sound of the confusion and alarm that prevailed in the city could be plainly heard, although the evening had set in rough and tempestuous. The shouts of the excited mob mingled with the clanging of the church bells.

"That does not sound like confidence in victory," Terence remarked.

"Quite the other way, sir. I should say that after all their bragging every man in the place is in a blue funk."

A great many people, especially women with children, were making their way across the bridge. About nine o'clock a little knot of five or six men, following a tall figure, passed them.

"That is the bishop," Terence whispered, and in pursuance of the orders that he had previously given them, the two men followed him as he fell in at a short distance behind the group. These turned off from the main road and took one that led up to the Serra Convent, standing on the crest of a rugged hill. As soon as they had passed beyond the houses at the foot of the hill, and the road was altogether deserted, Terence said to the men:

"Now is our time. Do you take the attendants; I will manage the bishop."

They moved forward quickly and silently until they were close to the group, then they dashed forward. As the startled attendants turned round the troopers fell upon them, and with heavy blows from their fists knocked them to the ground like nine-pins. The bishop turned round and shouted:

"Villains, I am the bishop!"

"I know that!" Terence exclaimed, and sprang at him.

The prelate reeled and fell. Terence threw himself upon him, and seizing his hand wrested from it the episcopal ring. Then, upon seeing that the bishop had fainted, probably from fright, Terence leapt to his feet. The five attendants were lying on the ground.

"All right, lads," he said, "we have got what we wanted, but just strip off one of these fellows' clothes. Take this one, he is a priest."

It took but a minute for the two troopers to strip off the garment and pick up the three-cornered hat.

"Now, come along, men."

They reached the houses again without hearing so much as

a cry from the astounded Portuguese, who as yet had but a vague idea of what had happened to them. The capture of the clothes had been rendered necessary by Herrara's report, two days before, that the young lady had failed to get the clothes, for the shopman had asked so many questions concerning them that she had said carelessly that it made no matter. She had intended to give them as a present and a surprise, but as there seemed a difficulty about it she would give money instead, and let the priest choose his own clothes. She had purposely entered a shop in the opposite end of the town from that in which her father lived, so that there would be less chance of her being recognized.

Herrara said that she would try elsewhere, but Terence at once begged him to tell her not to do so.

"The bishop is sure to have some of his priests with him," he said, "and if I rob him of his ring, I might just as well rob one of them of his clothes."

On returning to the camp Terence found that his comrade had already arrived with a gentleman and three ladies. The tent had been given up for the use of the latter. Herrara had warned him not to say a word to the old gentleman of his adventure.

"He and the others know nothing about it," he said, "and it is just as well that they shouldn't, for he is somewhat rigid in his notions, and might be rather horrified at your assaulting a bishop, however great a scoundrel he might be, and would be specially so at the borrowing of his ring."

At twelve o'clock heavy peals of thunder were heard, followed by a tremendous outbreak of firing from the intrenchments, two hundred guns and a terrific musketry fire opening suddenly.

"The French are attacking!" Herrara exclaimed.

"I don't think so," Terence replied. "It is more likely

to be a false alarm. The troops may have thought that the thunder was the roar of French guns. Soult would hardly make an attack at night, or, not knowing the nature of the ground behind the intrenchments, his men would be falling into confusion, and perhaps fire into each other."

As, after a quarter of an hour of prodigious din, the fire slackened and presently ceased altogether, it was evident that this supposition was a correct one. The morning broke bright and still, and an hour later the cannonade began again. Terence at once, after telling Herrara to form the troops up and march them down to the end of the bridge, left the camp, and after proceeding a short distance took off his uniform and donned the attire of the ecclesiastic, and then hurried down into the town. He was accompanied by the two troopers in their peasant dress. These left him at the bridge. The din was now tremendous, every church bell was ringing furiously, and frightened women were already crowding down towards the bridge.

Their point of crossing had already been decided upon—it was at the end of a street close to the convent, and when Terence reached the convent the two men were already standing at the end of the street, awaiting him.

"Now, you do your part of the business and I will do mine," Terence said, and he moved forward to the door of the convent, where he would be unseen should anyone look out.

The two troopers went to the middle of the street, opposite the window which the officer had described to Terence, and both shouted in a stentorian voice:

"Mary O'Connor!"

The shout was heard above the tumult of the battle and the din in the city, and a head appeared at the window and looked down with a bewildered expression.

"Mary O'Connor," Bull shouted again, "a friend is here to rescue you. You will leave the convent directly with the rest. Look out for us."

Then they walked on, and passed Terence.

"Have you seen her face?"

"We have, sir. We shall know her again, never fear."

Terence now seized the bell and rung it vigorously. The door opened, and a terrified face appeared at the window.

"I have a message from the bishop to the lady superior."

The door was opened, and was at once closed and barred behind him. He was led along some passages to the room where the lady superior, pale and agitated, was awaiting him.

"Have the French entered the intrenchments?" she asked.

"I trust they have not entered yet, but they may do so at any moment. The bishop is at the Serra Convent, and from there has a view over the town to the intrenchments. He begs you to instantly bring the nuns across, for they will be in safety there, whereas no one can say what may happen in the town. Here is his episcopal ring in proof that I am the bearer of his orders. I pray you to hasten, sister, for a crowd of fugitives are already pouring over the bridge, and there is not a moment to be lost."

"The nuns are just coming down to prayer in the chapel, and we will start instantly."

In two minutes upward of a hundred frightened women were gathered in the courtyard.

"Are all here?" Terence asked the lady superior.

"All of them."

"I asked because I know that he is specially anxious that one, who is a sort of prisoner, should not fall into the hands of the French, as that might cause serious trouble."

"I know whom you mean," and she called out "Sister Theresa!" There was no answer.

"It is well you asked," she said. "They have forgotten her." She gave orders to one of the sisters, who at once entered the house, and returned in a minute with a young nun. The door was now opened, and they moved out in procession. Terence could hear regular volleys amidst the roar of guns and the incessant crack of muskets.

"I fear that they have entered the intrenchments," he said. "Hasten, sister, or we shall be too late."

With hurried steps they passed along the deserted streets. As they neared the bridge a crowd of fugitives were hastening in that direction, and when they approached its head they found it blocked by a struggling mass.

"What is to be done?" the lady superior asked in consternation.

"We must wait a minute or two; they may clear off."

But every second the crowd increased, and was soon thick behind them. Already the line of nuns was broken up by the pressure. Terence had kept his eyes on the two tall figures who had followed, at first behind them, and had then quickened their footsteps until abreast of the centre of the line, and to his satisfaction saw that they had one of the nuns between them, and were forcing their way with her through the crowd behind. At this moment a terrible cry arose from the crowd. A troop of Portuguese dragoons rode furiously down the street leading to the bridge, and dashed into the crowd, trampling down all in their way in their reckless terror, until they gained the end of the bridge. As they rode on to it, two of the boats, already low in the water from the weight upon them, gave a surge and sank, carrying with them hundreds of people. The crowd recoiled with a cry of horror.

"There is no escape now, sister," Terence said; "go back to the convent."

"Home, sisters!" she cried in a loud, shrill voice, that

made itself heard even over the screams of the drowning people and the wails and cries of the mob.

Terence placed himself before the lady superior, and by main force made a way through the crowd; which was the more easy as, seeing their only escape cut off, numbers were now beginning to disperse to their homes. The movement was converted into a wild rush when a troop of French cavalry came thundering down to the bridge. In a moment all was mad confusion and fright. The nuns followed their superior, and all thought of decorum being now lost, fled with her like a flock of frightened sheep along the street leading to the convent. Terence paused a moment. He saw that the French troopers threw themselves from their horses, and, all animosity being for the moment forgotten in the horror of the scene, set to work to endeavour to save the drowning wretches, regardless of the fire which, as soon as the French appeared, was opened by the battery on the height of Villa Nova.

Then he sped away after the nuns, whom he soon passed. He turned down the street next to the convent, and, on reaching the end, saw the two troopers with a nun in a boat ten yards away. Macwitty was standing covering the two boatmen with his pistols.

"Row back to the shore again," he roared out in English, "and take off that gentleman there." The men did not understand his words, but they understood his gestures, and a stroke or two took them alongside. Terence leapt in and told the men to row across the river.

"This is an unexpected meeting, cousin," he said to the girl.

"They have been telling me who you are, and how you have effected my rescue," she said, bursting into tears. "How can I thank you?"

"Well, this is hardly a time for thanks," he said, "and I

"MACWITTY WAS STANDING COVERING THE TWO BOATMEN WITH HIS PISTOLS."

am as glad as you are that it has all turned out well. I will tell you all about it as soon as we are across."

They were nearly over when he exclaimed to the troopers:

"The French have repaired the bridge with planks. See, they are crossing!"

They sprang out on reaching the opposite shore. A moment later a rattle of musketry broke out.

"Macwitty," he said, "I will give this young lady into your charge. Take her straight up to the camp. There are three ladies there," he said to his cousin, "and in the tent they have some clothes for you to change into. It will not be long before I shall rejoin you. But I must join my regiment now; they are engaged with the enemy."

As he hurried along with Bull, he could hear above the sound of the musketry the sharp crack of the field-guns from the opposite side of the river.

"They are covering the passage, Bull."

As he came up he found that Herrara had taken possession of the houses near the end of the bridge. A part of his troops filled the windows, while the main body lined the quay. The French were recoiling, but a mass of their troops could be seen at the further end of the bridge, and two field batteries were keeping up an incessant fire. Herrara was posted with a company at the end of the bridge.

"We had better fall back, Herrara, before they form a fresh column of attack. We might repulse them again, but they will be able to cross by boats elsewhere, and we shall be taken in front and rear. Let us draw off in good order. The infantry will be sure to march straight against the battery on the hill behind, and it will be half an hour before the cavalry can cross, and by that time we shall be well on our way; whereas, if we stop here until we are taken in flank and rear, we shall be cut to pieces."

"I quite agree with you," Herrara said, and ordered the man with the horn standing beside him to sound the retreat.

The men near at once formed up and got in motion, those in the houses poured out, and in two minutes the whole force were going up the hill at a trot, but still preserving their order. Five minutes later the head of the French column poured over the bridge. Just as the troops reached the place of encampment the fire of the battery ceased suddenly.

CHAPTER XVIII

MARY O'CONNOR

NEVER was a large force of men driven from a very strong position, carefully prepared and defended by a vast number of guns, so quickly and easily as were the Portuguese before Oporto. The bishop, after rejecting Soult's summons and disregarding his prayers to save the city from ruin, suddenly lost heart, and after all his boasting, slipped away after dark to the Serra Convent, leaving the command to the generals of the army. The feint which Soult had made with Merle's division the night before against the Portuguese left succeeded perfectly, the Portuguese massing their forces on that side to resist the expected attack.

Soult's real intentions, however, were to break through the centre of the line and then to drive the Portuguese right and left away from the town, while he pushed a body of troops straight through the city to seize the bridge and thus cut off all retreat. Accordingly he commenced the attack on both wings. The Portuguese weakened their centre to meet these, and then the central division of the French rushed forward, burst through the intrenchments, and carried at once the two principal forts. Then two battalions marched into the town and made for the bridge, while the rest fell on the Portuguese rear. The French right carried in succession a number of forts, took fifty pieces of artillery, and drove off a great mass of the Portuguese from the town, while Merle met with equal success on the other flank. Half the Portuguese, therefore, were driven up the valley of the Douro, and the other half down towards the sea.

Maddened by terror, some of them strove to swim across, others to get over in small boats. Lima, their general, shouted to them that the river was too wide to swim, and that those who took to boats would be shot down by the pursuing French. Whereupon his own troops turned upon him and murdered him, although the French were but a couple of hundred yards away; they then renewed their attempt to cross, and many perished. Similar scenes took place in the valley above the town, but here the French cavalry interposed between the panic-stricken fugitives and the river, and so prevented them throwing away their lives in the hopeless attempt to swim across. In the meantime incessant firing was going on in the city. The French column arriving at the bridge, after doing their best to rescue the drowning people, sacrificed to the heartless cowardice of the Portuguese cavalry, speedily repaired the break caused by the sinking boats and prepared to cross the river, while others scattered through the town.

The inhabitants fired upon them from the roofs and windows, and two hundred men defended the bishop's palace to the last. Every house was the scene of conflict. The French on entering one of the principal squares found a number of their comrades, who had been taken prisoners and sent to the town, still alive but horribly mutilated, some of them having been blinded, others having legs cut off, and all mutilated in various ways. This terrible sight naturally goaded them to such a state of fury that Soult in vain endeavoured to stop the work of slaughter and pillage. This continued for several hours, and altogether the number of Portuguese who perished by drowning and slaughter in the streets was estimated at ten thousand, of which the number killed in the defence of the works formed but an insignificant portion.

Terence on his arrival at the camp in the wood resumed his uniform. Herrara had, on the previous day, purchased a light waggon and two horses for the use of the ladies, and as soon as the men had strapped on the cloaks and blankets which they had left behind them when they advanced to the defence of the bridge, the retreat began. Not until he had seen the column fairly on its way did Terence ride up to speak to the occupants of the waggon. He had not been introduced by Herrara to his friends, for on his return from his encounter with the bishop the ladies had already retired to their tent.

"I must introduce myself to you, Don Jose. I am Terence O'Connor, an ensign in his Britannic Majesty's regiment of Mayo Fusiliers and an aide-de-camp of General Cradock, a very humble personage, though at present in command of these troops—irregular regiments of the Portuguese army."

"Lieutenant Herrara has told us so much about you, Señor O'Connor, that we have been looking forward with much pleasure to meeting you. Allow me to present you to my wife and daughters, who have been as anxious as myself to meet an officer who has done such good services to the cause, and to whom it is due at the present moment that we are here, instead of being in the midst of the terrible scenes that are no doubt at this moment being enacted in Oporto."

Terence bowed deeply to the ladies, and then said to his cousin:

"I almost require introducing to you, for I caught but a

glimpse of you as we crossed the river, and you look so different now that you have got rid of that hideous attire that I don't think that I should have known you."

"You have changed greatly, too, Señor O'Connor."

Terence burst into a laugh.

"My dear cousin, it is evident that you know very little of English customs, though you speak English so well. We don't call our cousins Mr. and Miss; you will have to call me Terence and I shall certainly call you Mary. Macwitty brought you back to camp all right?"

"Yes; but it was terrible to hear all that firing, and I was wondering all the time whether you were being hurt."

"There is a great deal of powder fired away to every one that gets hit."

"Do you know what has happened in the town?" Don Jose asked.

"I know no more than what my cousin has no doubt told you of that terrible scene at the bridge. It is evident that the French burst through the lines without any difficulty, as we saw no soldiers, except those cowardly cavalrymen, before the French arrived. It is probable that the intrenchments were carried in the centre, and Soult evidently sent a body of soldiers straight through the town to secure the bridge. I think he must have cut off the main body of the defenders of the intrenchments from entering the town and must either have captured them or driven them off. The fire of cannon had ceased over there before we retired, and it is clear from that that the whole of the intrenchments must have been captured. There was, however, a heavy rattle of musketry in the town, and I suppose that the houses, and perhaps some barricades, were being defended. It was a mad thing to do, for it would only excite the fury of the French troops, and get them out of hand altogether. If there had been no resistance the columns might have marched in in good order; but even then I fear there might have been trouble, for unfortunately, your peasants have behaved with such merciless cruelty to all stragglers who fell into their hands, that the thirst for vengeance would in any case have been irrepressible. Still, the officers might possibly have preserved order had there been no resistance."

"Shall we be pursued, do you think, señor?" Don Jose's wife asked.

"I do not think so. Possibly parties of horse may scour the country for some distance round, to see if there is a body of troops here, but we are too strong to be attacked by any but a very numerous body of horse; and if they should attempt it, you may be sure that we can render a very good account of ourselves. We have beaten off the French horse once, and, as since then we have had some stiff fighting, I have no fear of the men being unsteady, even if all Franceschi's cavalry came down upon us. Of that, however, there will be little chance; the French have their hands full for some days, and a few scouting parties are all that they are likely to send out."

"You speak Portuguese very well, Terence," Mary O'Connor said, in that language, hesitating a little before she used his Christian name.

"I have been nearly nine months in the country, during most of which I have been on the staff, and have had to communicate with peasants and others, and for the past two months I have spoken nothing else; necessity is a good teacher. Besides which, Lieutenant Herrara has been good enough to take great pains in correcting my mistakes and teaching me the proper idioms; another six months of this work and I have no doubt I shall be able to pass as a native."

After marching fifteen miles the column halted, Terence feeling assured that the French would not push out their scouting parties more than three or four miles from Villa Nova. They halted at the edge of a forest, and a party under one of the officers was at once despatched to a village two miles away, and returned in an hour with a drove of pigs that had been bought there, and a cart laden with bread and wine. Fires had already been lighted, and after seeing that the rations were divided among the various companies, Terence went to the tent. Herrara was chatting with his friends, and Mary O'Connor came out at once and joined him.

"That is right, Mary; we will take a stroll in the wood and have a talk together. Now tell me how you have got on. I had expected to find you quite thin and almost starving."

"No, I have had plenty of bread to eat," she laughed; "the sisters kept me well supplied. I am sure that most of them were sorry for me, and they used to hide away some of their own bread and bring it to me when they had a chance. The lady superior was very hard, and if I had had to depend entirely on what she sent me up I should have done very badly. I always ate as much as I could, as I wanted to keep up my strength; for I knew that if I got weak I might give way and do what they wanted, and I was quite determined that I would not, if I could help it."

"Macwitty told you, I suppose, how I came to hear where you were imprisoned?"

"Yes; he said that the officer had given you the letter that I dropped to him; yet how did he come to know that you were my cousin?"

"It was quite an accident; just the similarity of name. We were chatting, and he said, casually, 'I suppose that you have no relatives at Oporto,' and I at once said I had, for fortunately my father had been telling me about your father and you, the last time I saw him, that is four months ago. He was badly wounded at Vimiera and invalided home. Then Captain Travers told me about getting your letter and what was in it, and I felt sure that it was you, and of course made up my mind to do what I could to get you out, though at the time I did not think that I should be in Oporto until I entered with the British army."

"But I cannot think how you got us all to start, and walked along with the lady superior as if you were a friend of hers. Macwitty had not time to tell me that. I was so frightened and bewildered with the dreadful noise and the strangeness of it all that I could not ask him many questions."

"It was by virtue of this ring," he said, holding up his hand.

"Why," she exclaimed in surprise, "that is the bishop's! I noticed it on his finger when he came one day to me and scolded me, and said that I should remain a prisoner if it was for years until my obstinate spirit was broken. But how did you get it?"

"Not with the bishop's good-will, you may be sure, Mary," Terence laughed; and he then told her how he had become possessed of it.

The girl looked quite scared.

"It sounds dreadful, doesn't it, Mary, to think that I should have laid hands upon a bishop, and such a bishop, a man who regards himself as the greatest in Portugal. However, there was no other way of getting the ring, and I could not see how, without it, I could persuade the lady superior to leave her convent with you all; and to tell you the truth, I would rather have got it that way than any other. The bishop is, in my opinion, a man who deserves no respect. He has terrorized all the north of Portugal, has caused scores of better men than himself to be imprisoned or put to death, and has now by his folly and ignorance cost the lives of no one knows how many thousand men, and brought about the sack of Oporto."

"Did you hear anything of my mother?" the girl asked.

"No; my Portuguese was not good enough for me to ask questions without risking being detected as a foreigner at once. She has behaved shamefully to you, Mary."

"She never liked me," the girl said, simply. "She and father never got on well together, and I think her dislike began by his taking to me, and my liking to be with him and getting to talk English. There was a terrible quarrel between them once because she accused him of teaching me to be a Protestant, although he never did so. He did give me a Bible, and I used to ask him questions and he answered them, that was all; but as it did seem to me that he was much wiser in all things than she was, I thought that he might be wiser in religion too. I would have given up the property directly they wanted me to, if they would have let me go away to England; but when they took me to the convent and cut off my hair, and forced me to become a nun, I would not give way to them. I never took the vows, Terence; I would not open my lips, but they went on with the service just the same. I was determined that I would not yield. I thought that the English would come some day, and that I might be freed then."

"What would you have done in England if you had gone there, Mary?"

"I should have found your father out, and gone to him. Father told me that your father was his greatest friend, and just before he died he told me that he had privately sent over all his own money to a bank at Cork, and ordered it to be put in your father's name. It was a good deal of money, for he would not give up the business when he married my mother, though she wanted him to; but he said that he could not live in idleness on her money, and that he must be doing something. And I know that he kept up the house in Oporto, while she kept up her place in the country. He told me that the sum he had sent over was £20,000. That will be enough to live on, won't it?"

"Plenty," Terence laughed. "I had no idea that I was rescuing such an heiress. I was sure that there was no chance of your getting your mother's money, at any rate, as long as the bishop was leader of Oporto. However just your claim, no judge would decide in your favour."

"Now tell me about yourself, Terence, and your home in Ireland, and all about it."

"My home has been the regiment, Mary. My father has a few hundred acres in County Mayo, and a tumble-down house; that is to say, it was a tumble-down house when I saw it four years ago, but it had been shut up for a good many years, and I should not be surprised if it has quite tumbled down now. However, my father was always talking of going to live there when he left the army. The land is not worth much, I think. There are five hundred acres, and they let for about a hundred a year. However, my father has been in the regiment now for about eighteen years; and as I was born in barracks I have only been three or four times to Ballinagra, and then only because father took a fancy to have a look at the old house. My mother died when I was ten years old, and I ran almost wild until I got my commission last June."

"And how did you come to be a staff-officer of the English general?" she asked.

"I have had awfully good luck," Terence replied. "It happened in all sorts of ways."

"Please tell me everything," she said. "I want to know all about you."

"It is a long story, Mary."

"So much the better," she said. "I know nothing of

what has passed for the last year, and I dare say I shall learn about it from your story. You don't know how happy I am feeling to be out in the sun and in the air again, and to see the country after being shut up in one room for a year. Suppose we sit down here and you tell me the whole story."

Terence accordingly related the history of his adventures since he had left England. The girl asked a great many questions, and specially insisted upon hearing his own adventures very fully.

"It is no use your keeping on saying that it is all luck," she said when he had finished. "Your colonel could not have thought that it was luck when he wrote the report about that adventure at sea, and your general could not have thought so, either, or he would not have praised you in his despatch. Then, you know, General Fane must have thought that it was quite out of the way or he would not have chosen you to be on his staff. Then afterwards the other general must have been pleased with you, or he would not have put you on his staff and sent you off on a mission to General Romana. It is quite certain that these things could not have been all luck, Terence. And anyhow, you cannot pretend that it was luck that this regiment of yours fought so well against the French, while none of the others seem to have fought at all. I suppose that you will say next that it was all luck that you got me out of the convent."

"There was a great deal of luck in it, Mary. If that cowardly bishop hadn't left Oporto secretly, after declaring that he would defend it until the last, I could never have got his ring."

"You would have got me out some other way if he hadn't," the girl said, with confidence. "No, Terence, you can say what you like, but I shall always consider that you have been wonderfully brave and clever."

"Then you will always think quite wrong," Terence said, bluntly.

"I shall begin to think that you are a tyrant, like the Bishop of Oporto, if you speak in that positive way. How old are you, sir?"

"I was sixteen six months ago."

"And I was sixteen three days ago," she said. "Fancy your commanding two thousand soldiers and only six months older than I am."

"It is not I, it is the uniform," Terence said. "They obey me when they won't obey their own officers, because I am on the English general's staff. They know that we have thrashed the French, and that their own officers know nothing at all about fighting, and they have no respect whatever for them. More than that, they despise them because they know that they are always intriguing, and that really, although they may be called generals, they are but politicians. You will see, when they get English officers to discipline them, they will turn out capital soldiers; but they think so little of their own, that if anything goes wrong their first idea is that their officers must be traitors, and so fall upon them and murder them.

"You look older than I do, Mary. You seem to me quite a woman, while, in spite of my uniform and my command, and all that, I am really only a boy."

"I suppose I am almost a woman, Terence, but I don't feel so. You see out here girls often marry at sixteen. I know father said once that he hoped I shouldn't marry until I was eighteen, and that he wanted to keep me young. I never thought about getting almost a woman until the bishop told me one day that if I chose to marry a señor that he would choose for me, he would get me absolution from my vows, and that I need not then resign my property."

"The old blackguard!" Terence exclaimed, angrily. "And what did you say to him?"

"I said that, in the first place, I had never thought of marrying; that in the second place, I had not taken any vows; and in the third place that when I did marry I would choose for myself. He got into a terrible rage, and said that I was an obstinate heretic, and that some day when I was tired of my prison I would think better of it."

"I would have hit the bishop hard if I had known about that," Terence grumbled. "If ever I fall in with him again I will pay him out for it. Well, anyhow, I may as well take off his ring; it might lead to awkward questions if anyone noticed it."

"I think that you had certainly better do so, Terence; it might cost you your life. The bishop is a bad man, and he is a very dangerous enemy. If he heard that an English officer was wearing an episcopal ring, and upon inquiring found that that officer had been in Oporto at its capture, he would know at once that it was you who assaulted him, and he would never rest until he had your life. You had better throw it away."

"All right, here goes!" Terence said, carelessly, and he threw the ring into a clump of bushes. "Now, Mary, it is getting dark, and I should think supper must be waiting for us."

"Yes, it is late; we have been a long while, indeed," the girl said, getting up hastily. "I forgot all about time."

"We are in plenty of time," Terence said, looking at his watch. "As we all had some cold meat for lunch as soon as we arrived, I ordered dinner at six o'clock, and it wants twenty minutes of that time now."

"It is shocking, according to our Portuguese ideas," she said, demurely, "for a young lady and gentleman to be talking together for nearly three hours without anyone to look after them."

"It is not at all shocking, according to Irish ideas," Terence said, laughing, "especially when the young lady and gentleman happen to be cousins."

They walked a short time in silence, then she said:

"I have obeyed you, Terence, and haven't uttered a word of thanks for what you have done for me."

"That shows that you are a good girl," Terence laughed.

"Good girls always do as they are told; at least they are supposed to, though as to the fact I never had any experience, for I have no sisters, and there were no girls in barracks; still, I am glad that you kept your promise, and hope that you will always do so. Being a cousin, of course it was natural that I should try to rescue you."

"And you would not if I hadn't been a cousin?"

"No, I don't say that. I dare say I should have tried the same if I had heard that any English or Irish girl was shut up here. I am sure I should if I had seen you beforehand."

She coloured a little at the compliment, and said, lightly:

"Father told me once that Irishmen were great hands at compliments. He told me that there was some stone that people went to an old castle to kiss—I think that he called it the Blarney Stone—and after that they were able to say all sorts of absurd things."

"I have never kissed the Blarney Stone," Terence said, laughing. "If I wanted to kiss anything, it would be something a good deal softer than that."

They were now entering the camp, and in a few minutes they arrived at the tent.

"I began to think that you were lost, O'Connor," Herrara said, as they came up.

"We had a lot to talk about," Terence replied. "My cousin has been insisting upon my telling her my whole history, and all about what has passed here since she was shut up a year ago, and, as you may imagine, it was rather a long story."

A few minutes later they sat down on the ground to a meal in which roast pork was the leading feature.

"This is what we call in England a picnic, señora," Terence said to Don Jose's wife.

"A picnic," she repeated; "what does that mean? It is a funny word."

"I have no idea why it should be called so," Terence said. "It means an open-air party. The ladies are supposed to bring the provisions, and the gentlemen the wine. Sometimes it is a boating party; at other times they drive in carriages to the spot agreed upon. It is always very jolly, and much better than a formal meal indoors, and you can play all sorts of tricks."

"What sort of tricks, señor?"

"Oh, there are lots of them. I was always having fun before I became an officer. My father was one of the captains of the regiment, and I was generally in for any amusement that there was. Once at a picnic, I remember that I got hold of the salt-cellars and mustard-pots beforehand, and I filled up one with powdered Epsom salts, which are horribly nasty, you know, and I mixed the mustard with cayenne pepper. Nobody could make out what had happened to the food. They soon suspected the mustard, but nobody thought of the salt for a long time. The colonel was furious over it, but fortunately they could not prove that I had any hand in the matter, though I know that they suspected me, for I did not get an invitation to a picnic for a long time afterwards."

The three girls laughed, but Don Jose said, seriously: "But you would have got into terrible trouble if you had been found out, would you not?"

"I should have got a licking, no doubt, señor; but I was

pretty accustomed to that, and it did not trouble me in any way. At any rate, it did not cure me of my love for mischief. I am afraid I never shall be cured of that. I used to have no end of fun in the regiment, and I think that it did us all good. It takes some thinking to work out a bit of mischief properly, and I suppose if one can think one thing out well, one can think out another."

"It seems to have succeeded well in your case, anyhow," Herrara laughed. "Perhaps if it had not been for your playing that trick at the picnic you would never have taken command of that mob, and we should never have gone to Oporto, and my friends and your cousin would be there now—that is, if they had not been killed."

"It may have had something to do with it," Terence admitted.

"And now, señor," Don Jose said, "which way are you going to take us?"

"We shall go straight on to Coimbra," Terence said, "unless we come upon a British force before that. Two long days' march will take us there. After that I must do as I am ordered; my independent command will come to an end there. I hope that I shall soon hear that my regiment has returned from England."

"And what is to become of me? I have not thought of asking," Mary O'Connor said.

"That must depend upon circumstances, Mary. If I go down to Lisbon, I hope that we shall all travel together, and I can then put you on board a transport returning to England. I am sure to find letters from my father there, telling me where he is and whether he is coming back with the regiment."

"We shall be very happy, señor," Don Jose said, courteously, "to take charge of the señora, until there is an opportunity for sending her to England. I have, of course, many friends in Lisbon, and shall take a house there the instant I arrive, and Donna O'Connor will be as one of my own family."

"I am extremely obliged to you, Don Jose. I have been wondering all day as I rode along what I should do with my cousin if, as is probable, I am obliged to stay at Coimbra until I receive orders from Lisbon. Your kind offer relieves me of a great anxiety. I think that it will be prudent for her to take another name while she is at Lisbon. There will certainly be no inquiries after her, for the lady superior of her convent will, of course, conclude that she was accidentally separated from the others in the crush, and that she was trampled on, or killed; and, indeed, there will be such confusion in Oporto that the loss of a nun more or less would fail to attract attention. At any rate, it is likely to be a long time before any report the lady superior will make to the bishop will reach him—months, perhaps, for she is not likely to take any particular pains to tell him news that would certainly anger him.

"Still, if he goes to Lisbon, as no doubt he will, and by any chance happens to hear that Miss O'Connor was one of those who had escaped from the sack of Oporto, he might make inquiries, and then all sorts of trouble might arise, even if he did not have her carried off by force, which would be easy enough in a place so disturbed as Lisbon at present is."

"I think that you are right, señor," Don Jose said, gravely. "At any rate it would be as well to avoid any risk. What name shall we call her?"

"You can call her Miss Dillon, señor, that is the name of an officer in our regiment."

"But the bishop might meet her in the street by chance; what then?"

"I don't think that he would know me," Mary O'Connor

put in. "I have seen him, but I don't suppose that he ever noticed me until he saw me in my nun's dress, and, of course, I look very different now. Still, he is very sharp, and I will take good care never to go out without a veil."

"That will be the safest plan, Mary," Terence said, "though I don't think anyone would recognize you. Of course, he supposes that you are still snugly shut up in the convent; still, it is just as well not to run the slightest risk."

They made two long marches and reached Coimbra early on the third morning, bringing the first news that had been received there of the storming of Oporto. Terence at once reported himself to the commanding officer.

"I was wondering where these two regiments came from, Mr. O'Connor," the colonel said. "I watched them march in, and thought that they were the most orderly body that I have seen since we came out here. Whose corps are they?"

"Well, Colonel, they are my corps. I will tell you about it presently; it is a long story."

"How strong are they?"

"The field state this morning made them two thousand three hundred and fifty-five. They were two thousand five hundred to begin with; the rest are either killed or wounded."

"Oh, you have had some fighting then."

"We have had our share, at any rate, Colonel, and I think I can venture to say that no other Portuguese corps shows so good a record."

"We have a large number of tents in store, and I will order a sufficient number to be served out to put all your men under canvas, with the understanding that if the army advances this way the tents must be handed back to us. There are quantities of uniforms also. There have been ship-loads sent over for the use of the Portuguese militia, who were to turn out in their hundreds of thousands, but who have yet to be discovered. Would you like some of them?"

"Very much, indeed, Colonel. It would add very greatly to their appearance; though, as far as fighting goes, I am bound to say that I could wish nothing better."

"Really! Then all I can say is you have made a very valuable discovery. Hitherto the fighting powers of the Portuguese have been invisible to the naked eye. But if you have found that they really will fight under some circumstances, we may hope that, now Lord Beresford has come out to take command of the Portuguese army, and is going to have a certain number of British officers to train and command them, they will be of some utility, instead of being simply a scourge to the country and a constant drain on our purse."

"Have you heard that Oporto is captured, sir?"

"No, you don't say so!"

"Captured in less than an hour from the time that the first gun was fired."

"Just what I expected. When you have political bishops who not only pretend to govern a country, but also assume the command of armies, how can it be otherwise? However, you shall tell me about it presently. I will go down with you at once to the stores and order the issue of the tents and uniforms. My orders were that the uniforms were to be served out to militia and ordenanças; under which head do your men come?"

"The latter, sir; that is what they really were, but they hung the three men the Junta sent to command them, and placed themselves in my hands, and I have done the best I could with them, with the assistance of Lieutenant Herrara—who, as you may remember, accompanied me in charge of the escort—and my own two troopers and his men, and between us we have really done much in the way of disciplining them."

Two hours later the tents were pitched on a spot half a mile distant from the town. By the time that this was done the carts with the uniforms came up, to the great delight of the men.

"I have to go to the commandant again now, Herrara; let the uniforms be served out to the men at once. Tell the captains to see to their fitting as well as possible. I have no doubt that the colonel will come down to inspect them this afternoon, and will probably bring a good many officers with him, so we must make as good a show as possible."

Herrara's friends and Mary O'Connor had, on arriving at Coimbra, hired rooms, as Don Jose had determined to stay for a few days before going on, because his wife had been much shaken by the events that had taken place, and his eldest daughter was naturally anxious to wait until she knew whether Herrara would be able to return to Lisbon, or would remain with the corps. By the time Terence returned to the colonel's quarters it was lunch time.

"You must come across to mess, Mr. O'Connor," the commandant said. "Everyone is anxious to hear your news, and it will save your going over it twice if you will tell it after lunch. I fancy every officer in the camp will be there."

CHAPTER XIX

CONFIRMED IN COMMAND

TERENCE, after lunch was over, first related to the officers all that he knew of the siege of Oporto, explaining why he did not choose to sacrifice the men under him by joining the undisciplined rabble in the intrenchments, but determined to keep the head of the bridge. They listened with breathless interest to his narrative of the attack and capture of Oporto.

"But how was it that that fifty-gun battery did not knock the bridge to pieces when the French tried to cross?"

"That is more than I can say, Colonel. I should fancy that they were so terrified at the utter rout on the other side, which they could see well enough, for they had a view right over the town to the intrenchments, that they simply fired wildly. I don't believe a single ball hit the bridge, though, of course, they ought to have sunk a dozen boats in a couple of minutes. My men could have held it for days, though they were suffering somewhat from the fire of two of the French field batteries; but I found that no steps whatever had been taken to remove the boats from the other side. There were great numbers of them all along the bank, and the enemy could have crossed a mile higher up, at the spot where I took my men over, and so fallen on our rear, therefore I withdrew to save them from being cut up or captured uselessly."

"Now tell us about those troops of yours, O'Connor."

Terence gave a somewhat detailed account of the manner in which he took the command and of the subsequent operations, being desirous of doing justice to Herrara and his troopers, and to his own two orderlies. There was much laughter among the officers at his assumption of command, and at the subsequent steps he took to form his mob of men into an orderly body; but interest took the place of amusement as he told how they had prevented the French from crossing at the mouth of the Minho, and caused Soult to take the circuitous and difficult route by Orense. His subsequent defence of the defile and the night attack upon the French, surprised them much, and when he brought his story to a conclusion there were warm expressions of approval among his hearers.

"I must congratulate you most heartily, Mr. O'Connor," the colonel said. "What seemed at first a very wild and hare-brained enterprise, if you don't mind my saying so, certainly turned out a singular success. It would have seemed almost impossible that you, a young ensign, should be able to exercise any authority over a great body of mere peasants, who have everywhere shown themselves utterly insubordinate and useless under their native officers. It is nothing short of astonishing; and it is most gratifying to find that the Portuguese should, under an English officer, develop fighting powers far beyond anything with which they have been hitherto credited. What are you going to do now?"

"I was intending to send my despatches on to Sir John Cradock, and wait here for orders."

"I think that you had better take your despatches on yourself, Mr. O'Connor. I do not suppose that they are anything like so full as the story you have told us, which, I am sure, would be of as much interest to the general as it has been to us."

"I will do so, sir, and will start this evening. My horse had three days' rest at Villa Nova, and is quite fit to travel."

"You must be feeling terribly anxious about your cousin," the officer who had first told him about her remarked; "there is no saying what may have happened in Oporto after it was stormed."

"I should indeed be, if she were there," Terence replied; "but I am happy to say that she is at present in Coimbra, having travelled with us under the charge of some Portuguese ladies, friends of Herrara."

"You don't mean to say that you persuaded the bishop to let her out of the convent?"

"Scarcely," Terence laughed, "though the bishop did unwittingly aid me."

"I congratulate you on getting her out," the colonel said.

"Travers was telling us the day after you left what a curious coincidence it was that the nun who threw him out a letter should turn out to be a cousin of yours. Will you tell us how you managed it?"

"I don't mind telling it, sir, if all here will promise not to repeat it. The Bishop of Oporto is a somewhat formidable person, and were he to lodge a complaint against me he might get me into serious trouble, and is perfectly capable of having me stabbed some dark night in the streets of Lisbon; therefore, I think it would be as well to omit any details of the share he played in the matter. Without that the story is simple enough. Having got a boat with two men in it at the end of the street in which stood the convent, I went there in the dress of an ecclesiastic, just as the French burst into the town. The bishop had fled on the night before to the Serra Convent on the other side of the river, and I was able to produce an authority from him which satisfied the lady superior that I was the bearer of his order for her and the nuns to make for the bridge, and to cross the river at once.

"Of course, I accompanied them. The crowd was great and they naturally got separated. In the confusion my orderlies managed to get my cousin out of the crowd, and took her straight to the boat. As soon as I saw that they had gone, I persuaded the lady superior to take the rest of the nuns back to the convent at once, as the bridge was by this time broken, and the French had made their appearance. She got the nuns together and made off with them as fast as they could run, and after seeing that they were all nearly back to their convent without any signs of the French being near, I joined the others in the boat, and we rowed across the river. It was a simple business altogether, though at first it seemed very hopeless."

"Especially to get the authority of the bishop," the colonel said, with a smile.

"That certainly seemed the most hopeless part of the business," Terence replied; "but happily I was able to manage it somehow."

"Well, you certainly have had a most remarkable series of adventures, Mr. O'Connor. Now we will go and inspect your corps. Of course they will be rationed while they are here, and will be under my general orders until I hear from Cradock."

"Quite so, Colonel; I am sure they will be proud of being inspected by you. Of course, they are unable to do any complicated manœuvres, but those they do know they know pretty thoroughly, and can do them in a rough and ready way that for actual work is, I think, just as good as a parade-ground performance. I will go on ahead, sir, and form them up."

"I would rather, if you don't mind, that they should have no warning," the colonel said; "we will just go down quietly, and see how quickly they can turn out."

"Very well, sir."

All there expressed their wish to go, and as all were provided with horses or ponies of some kind, in ten minutes they rode off in a body. His officers had been very busy all the time that Terence had been away, serving out the uniforms and seeing that they were properly put on. The work was just over, and the men were sauntering about round their tents when the party arrived. Herrara came up and saluted. He was known to the colonel, as he had dined with Terence at the mess on their way through.

After a few words, Terence said to Herrara:

"Have the assembly blown, and let the men fall in."

Herrara walked back to the tents, and a moment later a

horn blew. It had an uncouth sound, and bore no resemblance to the ordinary call, but it was promptly obeyed. The men snatched their muskets from the piles in front of the tents, and in a wonderfully short time the whole were formed up in their ranks, stiff and immovable.

"Excellently done!" the colonel said; "no British regiment could have fallen in more smartly."

Accompanied by Terence, and followed by the rest of the officers, he rode along the line. The evening before Terence had impressed upon the captains of companies the necessity for having the rifles perfectly clean, as they were about to join a British camp, so that the pieces were all in perfect order. When the inspection was over the mounted group drew off a little.

"The troops will form up in columns of companies," Terence said, and Bull and Macwitty, who were at the head of their respective regiments, gave the orders. The movements were well executed. The men, proud of their uniform, and on their mettle at being inspected by British officers, did their best, and that best left little to be desired. After marching past, they formed into company squares to resist cavalry, then retired by alternate companies, and then formed into line.

"Excellently done!" said the colonel. "Indeed, I can hardly believe it possible that a party of peasants have in a month's time been formed into a body of good soldiers. I should like the officers to come up."

"Call the officers."

There was an officers' call, and this now sounded, and the twelve captains with their two majors rode to the front and saluted. "Mr. Herrara," the colonel said, "I have seen with surprise and the greatest satisfaction the movements of the men under you; they do you the greatest credit, and I shall have pleasure in sending in a most favourable report to the general, the result of my inspection of the regiments. I hear from Mr. O'Connor that your men have shown themselves capable of holding their own against the French, and I can say that I should feel perfectly confident in going into action with my regiment supported by such brave and capable troops. Would that instead of 2,000 we had 100,000 Portuguese troops equally to be trusted, we should very speedily turn the French out of Portugal and drive them from the Peninsula."

The officers bowed and rode off. The troops had not learned the salute, and when the horn sounded they were at once dismissed drill.

"Well, Mr. O'Connor, I must congratulate you most heartily on what you have done. If nothing else, you have added to our army a couple of strong regiments of capable soldiers. If I had not seen it myself I should have thought it impossible that over 2,000 men could be converted into soldiers in so short a time, and that without experienced non-commissioned officers to work them up."

Returning to Coimbra with the colonel, Terence rode to the house where Herrara's friends had taken rooms, and told them that he was going to leave them. Don Jose at once wrote several letters of introduction to influential friends at Lisbon, telling them that he and his daughters had escaped from the sack of Oporto, and asking them to show every kindness to the officer, to whom they chiefly owed their safety.

Terence meanwhile returned to camp, arranged with Herrara and the two majors that everything was to go on as usual during his absence, urging them to work hard at their drill, and to impress upon the men the necessity, now that they were in uniform, of carrying themselves as soldiers, and doing credit to their corps.

Five days later he arrived at Lisbon, taking with him a report from the commandant of his inspection of the corps.

"I had begun to be afraid that you had been killed or taken prisoner, Mr. O'Connor," Sir John Cradock said, as Terence presented himself, "or that you must have fallen back with Romana into Spain. He seems to have behaved very badly, for, as I hear, although he had 10,000 men with him, half of them regular troops, he retired without a shot being fired—except by two regiments who were mauled by the French cavalry—and left Silveira in the lurch."

"I was on other business, General, and I fear that you will think that I exceeded my orders; but I hope that you will consider that the result has justified my doing so. Will you kindly first run your eye over this report by the officer commanding at Coimbra?"

Sir John Cradock read the report with a puzzled expression of face, then he said: "But what regiments are these that Colonel Wilberforce speaks of in such high terms? Were they part of Romana's force? He speaks of them as a corps under your command, and as being 2,300 strong."

"They were not Romana's men, sir, but a body of ordenanças, of whom, as my report will inform you, I came by a combination of circumstances to take the command, appointing Lieutenant Herrara, who commanded my escort, colonel, my two orderlies as majors, and the Portuguese troopers of my escort as captains of companies. We have been several times engaged with the French, and I cannot speak too highly of the behaviour of officers and men."

Sir John Cradock burst into a laugh. "You certainly are a cool hand, Mr. O'Connor. Assuredly I did not contemplate when I sent you off that you would return as colonel of two regiments."

"Nor did I, sir. But, you see, you gave me general instructions to concert measures with Romana for the defence of the frontier. I saw at once that Romana was hopeless, and was therefore myself driven to take these measures. As Oporto has fallen I cannot say they were successful, but at least I may say that we gave Oporto fourteen days' extra time to prepare her defence, and if she did not take advantage of the time it was not my fault."

The look of amusement on the general's face turned to one of interest.

"How did you do that, sir?"

"My corps prevented Soult from crossing at the mouth of the Minho, General, killing some two hundred of his men and driving his boats back across the river. When the French general saw that he could not cross in face of such opposition, he was obliged to march his army round by Orense and down by the passes, which ought to have been successfully defended by the Portuguese."

"That was good service, indeed, Mr. O'Connor. I received despatches from our agents at Oporto, saying that Soult's landing had been repulsed by armed peasants."

"My men were little more than armed peasants then, sir, though they had had a few days' hard drill; still, a British officer would scarcely have called them soldiers."

"Well, I think that Wilberforce's report shows that they have a right to that title now. Take a seat, Mr. O'Connor, and a newspaper—there are some that arrived two days ago—while I look over your report."

Terence had written in much greater detail than is usual in official reports, as he wished the general to see how well the men and their officers had behaved. It was twenty minutes before the general finished it.

"A very remarkable report, Mr. O'Connor; very remarkable. You must dine with me this evening. I have many questions to ask you about it, and also about the storming of Oporto, of which we have, as yet, received no details, although a messenger from the bishop brought us the news some days ago. He seems to have made a terrible mess of it."

"He ought to be hung, sir!" Terence said, indignantly. "After getting all those unfortunate peasants together he sneaked off and hid himself in a convent on the other side of the river, on the very night before the French attacked."

"Unfortunately, Mr. O'Connor, we cannot give all men their deserts, or we should want all the rope on board the ships in the harbour for the purpose. The bishop is a firebrand of the most dangerous kind; and I suppose we shall have him here in a day or two, for he said in his letter that he was on his way. There is one comfort: he will be too busy in quarrelling with the authorities to have any time to spend on his quarrels with us. Then I shall see you in an hour's time. Please ask Captain Nelson to come in here; I have some notes for him to write."

Terence bowed and retired.

"What a nuisance!" Captain Nelson said. "I was wanting to hear all that you had been doing."

"I am to dine with the general," Terence said. "Perhaps I shall meet you there."

Captain Nelson found that he was wanted to write notes of invitation to such of the officers who were still at Lisbon as had dined there when Terence was last the general's guest; and as the general's invitations overrode all other engagements, most of them were present when Terence returned.

"Mr. O'Connor has another story for you, gentlemen," the general said, when the cloth was removed and the wine put upon the table. "I am not sure whether I am right in calling him Mr. O'Connor, for he has been performing the duties of a colonel, commanding two regiments in the Portuguese service. I will preface his story by reading the report of Colonel Wilberforce, commanding at Coimbra, of the state of efficiency of his command."

There was a look of surprise at the general's remarks, and that surprise was greatly heightened on the reading of Colonel Wilberforce's report.

"Now, Mr. O'Connor," the general said, when he had finished, "I am sure that we shall all be obliged by your giving us a detailed statement of the manner in which you raised those regiments, and of the operations that you undertook with them; and the more details you give us the better, for it is well that we should understand how the Portuguese can be best handled. I may say at once that, personally, we are greatly indebted to you for having proved that, when even partially disciplined and well led, they are capable of doing very good service, a fact of which, I own, I have been hitherto very doubtful."

Smiles were exchanged among the auditors when Terence described the manner in which he came to command the body of undisciplined ordenanças. When he spoke of the state in which he found Romana's army, and the reason for his determination to keep his column intact, they listened more attentively, and exchanged looks of surprise when he described his rapid march to the mouth of the Minho, and the repulse of Soult's attempt to cross from Tuy. He then described how he had joined Silveira, and the mutiny of that general's troops. Still more surprise was manifested when he related the action in the defile and the bravery with which his troops had behaved, and the manner in which they had been handled by the troopers that he had appointed as their officers. The night attack on the cavalry and infantry of the head of Soult's column was equally well received. His reasons for not joining the army at Braga, and of keeping aloof from the mob of peasants at Oporto were as much approved as was the holding of the bridge for a while, and his reasons for withdrawing.

"Well, gentlemen," the general said, when Terence had finished, "I think you will allow that my aide-de-camp, Mr. O'Connor, has given a good account of himself, and that if he went outside my orders, his doing so has been most amply justified."

"It has, indeed, General," one of the senior officers said, warmly. "I can answer for myself, that I should have been proud to have been able to tell such a story."

A murmur of approval ran round the table.

"It is difficult to say whether Mr. O'Connor's readiness to accept responsibility, or the manner in which, in the short space of a month, he turned a mob of peasants into regular soldiers, or the quickness with which he marched to the spot threatened by Soult, and so compelled him to entirely change the plan of his campaign, or his conduct in the defence of the defile, and in his night attack, are most remarkable."

"I should wish to say, General, that in telling this story I have been chiefly anxious to do justice to the hearty co-operation of Lieutenant Herrara, and the services rendered by my own two orderlies and his troopers. By myself, I could have done absolutely nothing. Their work was hard and incessant, and the drill and discipline of the troops was wholly due to them."

"I understand, Mr. O'Connor; it is quite right for you to say so, and I thoroughly recognize that they must have done good service; but it is to the man that plans, organizes, and infuses his own spirit into those under his command, that everything is due. Now, Mr. O'Connor, I think I will ask you to leave us for a few minutes; the case is rather an exceptional one, and I shall be glad to chat the matter over with the officers present. Well, gentlemen, what do you think that we are to do with Mr. O'Connor?" he went on, with a smile, as the door closed behind Terence.

"My experience affords me no guide, General," another of the senior officers said. "It is simply amazing that a lad of seventeen—I suppose he is not much over that—should have conceived and carried out such a plan. It sounds like a piece of old knight-errantry. Clive did as much, but Clive was some years older when he first became 'a thorn in the side of the French. What is your opinion, sir?"

"He is already a lieutenant," the general said. "I sent home a strong recommendation that he should be promoted, when he was last here, and received an intimation three days ago that he had been gazetted lieutenant and transferred to my staff. This time I shall simply send home a copy of the report he has furnished me with, and that of Colonel Wilberforce, and say that I leave the reports to speak for themselves, but that in my opinion it is a case altogether exceptional. That is all I can do now. The question of course is, whether he shall return to staff service again, or shall continue in command of the corps with which he has done so much. If he does the latter he must have local rank, otherwise he would be liable to be overruled by any Portuguese officer of superior rank. I think that the best way would be to send a copy of the reports to Lord Beresford, saying that my opinion is very strong that Lieutenant O'Connor should be allowed to retain an independent command of the corps that he has raised and disciplined; and that I will either myself bestow local rank upon him, and treat the corps as forming a part of the British army, like that of Trant, or that he should give him local rank as its colonel, in which case he would operate still independently, but in connection with Beresford's own force."

"I should almost think that the first step would be best, General, if I might say so. In the first place, Beresford will have any number of irregular parties operating with him, while such a corps would be invaluable to us. They are capable of taking long marches, they know the mountains and forests, and would keep us supplied with news, while they harassed the enemy. As an officer on your staff, O'Connor would have a much greater power among the Portuguese population than he would have on his own account in their own army, and he would be very much less likely to be interfered with by the leaders of other parties and corps."

"Perhaps that would be the best way, Colonel. I will send the reports to Beresford, and say that I have appointed Lieutenant O'Connor to remain in command of this corps, which I shall attach to my own command; and saying that I shall be obliged if he will have a commission made out for him, giving him the local rank of colonel in the Portuguese army. Beresford is himself a gallant soldier, and will appreciate, as you do, the work that O'Connor has done; and as he knows nothing of the lad's age he will comply, as a matter of course, with my request. I shall, in writing home, strongly recommend his two cavalrymen for commissions. As to Herrara, I shall ask Beresford to give him the rank of lieutenant-colonel. I shall suggest to Beresford that his troopers should all receive commissions in his army. They have all earned them, which is more than I can say of any other Portuguese soldiers, so far as I have heard."

Terence was then called in again.

"In the first place, I have a pleasant piece of news to give you, Mr. O'Connor, namely, that I have received from home an official letter, that on my recommendation you have been gazetted to the rank of lieutenant and transferred to my staff; in the second place, I have decided, that while still retaining you on my staff, you will be continued in your present command; I shall obtain for you a commission as colonel in the

Portuguese service, but your corps will form part of my command, and act with the British army. I shall request Lord Beresford to appoint Mr. Herrara to the rank of lieutenant-colonel, and shall recommend that commissions be given to his troopers. The two orderlies, of whose services you spoke so highly, I shall recommend for commissions in our army, and shall request Lord Beresford to give them local rank as majors."

Terence coloured with pleasure and confusion.

"I am greatly obliged to you, General," he said; "but I do not at all feel that the services that I have tried to perform——"

"That is for me to judge," the general said, kindly. "All the officers here quite agree with me, that those services have been very marked and exceptional and are at one with me as to how they should be recognized. Moreover, in obtaining for you the rank of colonel in the Portuguese army, I am not only recognizing those services, but am adding to the power that you will have of rendering further services to the army. Although attached to our forces, you will receive your colonel's commission from Lord Beresford, who is now the general appointed by the Portuguese government to command their army."

It was now late, and the party rose. All of them shook hands warmly with Terence, who retired with his friend Captain Nelson. The latter told him before they went in to dinner that he had had a bed put up for him in his own room.

"Well, Colonel O'Connor," Nelson laughed, "you must allow me to be the first to salute you as my superior officer."

"It is absurd altogether," Terence said, almost ruefully. "Still, Captain Nelson, though I may hold a superior rank in the Portuguese army, that goes for very little. I have seen enough of Portuguese officers to know that even their own soldiers have not got any respect for them, and in our own army I am only a lieutenant."

"That is so, lad; however, there was never promotion more deserved. And as you hung, or rather left to be hung, a Portuguese colonel, it is only right that you should supply the deficiency."

"I hope I shall not have to wear a Portuguese uniform," Terence said, earnestly.

"I should think not, O'Connor, but I will ask the general in the morning. Of course, you will not wear your present uniform, because you are now gazetted into the staff and out of your own regiment. Now we will smoke a quiet cigar before we turn in. Have you any other story to tell me that you have not already related?"

"Well, yes, I have one, but it is only of a personal interest;" and he then gave an account of his discovery of his cousin in the convent at Oporto, and how he had managed to rescue her, ending by saying: "I have told you the story, Nelson, so that if by any unexpected accident it is found out that she is an escaped nun, and her friends appeal to the general for protection, you may be aware of the circumstances, and help."

"Certainly I will do so," Captain Nelson said, warmly. "You certainly have a wonderful head for devising plans."

"I began it early," Terence laughed. "I was always in mischief before I got my commission, and I suppose that helps me; but you see I had wonderful luck."

"I don't say anything against your luck; but good luck is of no use unless a fellow knows how to take advantage of it, and that is just what you have done. I suppose that you will stay here for a day or two."

"My horse wants a couple of days' rest, and I have my

uniform to get. I suppose I can get one made in a couple of days, whether it is a Portuguese or an English one."

"Yes, I dare say you will be able to manage that."

The next morning, to his great satisfaction, Terence learned that the general said he had better wear staff uniform, and he accordingly went with Captain Nelson and was measured.

"Your Portuguese seems to have improved amazingly in the two months you have been away," the latter said, as they came out from the shop; "you seem to jabber away quite fluently."

"I have been talking nothing else, and Herrara has acted as my instructor, so I get on very fairly now."

At this moment a carriage drove past them.

"That is the Bishop of Oporto," said Terence; "I suppose he has just arrived."

"It is a good thing that he does not know you as well as you know him," Captain Nelson said, dryly; "if he did, your adventures would be likely to be cut short by a knife between your shoulders some dark night."

"He does not know me at all," Terence laughed; "the advantages are all on my side in the present case."

"It is an advantage," Captain Nelson laughed. "When I think that you have raised your hand against that venerable but somewhat truculent prelate, I shudder at your boldness. I only caught a glimpse of him as he passed, but I could see that he looks rather scared."

"Perhaps he hasn't recovered yet from the fright I gave him," laughed Terence; "I have seen and heard enough of his doings, and paid him a very small instalment of the debt due to him."

The uniforms were promised for the next evening, and Terence felt when he put them on that they were a considerable improvement upon his late one, stained and discoloured as it was by wet, mud, and travel. After paying a visit to the general to say good-bye, Terence mounted and started for Coimbra.

Upon his arrival there four days later he at once reported himself to the commandant.

"I received a copy of the general order of last Tuesday," the latter said, "and congratulate you warmly on being confirmed in your rank. I thought that it would be so, for one could not reckon that, had another taken your place, your corps would have maintained its present state of efficiency."

"You are very good to say so, Colonel, but any British officer appointed to command it would do as well or better than I should."

"I don't think that he would in any way; but certainly he would not be followed with the same confidence by his men as they would follow you, and with troops like these everything depends upon their confidence in their commander."

"The corps is now attached to our army, Colonel; you were good enough to order them to be rationed before, but I have now an order from the general for them to draw pay and rations the same as the British troops."

"That is all right," the colonel said, examining the document; "I will take a copy of it, but as it is a general order you must keep the original yourself. I see that you have now adopted the uniform of the staff. It is certainly a great improvement upon that of an infantry officer, and appearances go for a good deal among these Portuguese. I see, by the way, that you have got your step in our army."

"Yes, Colonel, the general was good enough to recommend me. Of course I am glad in one way, but I am sorry that it has put me out of the regiment that I have been brought up with. But, of course, it was necessary, for I could not have gone over other men's heads in it."

"No, when a man gets special promotion it is always into another regiment for that reason. You will be glad to hear that your men have been behaving extremely well in your absence, and that I have not heard of a single case of drunkenness or misconduct among them. I have been down there several times, and always found them hard at work drilling; they seem to me to improve every time I see them."

On leaving the colonel's quarters Terence rode to his cousin's. Mary rose with an exclamation of surprise as he entered.

"What a handsome uniform, Terence! How is it that you have changed it?"

"I am now regularly on the general's staff, Mary, and this is the uniform."

"You look very well in it," she said; "don't you think so, Lorenza?"

"I do, indeed," her friend agreed; "it does make a difference."

"Well, to begin with, it is clean and new," Terence laughed; "and though the other was not old, it had seen its best days. But I have more news, Mary; you have now to address your cousin as colonel."

Mary clapped her hands, and Don Jose and his family uttered exclamations of pleasure.

"It is quite right," Mary said; "it is ridiculous that Señor Herrara should be colonel and you only Mr. O'Connor."

"It does not matter much about a name," he said. "I commanded before and I shall do so now, but I have got Portuguese rank."

"Why did not they make you an English colonel?" Mary asked, rather indignantly.

Terence laughed. "I shall be lucky if I get that in another twenty years, Mary. I am a lieutenant now—I have got the step since you saw me last—but I am to rank as a colonel in the Portuguese army as long as I command this corps, which I am glad to say is now to form a part of the British army. Herrara is to have the rank of lieutenant-colonel. Bull and Macwitty will, I hope, get their commissions as ensigns in the British army, with local rank of majors. The general will recommend that Herrara's troopers all get commissions in the Portuguese army."

"Ah, well! I am pleased that your services are appreciated, Terence. We are very glad that you have come back, Lorenza especially so, as, now you have returned, she thinks she will see more of Señor Herrara."

"The bishop is in Lisbon, Mary."

"That is not such good news, Terence. I will be very careful to keep out of his way."

"Do," he said. "I have spoken to Captain Nelson, one of the general's staff, about you, and if by any chance you should be recognized as an escaped nun, I hope that Don Jose will go to him at once and ask him to obtain the general's protection for you, which will, I am sure, be given. Your father was an Irishman. You are a British subject, and have a right to protection. You won't forget the name, Don Jose—Captain Nelson?"

"I will write it down at once," the Portuguese said, "but as Donna Mary will pass under the name of Dillon, and her dress has so changed her appearance, I do not think that there is the smallest fear of her being recognized. Indeed, no one could know her except the bishop himself."

"You may be sure that I shall not go out much in Lisbon," Mary said, "and if I do I will keep my promise to be always closely veiled."

CHAPTER XX

WITH THE MAYOS

THE news that Terence brought to the regiment gave great and general satisfaction. Herrara was delighted to hear that he was to be made a lieutenant-colonel in his army. Bull and Macwitty were overjoyed on hearing that they had both been recommended for commissions, and Herrara's troopers were equally pleased. The rank and file felt no less gratification, both at the honour of being attached to the British army, and at the substantial improvement in their condition that this would entail.

On the following day Herrara's friends and Mary O'Connor left for Lisbon, and the latter astonished Terence by bursting into tears as she said good-bye to him.

"I have said nothing yet of the gratitude that I feel to you, Terence, for all that you have done for me, for you have always stopped me whenever I have tried to, but I shall always feel it, always; and shall think of you and love you dearly."

"It has been just as fortunate for me as it has been good for you, Mary," he said. "I have never had a sister, and I seem to have found one now."

The girl looked up, pouting. "I don't think," she said, "I should particularly care about being a sister; I think that I would rather remain a cousin."

Terence looked surprised and a little hurt.

"You are only a silly boy," she laughed, "but will understand better some day. Well, good-bye, Terence," and the smile faded from her face.

"Good-bye, dear. Take great care of yourself in Lisbon, and be sure that you look out to see if the Mayo Fusiliers

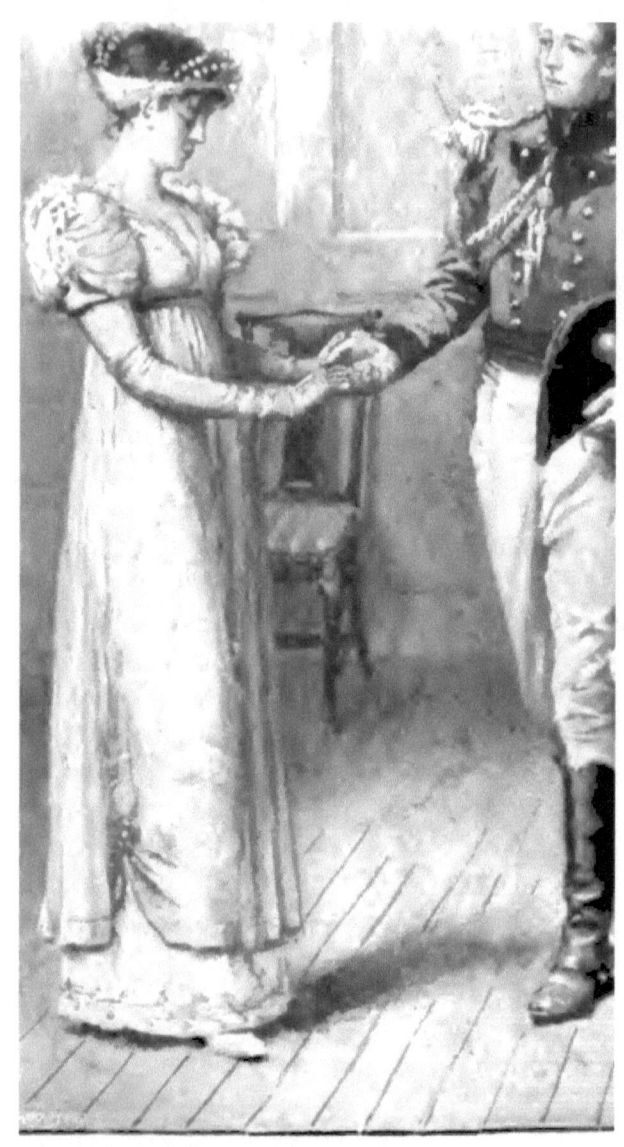

TERENCE BIDS GOOD-BYE TO HIS COUSIN, MARY

arrive while you are there. I heard that they were about to embark again with a force that General Hill is bringing out, but my father won't be with them, I am afraid. I have not heard from him, but I should hardly think that he will be fit for hard service again; yet, if he should be, he will tell you where to go to till we get back. At any rate, don't start for England until the regiment comes. I fancy that it will be at Lisbon before you are, and Don Jose can easily find out for you whether father is with it. If he is not, go to Ballinagra. I have written instructions how you are to travel, but you had better write to him there directly you land, and I have no doubt that he will come over and fetch you. I don't know anything about London, but you had better see Captain Nelson at Lisbon. Here is a note I have written to him, asking him where you had better go, and what you had better do when you get to London."

The day after the party had left, Terence marched with his corps north, and established himself at Carvalho, where the road from Oporto passed over the spurs of the Serra de Caramula, in order to check the incursions of French cavalry from Oporto. In the course of the next fortnight he had several sharp engagements with them. In the last of these, when making a reconnaissance with both regiments, he was met by the whole of Franceschi's cavalry. They charged down on all four sides of the square into which he formed his force, expecting that, as upon two previous occasions, the Portuguese would at once break up at their approach. They stood, however, perfectly firm, and received the cavalry with such withering volleys that Franceschi speedily drew off, leaving upwards of two hundred dead behind him.

The day after this fight Terence received a letter from Mary, saying that General Hill had arrived before they reached Lisbon, and that Don Jose had learned that Major O'Connor had retired on half-pay. Also that Captain Nelson had obtained a passage for her in one of the returning transports, and had given her a letter to his mother, who resided in London, asking her to receive her until she heard from the major.

A few days afterwards he learned from Colonel Wilberforce that the English army had marched for Leirya. General Hill's force of five thousand men and three hundred horses for the artillery arrived at an opportune moment. The storming of Oporto, the approach of Victor to Badajos, after totally defeating Cuesta's Spanish army, killing three-fifths of his men, and capturing thousands of prisoners, while Lapisse was advancing from the east, had created a terrible panic in Portugal. Beresford's orders were disobeyed, many of his regiments abandoned their posts, and the populace in Lisbon were in a state of furious turmoil. Hill's arrival to some extent restored confidence, the disorders were repressed, and Sir John Cradock now felt himself strong enough to advance.

Terence's report of the repulse of Franceschi's cavalry was answered by a letter from Cradock himself, expressing warm approval at the conduct of the corps.

"There is but little fear of an advance by Soult at present," he said. "He must know that we have received reinforcements, and he will not venture to march on Lisbon, as the force now gathering at Leirya could operate upon his flank and rear. I shall be glad, therefore, if you would march with your command to the latter town. The example of your troops cannot but have a good effect upon the raw Portuguese levies, and, in the event of our advancing to the relief of Ciudad-Rodrigo, could render good service by clearing the passes, driving in the French outposts, and keeping me well informed of the state of the roads, the accommodation available for the troops, and the existence of supplies."

Immediately on receipt of this Terence marched for Leirya,

where the British army was under canvas. On the way down they halted for a night at Coimbra.

"An official letter came for you last night, O'Connor," Colonel Wilberforce said. "I kept it until I should have an opportunity of forwarding it to you. Here it is, duly addressed, Colonel O'Connor, the Minho Regiment."

This was the name Sir John Cradock suggested to Terence, as a memorial of the service they had rendered in repulsing Soult at that river. It was the first time Terence had seen his name with the prefix of colonel.

"It looks like a farce," he said, as he broke the seal.

Inside was an official document, signed by Lord Beresford, to the effect that as a recognition of the very great services rendered by Lieutenant O'Connor, an officer on the staff of Sir John Cradock, when in command of the two battalions of the Minho Regiment, and in accordance with the strong recommendation of the British general, Lieutenant Terence O'Connor is hereby appointed to the rank of colonel in the Portuguese service, with the pay and allowances of his rank. Colonel O'Connor is to continue in command of the regiments, which will be attached to the British army, under the command of Sir John Cradock.

"Here is also a letter for your friend Herrara, and a much more bulky one; will you hand it to him?"

Herrara's letter contained his promotion to lieutenant-colonel, with an order to remain under Terence's command; also fourteen commissions, two giving Bull and Macwitty the Portuguese rank of major, the remaining being captain's commissions for the twelve troopers.

Two days later they reached Leirya. The April sun rendered shelter unnecessary for the Portuguese, and after establishing them, for the present, a quarter of a mile away from the British camp, he went and reported his arrival to the officer in command, and was told that he could not do better than bivouac on the ground he had selected. Leaving the headquarters he soon found where the Mayo regiment was encamped, and made his way to the officers' marquee. They were just sitting down to lunch when, at the entry of an officer on the general's staff, the colonel at once rose gravely. O'Grady was the first to recognize the newcomer.

"Be jabers," he shouted, "but it is Terence O'Connor himself!" There was a general rush to shake hands with him, and a din of voices and a confusion of questions and greetings.

"And what in the world have you got that uniform on for, Terence?" O'Grady asked, when the din somewhat subsided. "We saw that the general had appointed you as one of his aides-de-camp when you got here after Corunna, but you would wear your own uniform all the same."

"What matters about his uniform, O'Grady?" the others exclaimed. "What we want to know is how he saved his life at Corunna, when we all thought that he was either killed or taken prisoner."

"Wait till the lad has got something to eat and drink," the colonel said, peremptorily. "Pray take your seats, gentlemen. You take this chair by me, O'Connor; and now, while you are waiting for your plate, tell us in a few words how you escaped. Everyone made sure that you were killed. We heard that Fane had sent you to carry an order, that you had delivered it, and then started to rejoin him; from that time nobody saw you alive or dead."

"The matter was very simple, Colonel. My horse was hit in the head with a round shot. I went a frightful cropper on some stones in the middle of a clump of bushes. I lay there insensible all night, and coming-to in the morning, saw that the French had advanced, and the firing on the hill over the town told me that the troops had got safely on board ship.

I lay quiet all day, and at night made off, sheltered for a couple of days with some peasants on the other side of the hill, joined Romana, went to the Portuguese frontier with him, and then rode to Lisbon, where Sir John Cradock was good enough to put me on his staff."

"We heard you had turned up safely at Lisbon, and glad we were, as you may be sure, and a good jollification we had over it. As for O'Grady, it has served as an excuse for an extra tumbler ever since."

"Bad excuses are better than none," Terence laughed, "and if it hadn't been that, it would have been something else."

"Shut up, you young scamp," O'Grady said. "How is it that you have not answered my question? Why are you wearing staff-officer's uniform instead of your own?"

"Have you not heard, Colonel," Terence said, "that I no longer belong to the regiment?"

There was a chorus of expressions of regret round the table.

"And how has that happened, Terence?" the colonel asked. "That is bad news for us all, anyway."

"I was gazetted lieutenant a month ago, Colonel. I suppose you had sailed from England before the *Gazette* came out."

"I suppose so, lad. Well, you richly deserved your promotion, if it was only for that affair on board the *Sea-horse*, and you ought to have had it long ago."

"I am awfully sorry to leave the regiment. It has been my home as long as I can remember, and wherever I may be, I shall always regard it in that light."

"And so you remain on the staff at present, O'Connor?"

"Well, sir, I am on the staff still, but for the present I am on detached duty."

"What sort of duty, Terence?"

"I have the honour to command two Portuguese regiments that marched in an hour ago."

A shout of laughter followed the announcement.

"Bedad, Terence," O'Grady said, "that crack on your head hasn't changed your nature, thanks to your thick skull. I suppose it is poking fun at us that you are. But you won't take us in this time."

"I saw the regiments pass at a distance," the colonel said, "and they marched in good order, too, which is more than I have seen any other Portuguese troops do. Now you mention it, I did see an officer, in what looked like a British uniform, riding with the men, but it was too far off to see what branch of the service he belonged to. That was you, was it?"

"That was me, sure enough, Colonel."

"And what were you doing there? Tell us, like a good boy."

"Absurd as it may appear, and, indeed, absurd as it is, I am in command of those two regiments."

Again a burst of incredulous laughter arose. Terence took out his commission and handed it to the colonel.

"Perhaps, Colonel, if you will be kind enough to read that out loud, my assurance will be believed."

"Faith, it was not your assurance that we doubted, Terence, me boy!" O'Grady exclaimed. "You have plenty of assurance, and to spare; it is the statement that we were doubting."

The colonel glanced down the document, and his face assumed an expression of extreme surprise.

"Gentlemen," he said, rising, "if you will endeavour to keep silence for a minute, I will read this document."

The surprise on his own face was repeated on the faces of all those present, as he proceeded with his reading. O'Grady was the first to break the silence.

"In the name of St. Peter," he said, "what does it all mean? Are you sure that it is a genuine document, Colonel? Terence is capable of anything by way of a joke."

"It is undoubtedly genuine, O'Grady. It is dated from Lord Beresford's quarters, and signed by his lordship himself as commander-in-chief of the Portuguese army. How it comes about beats me as much as it does you. But before we ask any questions we will drink a toast. Gentlemen, fill your glasses; here is to the health of Colonel Terence O'Connor."

The toast was drank with much enthusiasm, mingled with laughter, for many of them had still a suspicion that the whole matter was somehow an elaborate trick played by Terence.

"Now, Colonel O'Connor, will you please to favour us with an account of how General Cradock and Lord Beresford have both united in giving you so big a step up."

"It is a long story, Colonel."

"So much the better," the colonel replied. "We have nothing to do, and it will keep us all awake."

Terence's account of his interview with the colonel of the ordenanças, the demand by Cortingos that he should hand over the money he was escorting, and the subsequent gathering to attack the house, and the manner in which the leaders were captured, the rioters appeased and subsequently advised to direct their efforts to obtain arms and ammunition, excited exclamations of approval; but the belief that the story was a pure romance still prevailed in the minds of many, and Terence saw Captain O'Grady and Dick Ryan exchanging winks. It was not until Terence spoke of his rapid march to the mouth of the Minho, as soon as he heard that the French were concentrating there, that he began to be seriously listened to; and when he told how Soult's attempt to cross had been defeated, and the French general obliged to change the whole plan of the campaign, and to march round by Orense, the conviction that all this was true was forced upon them.

"By the powers, Terence!" the colonel exclaimed, bringing his hand down on his shoulder, "you are a credit to the ould country. I am proud of you, me boy, and it is little I thought when O'Flaherty and myself conspired to get ye into the regiment that you were going to be such a credit to it. Gentlemen, before Colonel O'Connor goes further, we will drink his health again."

This time there was no laughter mixed with the cheers. Many of the officers left their seats and came round to shake his hand warmly, O'Grady foremost among them.

"Sure I thought at first that it was blathering you were, Terence; but, begorra, I see now that it's gospel truth you are telling, and I am proud of you. Faith, I am as proud as if I were your own father, for haven't I brought you up in mischief of all kinds? Be the poker, I would have given me other arm to have been with you."

The rest of the story was listened to without interruption. When it was concluded, Colonel Corcoran again rose.

"Gentlemen, we will for the third time drink to the health of Colonel O'Connor, and I think that you will agree with me that if ever a man deserved to be made a colonel it's himself."

This time O'Grady and three others rushed to where Terence was sitting, seized him, and before he knew what they were going to do, hoisted him onto the shoulders of two of them, and carried him in triumph round the table. When at length quiet was restored, and Terence had resumed his seat, the colonel said:

"By the way, Terence, there was a little old gentleman called on me three days after we landed to ask if Major O'Connor was with the regiment. I told him that he was not, having gone on half-pay for the present on account of a wound. He seemed rather pleased than otherwise, I thought, and I asked him pretty bluntly what he wanted to know for. He brought an interpreter with him, and said through him that he hoped that I would not press that question, especially as a lady was concerned in the matter. It bothered me entirely. Why, from the time we landed at the Mondego till your father was hit at Vimiera I don't believe we ever had the chance to speak to a woman. It may be that it was some lady that nursed him there after we had marched away, and who had taken a fancy to him. The ould man may have been her father, and was perhaps mighty glad to hear that the major was not coming back again."

Terence burst into a shout of laughter.

"My dear Colonel," he said, "the respectable old gentleman did not call on behalf of his daughter, but on behalf of a cousin of mine, who was wanting to find my father; and Don Jose, who was in charge of her, was glad to hear that he was going to remain in England."

"A cousin!" O'Grady exclaimed. "Why how in the name of fortune does a lady cousin of yours come to be cruising about in such an outlandish place as this?"

"That is another story, Colonel, and I have talked until I am hoarse now, so that that must keep until another sitting. It is quite time that I was off to see how my men are getting on."

"Of course you will dine with us?"

"Not to-night, Colonel; this has been a long sitting, and I would rather not begin a fresh one."

"Well, we will come and have a look at your regiments."

"I would rather you did not come until to-morrow, Colonel. The men have marched five-and-twenty miles a day for the last five days, and they want rest, so I should not like to parade them again. If you will come over, say at twelve o'clock to-morrow, I shall be proud to show them."

The corps now possessed five tents, Terence having obtained four more at Coimbra. Herrara and himself occupied one, while two were allotted to the officers of each regiment. Bull and Macwitty had both by this time picked up sufficient Portuguese to be able to get on comfortably, and had agreed with Terence that although they would like to remain together, it was better that each should stay with the officers of his own regiment.

At twelve o'clock next day Colonel Corcoran came over with nearly the whole of the officers of the Mayo regiment, and was accompanied by many others, as they had the night before given many of their acquaintances an outline of Terence's story.

The men had been on foot from an early hour after breakfast. There had been a parade. Every man's firelock, accoutrements, and uniform had been very closely inspected, and when they fell in again at a quarter to twelve a most rigid inspection would have failed to find any fault with their appearance. Terence joined the colonel as soon as he came on the ground.

"So your officers are all mounted, I see, Terence?"

"Yes, Colonel; you see the companies are over two hundred strong, for the losses we had have been filled up since, and one officer to each corps could do but little unless he were mounted."

"The men looked uncommonly well, Terence, uncommonly well. I should like to walk along the line before you move them."

"By all means, Colonel. Their uniforms do not fit as well as I should like, but I had to take them as they were served out, and have had no opportunity of getting them altered."

Since the inspection at Coimbra the men had been taught the salute, and as Terence shouted:

"Attention! General salute! Present arms!" the men executed the order with a sharpness and precision that would have done no discredit to a British line regiment. Then the colonel and officers walked along the line, after which the troops were put through their manœuvres for an hour, and then dismissed.

"Upon my word, it is wonderful," Colonel Corcoran said. "Why, if the beggars had been at it six months they could not have done it better."

There was a chorus of agreement from all the officers round.

"We could not have done some of those movements better ourselves, could we, O'Driscol?"

"That we could not," the major said, heartily. "Another three months' work and these two regiments would be equal to our best; and I can understand now how they stood up against the charge of Franceschi's cavalry regiments."

"Now, Colonel, I cannot ask you all to a meal," Terence said; "my arrangements are not sufficiently advanced for that yet; but I managed to get hold of some very good wine this morning, and I hope that you will take a glass all round before you go back to camp."

"That we will, and with pleasure, for the dust has well-nigh choked me. It is a different thing drilling on this sandy ground from drilling on a stretch of good turf. Of course, you will come back and lunch with us, and bring your friend Herrara."

Herrara, however, excused himself. He did not know a word of English, and felt that until he could make himself understood he would feel uncomfortable at a gathering of English officers. After lunch Terence was called upon to tell the story about his cousin. Among his friends of the regiment he had no fear of his adventure with the bishop getting abroad, and he therefore related the whole story as it happened.

"By my sowl," O'Grady said to him, afterwards, "Terence O'Connor, you take me breath away altogether. To think that a year ago you were just a gossoon, and here ye are a colonel—a Portuguese colonel, I grant, but still a colonel—fighting Soult, and houlding defiles, and making night attacks, and thrashing the French cavalry, and carrying off a nun from a convent, and outwitting a bishop, and playing all sorts of divarsions. It bates me entirely. There is Dicky Ryan, who, as I tould him yesterday, had just the same chances as you have had, just Dicky Ryan still. I tould him he ought to blush down to his boots."

"And what did he say, O'Grady?"

"The young spalpeen had the impudence to say that there was I, Captain O'Grady, just the same as when he first joined, and, barring the loss of an arm, divil a bit the better. And the worst of it is, it was true entirely. If I could but find a pretty cousin shut up in a convent you would see that I would not be backward in doing what had to be done; but no such luck comes to me at all, at all."

"Quite so, O'Grady; I have had tremendous luck. And it has all come about owing to my happening to think it would be a good thing to take possession of that French lugger."

"Don't you think it, me boy," O'Grady said, seriously. "No doubt a man may have a turn of luck, though it is not everyone who takes advantage of it when it comes. But when you see a man always succeeding, always doing something that other fellows don't do, and making his way up step by step, you may put it down that luck has very little to do with the matter, and that he has got something in him that other men haven't got. You may have had some luck to start with—enough, perhaps, to have got you your lieutenancy, though I don't say that it was luck; but you cannot put the rest of it down to that."

At this moment Dick Ryan came and joined them.

"Well, Dicky," Terence said, "have you had no fun lately in the regiment?"

"Not a scrap," Ryan said, dismally. "There was not much chance of fun on that long march; on board ship there was a storm all the way; then we were kept on board the transport at Cork nearly three months. Everyone was out of temper, and a mouse would not have dared squeak on board the ship. I have had a bad time of it since the day we lost you."

"Oh, well, you will have plenty of chances yet, Dicky."

"It has not been the same thing since you have gone, Terence," he grumbled. "Of course we could not always be having fun; but you know that we were always putting our heads together and talking over what might be done. It was good fun, even if we could not carry it out. I tried to stir up the others of our lot, but they don't seem to have it in them. I wish you could get me transferred to your regiment. I know that we should have plenty of fun there."

"I am afraid that it could not be done, Dicky, though I should like it immensely. But you see you have not learned a word of Portuguese, and you would be of no use in the world."

"There it is, you see," O'Grady said. "That is one of the points which had no luck in it, Terence. You were always trying to talk away with the peasants; and, riding about as you did as Fane's aide-de-camp, you had opportunities of doing so and made the most of them. Now there are not three other fellows in the regiment who can ask a simple question. I can shout *Carajo!* at a mule-driver who loiters behind, and can add two or three other strong Portuguese words, but there is an end of it. Cradock would never have sent you that errand to Romana if you could not have talked enough to have made yourself understood. You could never have jawed those mutineers and put them up to getting hold of the arms. If Dicky Ryan and I had been sent on that mission we should just have been as helpless as babies, and should, like enough, have been murdered by that mob. There was no luck about that, you see; it was just because you had done your best to pick up the language, and nobody else had taken the trouble to learn a word of it."

"I see that, O'Grady," Ryan said, dolefully. "I don't envy Terence a bit. I know that he has quite deserved what he has got, and that if I had had his start, I should never have got any farther. Still, I wish I could go with him. I know that he has always been the one who invented our plans. Still, I have had a good idea sometimes."

"Certainly you have, Dicky; and if I have generally started an idea, you have always worked it up with me. Well, if you will get up Portuguese a bit, and I see a chance of asking for another English officer, say as adjutant, I will see if I cannot get you; but I could not ask for you without being able to give as a reason that you could speak Portuguese well."

"I will try, Terence; upon my honour, I will try hard," Ryan said. "I will get hold of a fellow and begin to-day."

"Quite right, Dicky," O'Grady said. "Faith, I would do it meself, if it wasn't in the first place that I am too old to learn, and in the second place that I niver could learn anything when I was a boy. I used to get thrashed every day regularly, but divil a bit of difference did it make. I got to read and write, and there I stuck. As for the ancients, I was always mixing them up together; and whether it was Alexander or Cæsar who marched over the Alps and burnt Jerusalem, divil a bit do I know, and I don't see that if I did know it would do me a hap'orth of good."

"I don't think that particular piece of knowledge would, O'Grady," Terence agreed, with a hearty laugh; "still, even if you did learn Portuguese, I couldn't ask for you. I don't mind Dicky, because he is only a year senior to me; but if they made me commander-in-chief of the Portuguese army, I could never have the cheek to give you an order."

Three weeks later came the startling news that Sir Arthur Wellesley had arrived at Lisbon, and was to assume the command of the army. Sir John Cradock was to command at Gibraltar. There was general satisfaction at the news, for the events of the last campaign had given all who served under him an implicit confidence in Sir Arthur; but it was felt that Sir John Cradock had been very hardly treated. In the first place, he was a good way senior to Sir Arthur, and in the second place, he had battled against innumerable difficulties, and the time was now approaching when he would reap the benefit of his labours. To Terence the news came almost as a blow, for he felt that it was probable he might be at once appointed to a British regiment.

Personally he would not have cared so much, but he would have regretted it greatly for the sake of the men who had followed him. It was true that they might obey Herrara as willingly as they did himself, but he knew that the native officers did not possess anything like the same influence with the Portuguese that the English did, and that there might be a rapid deterioration in their discipline and morale. He remained in a state of uncertainty for a week, at the end of which time he received a letter from Captain Nelson, and tearing it open, read as follows:—

My Dear O'Connor,

I dare say you have been feeling somewhat doubtful as to your position since you heard that Sir Arthur has superseded Sir John Cradock. I may tell you at once that he has taken over the whole of Sir John's staff, yourself, of course, included. I ventured to suggest to Sir John that he should mention your case to Sir Arthur, and he told me that he had intended to take the opportunity of the first informal talk he had with him to do so. The opportunity came yesterday, and Sir John went fully into your case, showed him the reports, and mentioned how he came to appoint you because of the clear and lucid description you gave of the movements of every division of Moore's army.

Sir Arthur remembered your name at once, and the circumstances under which he had mentioned you in general orders for your conduct on board the transport coming out. Sir John told me that he said, ' There is no doubt that O' Connor is a singularly promising young officer, Sir John. The check he gave Soult on the Minho might have completely reversed the success of the Frenchman's campaign had he had any but Spaniards and Portuguese to oppose him. The report shows that O' Connor has done wonders with those two regiments of his, and I shall not think of removing him from their command. A trustworthy native corps of that description would be of the greatest advantage, and will act, like Trant and Wilson's commands, as the eyes of the army. I am much obliged to you for your having brought the case before my notice, for otherwise, not knowing the circumstances, I might very well have considered that the position of a lieutenant on my staff as the commander of two native regiments was an anomalous one. I should, no doubt, have inquired how it occurred before I thought of superseding an officer you had selected, but your explanation more than justifies his appointment.' So you see, Terence, the change will make no difference in your position. And as I fancy Sir Arthur will not let the grass grow under his feet, you are likely to have a lively time of it before long. By the way, a Gazette *has arrived, and it contains the appointment of your two men to commissions.*

While waiting at Leirya, Terence had ordered uniforms for all the officers. He had, after consultation with Herrara, decided upon one approximating rather to the cavalry than to infantry dress, as being more convenient for mounted officers. It consisted of tight-fitting green patrol jacket, breeches of the same colour, and half-high boots and a gold-embroidered belt and slings. The two English officers wore a yellow band round their caps, and Herrara a gold one.

"I am sure, Colonel O'Connor," Bull said, when Terence told Macwitty and him that they had been gazetted to commissions, "we cannot thank you enough. Macwitty and I have done our best, but it has been nothing more than teaching drill to a lot of recruits."

"We had two or three hard fights, too, Bull; and I have very good reason for thinking most highly of you, for I should never have got the corps into an efficient state without your assistance. And, indeed, I doubt whether I should have ventured upon the task at all if I had not been sure that I should be well seconded by you."

"It is good of you to say so, Colonel," Macwitty said; "but at any rate, it has been a rare bit of luck for us, and little did we think when we were ordered to accompany you it was going to lead to our getting commissions. Well, we will do our best to deserve them."

"That I am sure you will, Macwitty; and now that the campaign is going to commence in earnest, and we may have two or three years' hard fighting, you may have opportunities of getting another step before you go home."

Three days later an order came to Terence to march north again with his corps, and to place himself in some defensible position north of the Mondego, and to co-operate, if necessary, with Trant and Silveira, also ordered to take post beyond the river. Cuesta, the Portuguese general, had gathered a fresh army of six thousand cavalry and thirty thousand infantry. The greater portion were in a position in front of Victor's outposts. Between the Tagus and the Mondego were 16,000 Portuguese troops of the line, under Lord Beresford, that had been drilled and organized to some extent by British officers. The British and German troops numbered 22,000 fighting men.

Sir Arthur Wellesley, at Lisbon, had the choice of either falling upon Victor or Soult. The former would be the most advantageous operation, but, upon the other hand, the Portuguese were most anxious to recover Oporto, their second city, with the fertile country round it.

Another fact which influenced the decision was that Cuesta was alike incapable and obstinate, and was wholly indisposed to co-operate warmly with the British. The British commander, therefore, decided in the first place to attack Soult, and the force at Leirya was ordered to march to Coimbra. Five British battalions and two regiments of cavalry, with 7,000 Portuguese troops, were ordered to Abrantes and Santarem to check Victor, should he endeavour to make a rapid march upon Lisbon. Four Portuguese battalions were incorporated in each British brigade at Coimbra, Beresford retaining 6,000 under his personal command. On the 2d of May Sir Arthur reached Coimbra and reviewed the force, 25,000 strong, 9,000 being Portuguese, 3,000 Germans, and 13,000 British.

Soult was badly informed of the storm that was gathering about him, or many of his officers were disaffected, and were engaged in a plot to have him supplanted; consequently, they kept back the information they received of the movements of the British.

"WHO ARE YOU, SIR, AND WHAT TROOPS ARE THESE?" SIR ARTHUR ASKED, SHARPLY.

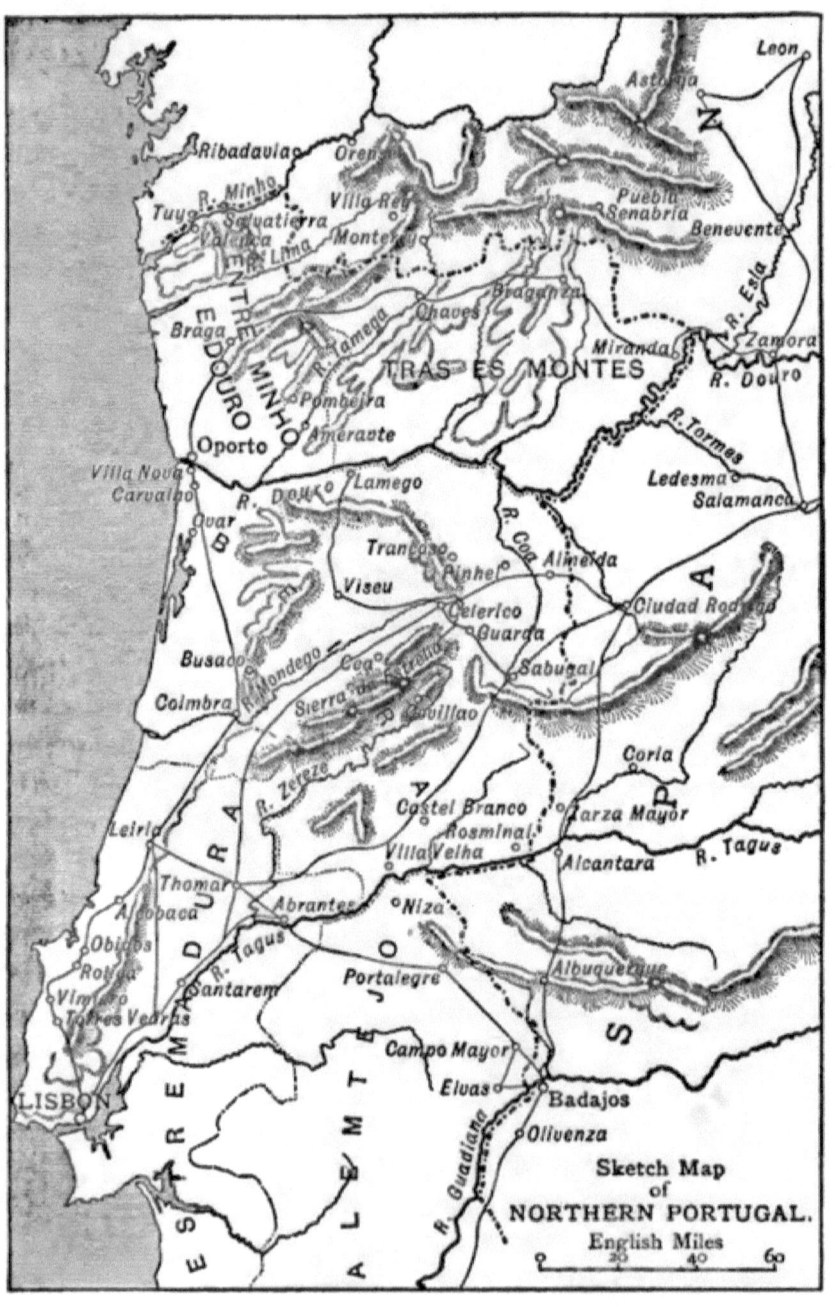

CHAPTER XXI

PORTUGAL FREED

ON the 9th of May Terence was directing the movements of his men, who were practising skirmishing among some rough ground at the bottom of the hill upon which he had taken up his position, to defend, if necessary, the road that crossed it. His men had thrown up several lines of breastworks along the face of the hill to a point where steep ravines protected the flank of his position. Presently he saw a party of horsemen riding down the hill behind him. They reined up suddenly when half-way down the hill and paused to watch what was being done; then they came on again. As they approached, Terence recognized the erect figure of the officer who rode at the head of the party. He cantered up and saluted.

"Who are you, sir, and what troops are these?" Sir Arthur asked, sharply.

"My name is O'Connor, sir. These men constitute the corps that I have the honour to command."

"Form them up in line," the general said, briefly.

Terence rode away at a gallop, and as soon as he reached the spot where his bugler was standing—for bugles had now taken the place of the horns that had before served the purpose—the latter at once blew the assembly, and then the order to form line. The men dashed down at the top of their speed, and in a very short time formed up in a long line with their officers in front.

"Break them into columns of companies," the general, who had now ridden with the staff to the front, said.

The manœuvre was performed steadily and well.

"Send out the alternate companies as skirmishers, while

the other companies form line and move forward in support."
When this had been done the order came: "Skirmishers, form into company squares to resist enemy's cavalry."

This had been so frequently practised that in a few seconds the six squares were formed up in an attitude to receive cavalry.

"That is very well done, Colonel O'Connor," Sir Arthur said, with more warmth than was usual with him. "Your men are well in hand and know their business. It is a very creditable display, indeed; you have proved your capacity for command. I have not forgotten what I have heard of you, sir, and it will not be long before your services are utilized."

So saying he rode on. Captain Nelson lingered behind for a moment to shake hands with Terence.

"You may feel proud of that, O'Connor," he said; "Sir Arthur is not given to praise, I can assure you. Good-bye, I must catch them up;" and, turning, he soon overtook the general's staff.

That the general was well satisfied was proved by the fact that three days later the following appeared in general orders:

"The officer commanding-in-chief on Thursday inspected the corps under the command of Lieutenant (with the rank of colonel in the Portuguese army) O'Connor. He was much pleased with the discipline and quickness with which the corps went through certain movements ordered by him. This corps has already greatly distinguished itself, and Sir Arthur would point to it as an example to be imitated by all officers having command of Portuguese troops."

Soult's position had now become very dangerous. The Spanish and Portuguese insurgents were upon the Lima, and the principal portion of his own force was south of the Douro.

Franceschi's cavalry, supported by infantry and artillery, and by Mermet's division, occupied the country between that river and the Vouga, and was without communication with the centre at Oporto, except by the bridge of boats.

Although aware that there was a considerable force gathering at Coimbra, the French general had no idea that the whole of the British army was assembling there. Confident that success would attend his operations, Sir Arthur directed the Portuguese corps to be in readiness to harass Soult's retreat through the mountain defiles and up the valley of the Tamega, and so to force him to march north instead of making for Salamanca, where he could unite with the French army there.

A mounted officer brought similar orders to Terence. Half an hour after receiving them the corps was on the march. The instructions were brief and simple:

"*You will endeavour to harass Soult as he retreats across the Tras-os-Montes, and try to head him off to the north. Act as circumstances may dictate.*"

The service was a dangerous one, and Terence felt that it was a high honour that the general should have appointed him to undertake it, for he assuredly would not have sent the corps on such a mission had he not considered that they could be relied upon to take care of themselves. They would be wholly unsupported save by parties of peasants and ordenanças; they would have to operate against an army broken, doubtless, by defeat, but all the more determined to push on, as delay might mean total loss.

He followed the line of the Vouga to the point where it emerged from the hills, crossed these, and came down upon the Douro some ten miles above San Joao, at nearly the same spot where he had before made the passage when on his way to join Romana.

He was now well beyond the district held by the French south of the Douro, and, obtaining a number of boats, crossed the river, and then made for Mirandella on the river Tua, and halted some distance from the town, having made a march of over seventy miles in two days. Learning from the peasants that there were no French troops west of the Tamega, he marched the next day to the crest looking down into the valley, and here halted until he could learn that Soult was retreating, and what road he was following. He had not long to wait for news, for, on the night of the 9th, while he was on his march by the Vouga, the British force had moved forward to Aveiro. Hill's division had there taken boats, and proceeding up the lake to Ovar, had landed at sunrise on the 10th, and placed himself on Franceschi's right.

In the meantime Paget's division had marched to Albergaria, while Cotton's division and Trant's command moved to turn Franceschi's position on its right. The darkness and their ignorance of the roads prevented the movement being attended with the hoped-for success. Had the operation been carried out without a hitch, Franceschi and Mermet would both have been driven off the line of retreat to the bridge of Oporto, and must have been captured or destroyed. As it was, Franceschi fell back fighting, joined Mermet's division at Crijo, a day's march in the rear, and although the whole were driven on the following day from this position, they retired in good order, and that night effected their retreat across the bridge of boats, which was then destroyed.

As Franceschi's report informed Soult that the whole force of the allies was now upon him, he at once sent off his heavy artillery and baggage by the road to Amarante. Mermet was posted at Valongo, with orders to patrol the river and to seize every boat. Those at Oporto were also secured. On the morning of the 12th the British force was concentrated behind the hill of Villa Nova, and Sir Arthur took his place on the top of the Serra Convent, from whence he commanded a view of the city and opposite bank. He saw that the French force was stationed for the most part below Oporto. Franceschi's report had led Soult to believe that Hill's division had come by sea, and he expected that the transports would go up to the mouth of the Douro, and that the British would attempt to effect a landing there.

The river took a sharp turn round the Serra Convent, and Sir Arthur saw that another large convent on the opposite bank, known as the Seminary, was concealed by the hill from Soult's position, and that it might be occupied without attracting the attention of the French. After much search a little boat was found; in this a few men crossed and brought back two large boats from the opposite side of the river. In these the troops at once began to cross, and two companies had taken possession of the convent before Soult was aware of what was going on. Then a prodigious din arose. Troops were hurried through the town, the bugles and trumpets sounded the alarm, while the populace thronged to the roofs of their houses wildly cheering and waving handkerchiefs and scarves, and the church bells added to the clamour.

Three batteries of artillery had been brought up close to the Serra Convent, and now that there was no longer need of concealment these were brought forward, and—as the French issued from the town and hurried towards the post held by the two companies that had crossed—opened a heavy fire upon them. The French pushed on gallantly in spite of this fire and the musketry of the soldiers, but the wall of the convent was strong, more boats had been obtained, and every minute added to the number of the defenders. The attack was, nevertheless, obstinately continued. The French artillery endeavoured to blow in the gate, and for a time the position of the defenders was serious, but the enemy's troops were now evacuating the lower part of the town, and immediately they did so the inhabitants brought boats over, and a brigade under Sherwood crossed there.

In the meantime General Murray had been sent with the German division to effect a passage of the river two miles farther up. Soult's orders to take possession of all the boats had been neglected, and it was not long before Murray crossed with his force. The confusion in the French line of retreat was now terrible. A battery of artillery, who brought up the rear, were smitten by the fire of Sherwood's men; many were killed, and the rest cut their traces and galloped on to join the retreating army. Sherwood's men pressed these in the rear, the infantry on the roof of the Seminary poured their fire on the retiring masses, and the guns on the Serra rock swept the long line.

Had Murray now fallen upon the disordered crowd their discomfiture would have been complete, but he held his force inactive, afraid that the French might turn upon him and drive him into the river. General Stewart and Major Harvey, furious at his inactivity, charged the French at the head of two squadrons of cavalry only, dashed through the enemy's column, unhorsed General Laborde and wounded General Foy. Receiving, however, no support whatever from Murray, the gallant little band of cavalry were forced to fight their way back with loss. Thus, as Franceschi had been saved from destruction from an error as to the road, Soult was saved the loss of this army by Murray's timidity, and in both cases Sir Arthur's masterly plans failed in attaining the complete success they deserved.

Terence had engaged several peasants to watch the roads

leading from Oporto, and as soon as he learned that a long train of baggage and heavy guns was leaving the city by the road to Amarante, he crossed the valley, took up a position on the Catalena hill flanking the road, and as the waggons came along opened a sudden and heavy fire upon them. Although protected by a strong guard the convoy fell into confusion, many of the horses being killed by the first volley. Some of the drivers leapt from their seats and deserted their charges, others flogged their horses, and tried to push through the struggling mass. An incessant fire was kept up, but just as Terence was about to order the whole corps to charge down and complete the work, a large body of cavalry, followed by a heavy body of infantry, appeared on the scene.

This was Merle's division, that had hastened up from Valonga on hearing the firing. The advance of the cavalry was checked by the musketry fire, but Merle at once ordered his infantry to mount the hill and drive the Portuguese off. The latter stood their ground gallantly for some time, inflicting heavy loss upon their assailants. Terence saw, however, that he could not hope to withstand long the attack of a whole French division, and leaving two companies behind to check the enemy's advance, he marched along the crest of the hill until he came upon the road crossing from Amarante to the Ave river.

By this time he had been joined by the rear-guard, who had retired in time to make their escape before the French reached the top of the hill. Merle posted a brigade along the crest of the ridge to prevent a repetition of the attack, and to cover Soult's line of retreat, if he were forced to fall back; while Terence took up his position near Pombeiro, whence he presently saw the convoy enter Amarante. He had the satisfaction, however, of noticing that it was greatly diminished in length, a great many of the waggons having been left behind owing to the number of horses that had been killed. His attack had had another advantage of which he was unaware, for it had so occupied Merle's attention that he had neglected to have all the boats taken across the river, which enabled Murray's command to cross the next day, an error which, had Murray been possessed of any dash and energy, would have proved fatal to the French army.

The next day Terence heard the sound of the guns on the Serra height, but the distance was too great for the crack of musketry to reach him, and he had no idea that the British were crossing the river until he saw the French marching across the mouth of the valley towards Amarante. Among such veteran troops discipline was speedly recovered, and they encamped in good order in the valley. That town was, however, in the hands of the Portuguese, Loison, either from treachery or incapacity, having disobeyed Soult's orders and retired before the advance of the Portuguese force under Lord Beresford, and, evacuating Amarante, taken the road to Guimaraens, passing by Pombeiro.

He had sent no news to Soult, and the latter general was altogether ignorant that he had left Amarante. Upon receiving the news from the head of the column he at once saw that the position had now become a desperate one. Beresford, he learned at the same time, had marched up the Tamega valley to take post at Chaves, where Silveira had joined him. A retreat in that direction, therefore, was impossible, and he at once destroyed his baggage, spiked his guns, and at nightfall, guided by a peasant, ascended a path up the Serra Catalena, and, marching all night, rejoined Loison at Guimaraens, passing on his way through Pombeiro. Terence had left the place a few hours before, believing that Soult must return up the valley of the Tamega, and, ignorant that Beresford and Silveira barred the way, he marched after nightfall towards

Chaves and took up a position where he could arrest, for a time, the retreat of the French army.

He had left two of his men at Pombeiro, and had halted but a short time after completing his long and arduous march when his two men came up with the news that Soult had passed by the very place he had a few hours before left. As there was more than one route open to Soult, Terence was unable to decide which he had best take. His men had already performed a very long march, and it was absolutely necessary to give them a rest; he therefore allowed them to sleep during the day. Towards evening he crossed the Serra de Cabrierra and came down upon Salamende, and sent out scouts for news. Destroying the guns, ammunition, and baggage of Loison's division, Soult reached the Carvalho on the evening of the 14th, drew up his army on the position that he had occupied two months before at the battle of Braga, reorganized his forces, and ordering Loison to lead the advance, while he himself took command of the rear, continued his march. The next day Sir Arthur Wellesley, who had been obliged to halt at Oporto until the whole army, with its artillery and train, had passed the river, reached Braga, having marched by a much shorter road.

Terence's scouts brought news that the whole of the French army were marching towards Salamende. Wholly unsupported as he was, ignorant of the position of Beresford and Silveira, and knowing nothing of Sir Arthur's march towards Braga, he decided not to attempt with his force to bar the way to Soult's twenty thousand men, but to hold Salamende for a time and then fall back up the mountains. Before doing so he sent a party to blow up the bridge at Ponte Nova across the Cavado, and also sent his second regiment to defend the passage at Riuvaens.

Thinking it likely that Soult would again cross the mountains to Chaves, he sent Herrara in command of the force at the bridge, while he himself remained at Salamende. Here he had the houses facing the road by which the enemy would approach, loopholed and the road itself barricaded. Late in the afternoon the French cavalry were seen approaching, and a heavy fire was at once opened upon them. The rapidity of the discharges showed Franceschi that the place was held by more than a mere party of peasants, and he drew off his cavalry and allowed the infantry to pass him. For half an hour the Portuguese held their ground and repulsed three determined assaults; then, seeing a strong body of troops ascending the hillside to take the position in flank, Terence ordered his troops to fall back. This they did in good order, and took up a position high up on the hill.

The French made but a short pause; a small body of cavalry that Soult had left near Braga brought him the news that the British army was entering that town. Scouts were sent forward at once, and their report that the bridge of Riuvaens was destroyed, and that 1,200 Portuguese regular troops were on the opposite bank, decided him to take the road by the Ponte Nova. The night was a terrible one; the rain had for two days been continuous, and the troops were drenched to the skin and impatient at the hardship that they had suffered. The scouts reported that the bridge here had also been destroyed, but that one of the parapets was still unbroken, and that the force on the other side consisted only of peasants. Soult ordered Major Doulong, an officer celebrated for his courage, to take a hundred grenadiers and secure the passage.

A violent storm was now raging, and their footsteps being deadened by the roar of the wind, the French crept up, killed the Portuguese sentry on their side of the bridge before he could give the alarm, and then crawled across the narrow line of masonry. Then they rushed up the opposite heights, shouting and firing, and the peasantry, believing that the whole French army were upon them, fled at once. The bridge was hastily repaired, and at four o'clock in the morning the whole of the French army had crossed. Their retreat was opposed at a bridge of a single arch over a torrent, by a party of Portuguese peasantry, but after two repulses the French, led by Major Doulong, carried it.

They were just in time, for in the afternoon the British came upon a strong rear-guard left at Salamende. Some light troops at once turned their flank, while Sherwood attacked them in front, and they fled in confusion to the Ponte Nova. As the general imagined that Soult would take the other road, their retreat in this direction was for some time unperceived, but just as they were crossing, the British artillery opened fire upon the bridge with terrible effect, very many of the enemy being killed before they could effect a passage. Their further retreat was performed without molestation. The British troops had made very long marches in the hopes of cutting Soult's line of retreat, and as the French, unlike the British, carried no provisions for their march, there was now little hope of overtaking them, especially as their main body was far ahead.

Sir Arthur halted for a day at Riuvaens, where Terence's corps was now concentrated, he having marched there the night he was driven out of Salamende. As soon as the British entered the place, the general inquired what corps was holding it, and at once sent for Terence.

"Let me hear what you have been doing, Colonel O'Connor."

Terence had, as soon as he heard that the army had arrived at Salamende, written out a report of his movements from the time that he had marched from Vouga. He now presented it. The general waved it aside.

"Tell me yourself," he said.

Terence related as briefly as possible the course he had followed, and the reasons of his movements.

"Good!" the general said, when he had finished. "Your calculations were all well founded; but, of course, you could not calculate on Soult's night march across the Catalena hills, and, as you knew nothing of the whereabouts of Beresford and Silveira, you had good reason to suppose that Soult would continue his march up the valley of the Tamega to Chaves. That was the only mistake you committed, and an older soldier might well have fallen into the same error. When you had found out your mistake, you acted promptly, and could not have done better than to proceed to Salamende. You did well to destroy both bridges, and to place half your force to defend the passage here, for you naturally supposed, as I supposed myself, that Soult would follow this road down to Chaves.

"You were again deceived, but were in no way to blame. Your position was most judiciously chosen on the Catalena hills on Soult's natural line of retreat, and I heard that the enemy's baggage train had been very severely mauled, and was only saved from destruction by Merle deploying his whole division against the force attacking it. Again I see you made a stout defence at Salamende. We saw a large number of French dead there as we marched in. If everyone else had done as well as you have done, young sir, Soult's army would never have escaped me."

Terence bowed, and retired deeply gratified, for he had been doubtful what his reception would be. He knew that he had done his best, but twice he had been mistaken, and each time the mistake had allowed Soult to pass unmolested; and he was, therefore, all the more pleased on learning that so skilful a general had declared that these mistakes, although unfortunate, were yet natural.

Soult reached Orense on the 20th, without guns, stores, ammunition, or baggage, his men exhausted with fatigue and misery, most of them shoeless, and some without muskets. He had left Orense seventy-six days before with 22,000 men, and had lately been joined by 3,500 from Tuy. He returned with 19,500, having lost 6,000 by sword, sickness, assassination, and capture. Of these 3,600 were taken in the hospitals at Oporto, Chaves, Vianna, and Braga. One thousand were killed in the advance, and the remainder captured or killed within the last eight days.

A day later the news arrived that Victor was at last advancing and a considerable number of the troops assembled at Salamende, among them Terence's corps, were ordered to march to join the force opposed to him. Terence started two hours before the bulk of the force got into motion, and traversing the ground at a high rate of speed, struck the road from Lisbon a day in advance of the British troops. There was, however, no occasion for action, for Victor, who had taken Abrantes, had, on receiving news of the fall of Oporto, at once evacuated that town and fallen back, and for a time all operations ceased on that side.

The British army had suffered but slight loss in battle, but the long marches, the terribly wet weather, and the effect of climate told heavily upon them, and upwards of 4,000 men were, in a short time, in hospital.

Fortunately, however, a reinforcement of equal strength arrived from England, and the fighting strength of the army was therefore maintained. There was still, however, a great want of transport animals; the commissariat were, for the most part, new to their duties, and ignorant of the language. Sir Arthur Wellesley was engaged in the endeavour to get Cuesta to co-operate with him, but the obstinate old man refused to do so unless his plans were adopted; and these were of so wild and impracticable a character that Sir Arthur preferred to act alone, especially as Cuesta's army had already been repeatedly beaten by the French, and the utter worthlessness of his soldiers demonstrated.

The pause of operations in Spain, entailed by the concentration of the commands of Soult, Ney, Victor, and Lapisse on the frontier, had given breathing time to Spain. Large armies had again been raised, and the same confident ideas, the same jealousy between generals, and the same quarrels between the Juntas had been prevalent. Once again Spain was confident that she could alone, and unaided, drive the French across the frontier altogether, forgetful of the easy and crushing defeats that had before been inflicted upon her. Like Moore, Sir Arthur Wellesley was to some extent deceived by these boastings, and believed that he should obtain material assistance in the way of transports and provisions, and that at least valuable diversions might be made by the Spanish army.

He accepted, too, to some extent, the estimate of the Spaniards as to the strength of the French, and believed that their fighting force in the Peninsula did not exceed 130,000 men, whereas in reality it amounted to over 250,000. The greatest impediment to the advance was the want of money, for while the British government continued to pour vast sums into Cadiz and Seville, for the use of the Spaniards, they were unable to find money for the advance of their own army. The soldiers consequently were unpaid, badly fed, almost in rags, and a large proportion of them shoeless; and to meet the most urgent wants, the general was forced to raise loans at exorbitant rates at Lisbon. And yet, while a great general and a victorious army were nearly starving in Portugal, the British government had landed 12,000 troops in Italy and had despatched one of the finest expeditions that ever sailed from England, consisting of 40,000 troops and as many seamen and marines of the fleet, to Walcheren, where no small proportion of them died of fever, and the rest returned home broken in health and unfit for active service, without having performed a single action worthy of merit.

The Mayo Fusiliers were among the regiments stationed at Abrantes, and Terence received orders to take up a position four miles ahead of that town, and hold it unless Victor again advanced in overwhelming strength, and then to fall back on Abrantes. This exactly suited his own wishes. It was pleasant to him to be within a short ride of his old regiment, while at the same time his corps were not encamped with a British division, for his own position was an anomalous one, and among the officers who did not know him he was regarded as a young staff-officer. He could not explain the position he held without constantly repeating the manner in which he had gained a commission as colonel in the Portuguese service.

During the month that had passed without movement, he continued his efforts to improve his corps, and borrowed a dozen non-commissioned officers from Colonel Corcoran to instruct his sergeants in their duty, and thus enable them to train others and relieve the officers of some of their work. He had in his first report stated that he had kept back £1,000 of the money he carried to Romana for the use of his corps, and as he had never received any comment or instructions as to the portion that had not been expended, he had still some money in hand. This he spent in supplementing the scanty rations served out. Frequently he rode into Abrantes and spent the evening with the Mayo Fusiliers. The first time he did so he requested the officers always to call him, as before, Terence O'Connor.

"It is absurd being addressed as colonel when I am only a lieutenant in the service. Of course when I am with the corps it is a different thing; I am its colonel, and must be called so; but it is really very annoying to be called so here."

"You must be feeling quite rusty," Colonel Corcoran said to him, "sitting here doing nothing, after nine months of incessant moving about."

"I am not rusting, Colonel, I am hard at work sharpening my blade; that is, improving my corps. Your men drill my sergeants four hours a day, and for the other eight each of them is repeating the instructions that he has received to three others. So that by the time we are in movement again I hope to have a sergeant who knows something of his duty to each fifty men. I can assure you that in addition to the great need for such men when the troops are out skirmishing, or otherwise detached in small parties, I felt that their appearance on parade was greatly marred by the fact that the non-commissioned officers did not know their proper places or their proper work, which neither Bull nor Macwitty, nor indeed the company officers, could instruct them in, all being cavalrymen."

"Yes, I noticed that when I saw them at Leirya," the colonel said. "Of course it was of no consequence at all as far as their efficiency went, but to the eye of an English officer, naturally, something seemed wanting."

"I should be glad of at least four more officers to each company, and at one time thought of writing to Lord Beresford to ask him to supply me with some, but I came to the conclusion that we had better leave matters as they were. In the first place young officers would know nothing of their work, and nothing of me; and in the second place, if they were men of good family they would not like serving under officers who have been raised from the ranks; and lastly, if they became discontented, they might render the men so. We have done very fairly at present, and we had better go on as we are; and when I get a sufficient number of trained men to furnish a full supply of non-commissioned officers, I shall do better than with commissioned ones, for the men are of course carefully selected, and I know them to be trustworthy, whereas those they sent me might be idle, or worse than useless."

"You spake like King Solomon, Terence," O'Grady said; "not that he can have known anything whatever about military matters."

A roar of laughter greeted this very doubtful compliment.

"Thank you, O'Grady," Terence said. "That is one of the prettiest speeches I have heard for a long time. I shall know where to come for a character."

"You are right there, Terence; but you may live a good many years before you get a chance of calling a whole British army under arms, as you did at Salamanca."

Terence was at once assailed with a storm of questions, for with the exception of O'Grady, no one had suspected the share that he and Dicky Ryan had had in that affair. Terence knew that the latter had kept the secret, for he had asked him only two or three days before, and he therefore assumed an expression of innocence.

"What on earth do you mean, O'Grady?"

"What do I mane? Why, that somehow or other you were at the bottom of that shindy when all the troops were turned out on a false alarm."

"Really, O'Grady, that is too bad. You know that every trick that was played at Athlone was your suggestion, and as we never could find out how that alarm originated, of course you put it down to me, whereas it is just as likely to have been your own work. Colonel Corcoran knows that Dicky and I were in the mess-room at the convent at the time when the alarm broke out."

"That was so," the colonel agreed, "for I know that you were talking to me when Hoolan ran in and told us that there was a row in the town. On what do you base your suspicions, O'Grady?"

"Just upon me knowledge of the two lads, Colonel. Faith, there never was a piece of mischief afloat that they were not mixed up with."

"If that is all you have to say, O'Grady," Terence replied, "I should advise you not to go hunting for mares' nests again. I know that you can see as far into a brick wall as most people, but you cannot see what is going on on the other side."

"All the same, Terence," O'Grady said, doggedly, "to the end of me life I will always believe that you had a hand in the matter. There is no one else that I know of except you and Ryan who would have had the cheek to do such a thing, and I don't believe that you can deny it yourself."

"I shall not trouble myself to plead not guilty, except before a regularly constituted court," Terence laughed. "At any rate, as when the march begins we shall go on first as scouts, it may be that I shall send in news which will turn out a British army again."

"I will forgive you if you do, for it is likely that we should have some divarsion after turning out, instead of marching out and back again like a regiment of omadhauns."

CHAPTER XXII

NEWS FROM HOME

A WEEK after arriving at Abrantes, seeing that there was no probability whatever of fighting for a time, Terence had suggested to Herrara that it would be a good opportunity for him to run down to Lisbon for a few days to see his fiancée and his friends in the town.

"I don't know who you really ought to apply to for leave," he said, "but as we are a sort of half-independent corps, it seems the simplest way for me to take the responsibility. Nobody is ever likely to ask any questions about it; and now that it will simply be a matter of hard drill till the army moves again, you can be very well spared. If it is company work, it is the captain's business. If the two regiments are manœuvring together, they will of course be under Bull and Macwitty, and I should be acting as brigadier."

"I should like to go very much," Herrara said. "I have not yet had the pleasure of introducing myself to my family and friends as a lieutenant-colonel. Of course, I wrote to my people when I received the commission from Lord Beresford; but it would be really fun to surprise some of my school-fellows and comrades, so if you think that it will not be inconvenient I should like very much to go."

"Then if I were you I should start at once. I will give you a sort of formal letter of leave in case you are questioned as you go down. You can get to Santarem to-night and to Lisbon to-morrow afternoon."

"Is there anything that I can do for you?"

"Yes; I wish you would ask Don Jose if he will, through his friends at Oporto, find out whether my cousin's mother was there at the time the French entered, and if she was, whether she got through that horrible business unhurt. I have been hearing about it from my friends, who were a couple of days there before the force marched to Braga. They tell me that, by all accounts, the business was even worse than we feared. The French came upon some of their comrades tied to posts in the great square, horribly mutilated, some of them with their eyes put out, still living, and after that they spared no one; and upon my word, I can hardly blame them, and in fact don't blame them at all, so long as they only wreaked their vengeance on men. The people made it worse for themselves by keeping up a desultory fire from windows and housetops when resistance had long ceased to be of any use; and, of course, seeing their comrades shot down in this way infuriated the troops still further.

"I don't suppose it will make the slightest difference in the world to my cousin whether her mother is dead or not, for I fancy from what Mary said that her mother never cared for her in the slightest. Possibly she was jealous that the child had the first place in the father's affections. However that may be, there was certainly no great love between them, and of course her subsequent treatment of my cousin destroyed any affection that might have existed. That either by some deed executed at the time of marriage, or by Portuguese law, Mary has a right to the estate at her mother's death, is clear from the efforts they made to get her to renounce that right. Still, there is no more chance of her ever inheriting it than there would be of her flying. As a nun she would naturally have to renounce all property, and no doubt the law of this priest-ridden country would decide that she had done so. She tells me—and I am sure, truly—that she refused to open her lips to say a single word when she was forced to go through the ceremony; but as, no doubt, a score of witnesses would be brought forward to swear that she answered all the usual questions and renounced all worldly possessions, that denial would go for nothing."

"Besides," Herrara said, "it would never do for her to set foot in Portugal. She would be seized as an escaped nun immediately, and would never be heard of again."

"I have no doubt that that would be so, Herrara; and as she has a nice fortune from her father, you may be sure that she will not trouble about the estates here, and her mother would be welcome to do as she likes with them, which is, after all, not unreasonable, as they are her property and descended to her from her father. Still, I should be glad to learn, if it does not give any great trouble, whether if, as is almost certain —for the people from all the country round took refuge there long before the French arrived—she was in Oporto, and if so, whether she got through the sack of the town unharmed. No doubt Mary would be glad to hear."

"I am sure Don Jose would be able to find out for you without any difficulty," Herrara said; "indeed I expect he will soon be going back there himself. Now that there is a British garrison in the town, that the bishop must be utterly discredited there, and a good many of his Junta must have been killed, while the rabble of the town has been thoroughly discomfited, the place will be more comfortable to live in than it has been for a long time past. Is there anything else I can do for you?"

"Nothing whatever."

A quarter of an hour later Herrara left for Lisbon, bearing many messages of kind regards on Terence's part to Don Jose and his family. Terence's last words were:

"By the way, Herrara, if you should be able to find at any store in Lisbon some Irish whisky, I wish you would get six dozen cases for me, or what would be more handy, a sixteen or eighteen gallon keg, and could get it sent on by some cart coming here, I should be very much obliged. It had better be sent to me, care of Colonel Corcoran, Mayo Fusiliers, Abrantes. I should like to be able to give a glass to my friends when they ride out to see me. But have the barrel or cases sewn up in canvas before the address is put on; I would not trust it to the escort of any British guard if they were aware of the nature of the contents. Wine would be safe with them, for they can get that anywhere, but it would be too much for the honesty of any Irishman if he were to see a cask labelled Irish whisky."

A week later Colonel Corcoran said when Terence rode in:

"By the bye, O'Connor, there is a cask of wine for you at my quarters; it was brought up by an ammunition train this morning. The officer said that a Portuguese colonel had begged him so earnestly to bring it up that he could not refuse."

"It was Herrara, no doubt, Colonel; he has gone down to Lisbon for a week."

"Ah! I suppose he sent you a keg of choice wine."

"You shall taste it next time you come out, Colonel. I have been wishing that I had something better than the ordinary wine of the country to offer when you come over to see me. I will send over a couple of men with a cart in the morning to bring it out to me."

On leaving that evening Terence invited all the officers who could get away from duty to come over to lunch the next day.

"Bring your knives and forks with you," he said; "and I think you had better bring your plates, too; I fancy four are all I can muster."

Early next morning Terence told Bull and Macwitty that he expected a dozen officers out to lunch with him. "And I want you to lunch with me too. I know that Captain O'Grady and others have asked you several times to go in and dine at mess, and that you have not gone. I hope to-day you will meet them at luncheon. I can understand that you feel a little uncomfortable at this first meeting with a lot of officers as officers yourselves; but, of course, you must do it sooner or later, and it would be much better doing so at once.

"The next thing is, what can I give them to eat? I should be glad if you will send out a dozen foraging parties in different directions; there must be little villages scattered among the hills that have so far escaped French and English plunderers. Let each party take four or five dollars with them. I want anything that can be got, but my idea is a couple of young kids, three or four ducks, or a couple of geese, as many chickens, and of course any vegetables that you can get hold of. My man Sancho is a capital cook, and he will get fires ready and two or three assistants. They will be here by one o'clock, so the foraging parties had better return by ten."

"If there is anything to be brought you shall have it, Colonel," Bull said; "Macwitty and I will both go ourselves, and we will get half a dozen of the captains to go too; between us it is hard if we don't manage to get enough."

By ten o'clock the officers rode in, almost every one of them having some sort of bird or beast hanging from his saddle-bow; there were two kids, a sucking pig, two hares, half a dozen chickens, three geese, and five ducks, while the nets which they carried for forage for their horses were filled with vegetables. Half a dozen fires had already been lighted, and Sancho had obtained as many assistants, so that by the time the colonel and fifteen officers rode up lunch was ready.

After chatting for a few minutes with them, Terence led the way to a rough table that was placed under the shade of a tree. Ammunition boxes were arranged along for seats. Although but a portion of what had been brought in had been cooked, the effect of the table was imposing.

"Why, O'Connor," the colonel said, "have you got one of the genii, like Aladdin, and ordered him to bring up a banquet for you? I have not seen a winged thing since we marched from Coimbra, and here you have got all the luxuries of the season. No wonder you like independent action, if this is what comes of it; there have we been feeding on tough ration beef, and here are the contents of a whole farm-yard."

Almost all the officers had been out before, and Bull and Macwitty had been introduced to them. They now all sat down to the meal.

"I am sorry Major O'Driscol is not here," Terence said.

"He could not get away," the colonel said, from the other end of the table. "If the general had come round and there hadn't been a field-officer left to meet him there would have been a row over it. I have brought pretty nearly all the officers with me, and I dared not stretch it further."

"O'Grady," Terence said, "I wish you would carve this hare for me, I have no idea how it ought to be cut. I can manage a chicken, or a duck, but this is beyond me altogether."

"I will do it gladly, Terence; faith, it is a comfort to find that there is something you can't do." And so, with much laughter and fun, the meal was eaten.

"You have not told us yet where you got all these provisions, O'Connor," the colonel said; "it is too bad to keep all the good things to yourself."

"It has been the work of eight officers, Colonel; they rode off this morning in different directions among the hills, and there was not one of them who returned empty-handed."

"The wine is fairly good," the colonel said, as he set down his tin mug after a long draught, "but it was scarce worth sending all the way up from Lisbon."

"That has to follow, Colonel; I thought you would appreciate it better after you had done eating."

"I have not had such a male since we left Athlone," O'Grady said, when at last he reluctantly laid down his knife and fork. "Be jabers, it would be all up with me if the French were to put in an appearance now, for faith I don't think I could run a yard to save me life."

The tin mugs were all taken away and washed when the table was cleared.

"You are mighty particular, O'Connor," the colonel said. "One mug is good enough for us. If we liquored-up a dozen times—which, by the way, we never do—one of these wines is pretty well like another, and if there was a slight difference it would not matter."

When the board was cleared a large jug was placed before Terence, and some water-bottles at various points of the table.

"I thought, Colonel, that you might prefer spirits even to the wine," Terence said.

"And you are right, O'Connor. A good glass of wine after a good dinner is no bad thing, but after such a meal as we have eaten I think that even this bastely spirit of theirs—which, after all, is not so bad when you get accustomed to it—is better than wine; it settles matters a bit."

Terence poured some of the spirit from a jug into his tin and filled it up with water. "Help yourself," he said, passing the jug to O'Grady, who sat next to him.

O'Grady was about to do so when he suddenly set the jug down.

"By the powers," he exclaimed, in astonishment, "but it is the real cratur!"

"Go on, O'Grady, go on, the others are all waiting while you are looking at it. If you feel too surprised to take it, pass the jug on."

O'Grady grasped it. "I will defind it wid me life!" he exclaimed. In the meantime the colonel had filled his mug.

"Gentlemen," he said, solemnly, after raising it to his lips, "O'Grady is right; it is Irish whisky, and good at that."

"It is a cruel trick you've played on us," O'Grady said, with a sigh, as he replaced the empty mug upon the table. "I had almost forgotten the taste, and had come to take kindly to the stuff here. Now I shall have to go through it all again. It is like holding the cup to the lips of that old heathen Tartarus, and taking it away again."

"Tantalus, O'Grady."

"Och, what does it matter, when he has been dead and buried thousands of years, how he spilt his name. Where did you get it from, Terence?"

"I asked Herrara to try and find some for me at Lisbon; I thought it was most likely that some English merchant there would have laid in a stock, and it seems that he has found one."

"Do you hear that, Colonel? There is whisky to be had at Lisbon, and us not know it."

"Well, Captain O'Grady, all I can say is that I shall at dinner this evening move a vote of censure upon you as mess president for not having discovered the fact before."

"Don't talk of dinner, Colonel; there is not one of us could think of sitting down to ration beef after such a male as we have had—and with whisky here, too! I move, Colonel, that no further mintion be made of dinner. I have no doubt that Terence will give us some divilled bones—there is as much left on the table as we have eaten—before we start home to-night."

"I will do that with pleasure. In fact, it is exactly what I reckoned upon," Terence replied.

"I think, O'Grady, we must send to Lisbon for some of this."

"Is it only think, Colonel? Faith, I would go down for it myself, if I had to walk with pays in my boots and to carry it back on me shoulders. Can I find Herrara there?" he asked.

"Yes, I can give you the address where he will be found."

"Anyhow, Colonel," O'Flaherty said, "I must—and I'm

sure all present will join me in the matter—protest against Captain O'Grady going down to Lisbon to fetch whisky for the mess. You must know, sir, as well as I do, that he would never return again, and we should probably hear some day that his body had been found by the side of the road with three or four empty kegs beside him."

There was a general burst of agreement.

"Perhaps, Doctor O'Flaherty," O'Grady said, in a tone of withering sarcasm, "it's yourself who would like to be the messenger."

"There might be a worse one," O'Flaherty said, calmly; "but as I believe that Captain Hall is going down on a week's leave to-morrow, I propose that he, being an Englishman, and therefore more trustworthy than any Irish member of the mess would be on such a mission, be requested to purchase some for the use of the mess, and to escort it back again. How much shall I say, Colonel?"

"That is a grave matter, and not to be answered hastily, Doctor. Let me see, there are thirty-two officers with the regiment. Now, what would you say would be a fair allowance per day for each man?"

"I should say half a bottle, Colonel. There are some of them won't take as much, but O'Grady will square matters up."

"I protest against the insinuation," O'Grady said, rising; "and, moreover, I would observe, that it is mighty little would be left for me after each man had taken his whack."

"That is sixteen bottles a day. For a continuance I should consider that too much; but seeing that we have been out of dacent liquor for a month, and may have but a fortnight after it arrives to make up for lost time, we will say sixteen bottles."

"Make it three gallons," O'Grady said, persuasively; "we

shall be having lots of men drop in when it gets known that we have got a supply."

"There is something in that, O'Grady. Well, we will say three gallons—that is, forty-two gallons for a fortnight. We will commission Captain Hall to bring back that quantity."

"If you say forty-five, Colonel, it will give us a drop in our flasks to start with, and we are as likely to be fifteen days as fourteen, anyway."

"Let it be forty-five then," the colonel assented. "Will you undertake that, Captain Hall?"

"Willingly, Colonel. I will get the whisky emptied into wine casks, and as I know one of the chief commissaries at Lisbon, I can get it brought up with the wine for the troops."

After sitting for a couple of hours, the colonel proposed that they should all go for a walk, while those who preferred it should take a nap in the shade.

"I move, O'Connor," he said, "that this meeting be adjourned until sunset."

"I think that will be a very good plan, Colonel."

The proposal was carried out. O'Grady and a few others declared that they should prefer a nap. The rest started on foot, and sauntered about in the shade of the wood for a couple of hours, then all gathered at the table again. At eight o'clock grilled joints of fowls and ducks were put upon the table, and at nine all mounted and rode back to Abrantes.

"How many of those quart jugs have been filled, Sancho?"

"Eight, sir."

"That is not so bad," Terence said to Macwitty. "That is twelve bottles; and as there were sixteen and our three selves, that is only about two bottles between three men."

"I call that vera moderate under the circumstances, Colonel," Macwitty said, gravely. "I have drank more myself many a time."

"They were a good many hours over it too," Terence added; "you may say it was two sittings. You will see that we shall have a great many callers from the camp for the next few days."

A fortnight later Terence received a letter from Don Jose, saying that he had heard from his friend at Oporto, and that they informed him that the Señora Johanna O'Connor had been killed at the sack of Oporto. She had left her own house and taken refuge at the bishop's. That place had been defended to the last, and when the infuriated French broke in, all within its walls had been killed.

Terence was not altogether sorry to hear the news. The woman had been a party to the cruel imprisonment of Mary. No doubt his cousin would feel her death, but her grief could not be very deep; and it was, he thought, just as well for her that her connection with Portugal should be altogether severed. Her mother might have endeavoured to tempt her to return there; and although he felt sure that she would not succeed in this, she might at least have caused some trouble, and it was better that there should be an end of it. As to the woman herself, she had been in agreement with the bishop, had been mixed up in his intrigues, and her death was caused by her misplaced confidence in him. Of course she had not known that he had left the town, and thought that under his protection she would be safe in the palace.

"She must have been a bad lot," he said to himself. "Evidently she did not make her husband happy, and persecuted her daughter, and I regret her death no more than any other of the ten thousand people who fell in Oporto."

A few days later he received letters both from his father and Mary. Being under eighteen he opened the former first.

My Dear Terence,

I have heard all about you and your doings from Mary, and I am proud of you. It is grand satisfaction that you should have won your lieutenancy, and that you should be on the general's staff; as to your being a colonel, although only a Portuguese one, it is simply astounding. I don't care so much about the rank, for the Portuguese officers are poor creatures, not one in fifty of them knows anything of his duty; but what I do value is your independent command. That will give you opportunities for distinguishing yourself that can never fall in the way of a subaltern of the line, and I fancy, now that you have got Wellesley at the head, there will be plenty of such opportunities.

I was delighted, as you may guess, when I got Mary's letter from London. I had just settled at the old house, and mighty lonely I felt with no one to speak to, and the wind whistling in at the broken windows, and the whole place in confusion. So putting aside Mary, I was glad enough to have some excuse for running away. I took the next coach for Dublin; found, by good luck, a packet just sailing for London; and got there a week later. She is a nice girl and a pretty one; but I suppose I need not tell you that. I told her it was a poor place I was going to take her to, but she would be as welcome as the flowers in May; but she only laughed and said, that after being shut up for a year in a single room, and having nothing but bread and water, it would not matter a pin to her what it was like.

She was in a grand house, and Mrs. Nelson insisted on my putting up there. We stopped three days and then we took ship to Cork. We had to prove that the money lying there belonged to me; that is to say, that I was the person in whose name it had been put. I had all sort of botheration about it, but luckily I knew the colonel of the regiment there, and he went to the bank with me and testified. Then we came down here, and

Mary hadn't been here a day before she began to spend money. I said I would not allow it; and she said I could not help it, the money was her own, and she could spend it as she liked, which was true enough; and at present the place is more topsy-turvy than ever.

I won't have anything to do with giving orders, but she has got a score of masons and carpenters over from Athlone, and she is turning the old place upside down. I sha'n't know it myself when she has done with it. There is not a place fit to sit down in, and we are living for the time at the inn at Kilnally, three miles away, and drive backwards and forwards to the house. Except that we quarrel over that, we get on first-rate together. She is never tired of talking about you, and when I hinted one day that it was ridiculous your being made a colonel, she spurred up like a young bantam, and more than hinted that if you had been appointed commander-in-chief instead of Sir Arthur it would not have been beyond your deserts.

My wound hurts me a bit sometimes, but I am able to get about all right, and the surgeon says in a few months I shall be able to walk as straight as anyone. And so, good-bye. I don't think I ever wrote such a long letter before, and as Mary will be telling you everything, I don't suppose I shall ever write such a long one again.

Terence laughed as he put the letter down and opened one from his cousin.

Dear Cousin Terence,
Here I am with your father as happy as a bird, and as free. I sing about the place all day, my heart is so light, and should be perfectly happy were it not that I am afraid that you will be fighting again soon, and then I shall be very anxious about you. Your father is just what I thought he would be

from what I know of you. He is as kind as if he was my own father, and reminds me of him. You told me it was a tumble-down old place, and it is. When we came it was only fit for owls to live in; so, of course, I set to work at once. Your father was very foolish about it, but, of course, I had my way. What is the use of having money and living in an owl's nest? So I have set a lot of men to work.

Your father won't interfere with it one way or the other. I had a builder down; he shook his head over it and said that it would be cheaper to pull it down and build a new one; but as it was an old family house I could not do that. However, between ourselves, I don't think there will be much of the old one left by the time we have finished. It looks awful at present. I am building a new wall against the old one, so that it will look just the same, only it will be new. The windows are going to be made bigger, and there will be a new roof put on. Inside it will all have to come down, all the woodwork was so rotten that it was dangerous to walk upstairs. It is great fun looking after the workmen. And though your father does keep on grumbling and saying that I am destroying the old place, I don't think he really minds.

As I tell him, one could live in a house without windows nine months in the year in Portugal, but it is not so in Ireland. One wants comfort, Terence; and, as I have plenty of money, I don't see why we should not have it. You can sleep on the ground, and go from morning till night in wet clothes, when you are on a campaign, but that is no reason why you should do it at other times. The weather is fine here now, at least your father says it is fine, and I want to get everything pushed on and finished before it changes to what even he will admit is wet. The people here seem all very nice and pleasant. They are delighted at having your father back again. I drive about with him a great deal, and we call upon the neighbours, who all seem very pleased that the house is going to be occupied again.

The poor people seem very poor. I don't know that they are poorer than they are in Portugal, but I think they look poorer; but they don't seem to mind much. I have made great friends with most of the children already, and always go about with a large bag of sweetmeats in what your father calls "the trap." I think of you very often, Terence, and your father and I generally talk about you all the evening. By what he says you must have been a very naughty boy, indeed, before you became a soldier. Do take care of yourself. We shall be very, very anxious about you as soon as we hear that fighting has begun again. I hope you think very often of your very loving cousin,

MARY O'CONNOR.

"She will do a world of good to my father," Terence said to himself as he put down the letters. "After being so long in the regiment he would have felt being alone in that old place horribly, especially as it has, of course, been a terrible trial to him to be laid aside just as a big campaign is beginning. She will keep him alive, and he won't have any time to mope. Even if for no other reason, it is a lucky thing indeed that I was able to get Mary out. I sha'n't feel a bit anxious about him now."

THE END.

A LIST OF BOOKS
FOR
YOUNG PEOPLE
By G. A. HENTY

BY CONDUCT AND COURAGE

A Story of Nelson's Days. Illustrated. $1.20 *net* (postage, 16c.).

This, the last of the celebrated Henty Books ever to be published, is a rattling story of the battle and the breeze in the glorious days of Parker and Nelson. The hero is brought up in a Yorkshire fishing village, and enters the navy as a ship's boy.

In the course of a few months after joining he so distinguishes himself in action with French ships and Moorish pirates that he is raised to the dignity of midshipman. His ship is afterward sent to the West Indies. Here his services attract the attention of the Admiral, who gives him command of a small cutter. In this vessel he cruises about among the islands, chasing and capturing pirates, and even attacking their strongholds. He is a born leader of men, and his pluck, foresight, and resource win him success where men of greater experience might have failed. He is several times taken prisoner: by mutinous negroes in Cuba, by Moorish pirates who carry him as a slave to Algiers, and finally by the French. In this last case he escapes in time to take part in the battles of Cape St. Vincent and Camperdown. His adventures include a thrilling experience in Corsica with no less a companion than Nelson himself.

WITH THE ALLIES TO PEKIN

A Tale of the Relief of the Legations. Illustrated by WAL PAGET. $1.20 *net*.

In this book the writer re-tells the story of the Siege of Pekin in a way that is sure to grip the interest of his young readers. The experience of Rex Bateman, the son of an English merchant at Tientsin, and of his cousins, two girls whom Rex rescues from the Boxers just after the first outbreak, offer a variety of heroic incident sufficient to fire the loyalty of the most indifferent lad.

THROUGH THREE CAMPAIGNS

A Story of Chitral, Tirah, and Ashanti. Illustrated by WAL PAGET. $1.20 *net*.

The exciting story of a boy's adventures in the British Army. Lisle Bullen, left an orphan, is to be sent home by the colonel of the regiment on the eve of the Chitral campaign. The boy's patriotism compels him, instead, to secretly join the regiment. He early distinguishes himself for conspicuous bravery. His disguise is discovered and his promotions follow rapidly.

BOOKS FOR YOUNG PEOPLE

By G. A. HENTY

"Among writers of stories of adventures for boys Mr. Henty stands in the very first rank."—*Academy* (London).

THE TREASURE OF THE INCAS

A Tale of Adventure in Peru. With 8 full-page Illustrations by WAL PAGET, and Map. $1.20 net.

Peru and the hidden treasures of her ancient kings offer Mr. Henty a most fertile field for a stirring story of adventure in his most engaging style. In an effort to win the girl of his heart, the hero penetrates into the wilds of the land of the Incas. Boys who have learned to look for Mr. Henty's books will follow his new hero in his adventurous and romantic expedition with absorbing interest. It is one of the most captivating tales Mr. Henty has yet written.

WITH KITCHENER IN THE SOUDAN

A Story of Atbara and Omdurman. With 10 full-page Illustrations. $1.20 net.

Mr. Henty has never combined history and thrilling adventure more skillfully than in this extremely interesting story. It is not in boy nature to lay it aside unfinished, once begun; and finished, the reader finds himself in possession, not only of the facts and the true atmosphere of Kitchener's famous Soudan campaign, but of the Gordon tragedy which preceded it by so many years and of which it was the outcome.

WITH THE BRITISH LEGION

A Story of the Carlist Uprising of 1836. Illustrated. $1.20 net.

Arthur Hallet, a young English boy, finds himself in difficulty at home, through certain harmless school escapades, and enlists in the famous "British Legion," which was then embarking for Spain to take part in the campaign to repress the Carlist uprising of 1836. Arthur shows his mettle in the first fight, distinguishes himself by daring work in carrying an important dispatch to Madrid, makes a dashing and thrilling rescue of the sister of his patron, and is rapidly promoted to the rank of captain. In following the adventures of the hero the reader obtains, as is usual with Mr. Henty's stories, a most accurate and interesting history of a picturesque campaign.

BOOKS FOR YOUNG PEOPLE

BY G. A. HENTY

"Mr. Henty might with entire propriety be called the boys' Sir Walter Scott."—*Philadelphia Press.*

IN THE IRISH BRIGADE

A Tale of War in Flanders and Spain. With 12 Illustrations by Charles M. Sheldon. 12mo, $1.50.

Desmond Kennedy is a young Irish lad who left Ireland to join the Irish Brigade in the service of Louis XIV. of France. In Paris he incurred the deadly hatred of a powerful courtier from whom he had rescued a young girl who had been kidnapped, and his perils are of absorbing interest. Captured in an attempted Jacobite invasion of Scotland, he escaped in a most extraordinary manner. As aid-de-camp to the Duke of Berwick he experienced thrilling adventures in Flanders. Transferred to the Army in Spain, he was nearly assassinated, but escaped to return, when peace was declared, to his native land, having received pardon and having recovered his estates. The story is filled with adventure, and the interest never abates.

OUT WITH GARIBALDI

A Story of the Liberation of Italy. By G. A. Henty. With 8 Illustrations by W. Rainey, R.I. 12mo, $1.50.

Garibaldi himself is the central figure of this brilliant story, and the little-known history of the struggle for Italian freedom is told here in the most thrilling way. From the time the hero, a young lad, son of an English father and an Italian mother, joins Garibaldi's band of 1,000 men in the first descent upon Sicily, which was garrisoned by one of the large Neapolitan armies, until the end, when all those armies are beaten, and the two Sicilys are conquered, we follow with the keenest interest the exciting adventures of the lad in scouting, in battle, and in freeing those in prison for liberty's sake.

WITH BULLER IN NATAL

Or, A Born Leader. By G. A. Henty. With 10 Illustrations by W. Rainey. 12mo, $1.50.

The breaking out of the Boer War compelled Chris King, the hero of the story, to flee with his mother from Johannesburg to the sea coast. They were with many other Uitlanders, and all suffered much from the Boers. Reaching a place of safety for their families, Chris and twenty of his friends formed an independent company of scouts. In this service they were with Gen. Yule at Glencoe, then in Ladysmith, then with Buller. In each place they had many thrilling adventures. They were in great battles and in lonely fights on the Veldt; were taken prisoners and escaped; and they rendered most valuable service to the English forces. The story is a most interesting picture of the War in South Africa.

www.ingramcontent.com/pod-product-compliance
Lightning Source LLC
Chambersburg PA
CBHW051721300426
44115CB00007B/412